# MUGABE'S
## WAR MACHINE

## Other related books by Paul Moorcraft

*A Short Thousand Years: The End of Rhodesia's Rebellion* (1979)

*Contact 2: The Struggle for Peace* (1981)

*Africa's Superpower* (1981)

*Stander: bank robber* (with Mike Cohen) (1984)

*African Nemesis: War and Revolution in Southern Africa, 1945-2010* (1990)

*What the hell am I doing here? Travels with an occasional war correspondent* (1995)

*Guns and Poses: Travels with an occasional war correspondent* (2001)

*Axis of Evil: The War on Terror* (with Gwyn Winfield and John Chisholm) (2005)

*The New Wars of the West* (with Gwyn Winfield and John Chisholm) (2006)

*Inside the Danger Zones: Travels to Arresting Places* (2010)

*Shooting the Messenger: The Political Impact of War Reporting* (with Phil Taylor) (2011)

*The Rhodesian War: A Military History* (with Peter McLaughlin) (2011)

# MUGABE'S
## WAR MACHINE

## PAUL MOORCRAFT

**JONATHAN BALL PUBLISHERS**
Johannesburg & Cape Town

Originally published in 2011 in hard cover in Great Britain by
Pen & Sword Military
An imprint of Pen & Sword Books Ltd

This edition published in trade paperback in South Africa in 2012 by
JONATHAN BALL PUBLISHERS (PTY) LTD
P O Box 33977
Jeppestown
2043

ISBN 978-1-86842-471-9

Set in Times New Roman by Chic Media Ltd
Printed and bound by Paarl Media, Paarl

# Contents

# About the Author

**Professor Paul Moorcraft** lived in Rhodesia and Zimbabwe from 1976-81. He covered the war, *inter alia*, for *Time* magazine, and also taught politics and history at the University of Rhodesia/Zimbabwe. His doctorate was on the intelligence and military failures of the Rhodesian government. He also served in the A Reserve of the BSAP/ZRP for eighteen months, after December 1979. In addition, he worked extensively as a journalist covering the conflicts throughout southern Africa from 1981-88, including reporting in both Angola and Mozambique. Later, he was the editor of a range of security and foreign policy magazines, including *Defence Review* and *Defence International*. He worked for most of the Western TV networks as a freelance producer/war correspondent as well as lecturing full-time around the world at ten major universities in journalism, politics and international relations. He was a Distinguished Radford Visiting Professor in Journalism at Baylor University, Texas. He has worked in thirty war zones in Africa, the Middle East, Asia and the Balkans, often with irregular forces, most recently in Afghanistan, Iraq, Palestine/Israel, Darfur and Nepal.

Paul Moorcraft is a former senior instructor at the Royal Military Academy, Sandhurst, and the UK Joint Services Command and Staff College. He also worked in Corporate Communications in the Ministry of Defence in Whitehall. In 2003 he was recalled temporarily to government service in Whitehall and Iraq. He still serves in various occasional MoD research groups.

In 2010, he was the head of mission for the British independent observer group comprising fifty observers at the Sudan elections. In January 2011, he returned to cover the referendum in South Sudan.

He is the author of a wide range of books on military history, politics and crime, as well as being an award-winning novelist. Paul Moorcraft is a regular broadcaster and contributor to UK and US newspapers (with frequent columns in the *Washington Times*, *Business Day* [Johannesburg], the *Guardian* etc) as well as a pundit on BBC TV and Radio, Al-Jazeera etc. His co-authored study, with Professor Phil Taylor, *Shooting the Messenger: The Political Impact of War Reporting*, was published in 2008; the paperback in 2011. Dr Moorcraft also co-authored the acclaimed *The Rhodesian War: A Military History* in 2008; paperback in 2011. His most recent military book is *Inside the Danger Zones: Travels to Arresting Places* (2010).

Dr Moorcraft is currently the director of the Centre for Foreign Policy Analysis, London, as well as being a Visiting Professor at Cardiff University's School of Journalism, Media and Cultural Studies.

# Abbreviations

The English versions are used here for consistency, not the Afrikaans or Portuguese original.

| | |
|---|---|
| AFZ | Air Force of Zimbabwe |
| ANC | African National Congress (South Africa) |
| AU | African Union |
| BMATT | British Military Advisory and Training Team |
| BOSS | Bureau for State Security |
| BSAP | British South Africa Police |
| CIO | Central Intelligence Organisation |
| COIN | Counter-insurgency |
| ComOps | Combined Operations HQ, Salisbury |
| DRC | Democratic Republic of the Congo |
| FPLM | FRELIMO's military wing |
| FRELIMO | Mozambique Liberation Front |
| GNU | Government of National Unity |
| GPA | Global Political Agreement |
| JOC | Joint Operations Command |
| JOMIC | Joint Monitoring Implementation Committee |
| KP | Kimberley Process |
| MDC | Movement for Democratic Change |
| MDC-M | Movement for Democratic Change - Mutambara |
| MDC-T | Movement for Democratic Change - Tsvangirai |
| MNR | See RENAMO |
| OAU | Organisation of African Unity |
| PAC | Pan-Africanist Congress |
| PF | Patriotic Front |
| PISI | Police Internal Security and Intelligence unit |
| RENAMO | Mozambique National Resistance |
| RAF | Rhodesian Air Force |
| RAR | Rhodesian African Rifles |
| RBC | Rhodesian Broadcasting Corporation |
| RF | Rhodesian Front |
| RLI | Rhodesian Light Infantry |

| | |
|---|---|
| SAAF | South African Air Force |
| SABC | South African Broadcasting Corporation |
| SADC | Southern African Development Community |
| SADF | South African Defence Force |
| SAP | South African Police |
| SAS | Special Air Service |
| SB | Special Branch |
| TRC | Truth and Reconciliation Commission |
| TTL | Tribal Trust Land |
| UANC | United African National Council |
| UDI | Unilateral Declaration of Independence |
| UNITA | National Union for the Total Liberation of Angola |
| ZANLA | Zimbabwe African National Liberation Army |
| ZANU | Zimbabwe African National Union |
| ZANU-PF | Zimbabwe African National Union - Patriotic Front |
| ZAPU | Zimbabwe African People's Union |
| ZDF | Zimbabwe Defence Forces |
| ZIPA | Zimbabwe People's Army |
| ZIPRA | Zimbabwe People's Revolutionary Army |
| ZNA | Zimbabwe National Army |
| ZNLWVA | Zimbabwe National Liberation War Veterans Association |
| ZRP | Zimbabwe Republic Police |

# List of Maps

# List of Illustrations

1. The Rhodesian historical view of the first *Chimurenga*: British South Africa Company forces about to be overwhelmed by Ndebele warriors in 1893.

2. Robert Mugabe campaigning just before he came to power.

3. On 11 December 1978, ZANLA guerrillas fired rockets and tracers at the central oil storage depot in Salisbury.

4. Guerrilla atrocity. On 23 June 1978, twelve men, women and children were variously raped, hacked and bludgeoned to death by ZANLA regulars at Elim Pentecostal Mission, near Umtali (Mutare).

5. ZANLA guerrillas in the bush with a fascinating array of arms.

6. Chinese-produced liberation posters used by ZANLA.

7. An early Soviet BTR-152 with a 12.7mm machine gun, used by FRELIMO.

8. South African troops. At the end of the liberation war, about 6,000 South African forces, some in Rhodesian uniform, were involved directly, with large reserves inside South Africa, ready to intervene.

9. A light ground support Impala, of the South African Air Force.

10. A ZANLA poster. *'Pamberi ne Chimurenga'* means 'Forward with the liberation struggle'.

11. Although ZANLA propaganda exaggerated the combat role of women, a considerable number of female guerrillas did see action.

12. Bishop Abel Muzorewa and his wife Maggie, just after he became the first black prime minister of the country (April 1979).

13. General Lookout Masuku, one of the most able ZIPRA military leaders, arriving in Salisbury just after the ceasefire (December 1979).

30. Worthless money. Zimbabwe managed the second highest inflation rate in modern history.

31. The two wings of the MDC. Left to right: Arthur Mutambara and Morgan Tsvangirai. (Ubuntu Hope.)

32. Morgan Tsvangirai has suffered much at he hands of his rival, Mugabe, but does he have the skills to lead and to reconstruct a devastated country? (Ubuntu Hope.)

33. Newspaper ad for Mugabe in the June 2008 election in which he was the only candidate.

# Introduction

Zimbabwe's military history is a fascinating tale, which has had an impact on the whole of Africa and far beyond. The story has not been told in a comprehensive fashion – until now. Yes, various historical accounts have examined separate conflicts from the pre-colonial period (the invasion of Zulus in the post-*Mfecane* period, for example) and resistance to the settler incursions of the 1890s (the so-called first *Chimurenga*, the Shona word for 'uprising'; the Ndebele called it *Umvukela*). The Rhodesian contributions to the two world wars have been chronicled. The canon also includes a series of books, often very partisan, on the 'war of liberation', the second *Chimurenga*, against Ian Smith's white regime. More recently, journalists and historians have written in a piecemeal manner about the various military interventions both inside Zimbabwe and in the southern African region as a whole.

This book will examine the totality of military power, especially since independence in 1980. This is the best way of making sense of how the current rogue dictatorship has undermined security in southern Africa. Zimbabwe's armed forces waged an almost genocidal war against its real and perceived enemies in Matabeleland in the early 1980s, but African leaders and politically correct Western politicians, enamoured of Mugabe as a great liberator, usually looked the other way. Also, in the early days of independence, Robert Mugabe's government was sucked into a secret war against apartheid South Africa. Simultaneously, the Zimbabwe Defence Forces (ZDF) were deployed in large numbers in the civil war in next-door Mozambique. Later, Mugabe's troops played an active role in the Congo, in what became known as 'Africa's First World War'. In the twenty-first century, Zimbabwe's security apparatus – military, police, intelligence and militias – waged a prolonged campaign against internal political challenges to the dictatorship in Harare. This became known as the 'third *Chimurenga*'. A part of this war was to reclaim the land from white farmers. The destruction of agriculture accelerated the implosion of the economy. As a result Zimbabwe witnessed one of the most dramatic and rapid collapses of any modern society.

The military-led wars and internal violence are interlinked. Zimbabwe's military history has never quite repeated itself, but it does rhyme, to adapt a quotation from Mark Twain. Zimbabwe certainly obeyed Clausewitz's dictum that war is politics by other means, as the key player, Mugabe's ruling party – the Zimbabwe African National Union-Patriotic Front (ZANU-PF) – has consistently used violence to attain political ends. Initially, the Shona-dominated ZANU and its military wing fought to break the back of white supremacy. Then it destroyed what it considered to be ethnic rivals, first the Ndebele and later white ownership of farms and businesses. The Mugabe administration was almost inevitably drawn into the conflicts created by the death throes of apartheid, as well as the fighting in Mozambique. In the latter, Mugabe played a constructive role in ending the long civil conflict. But the decision to send ZDF troops into the Democratic Republic of Congo further strained the Zimbabwean economy, while personally enriching some of Mugabe's generals. The total politicization of the security apparatus resulted from ZANU-PF's determination to keep Mugabe, and his party, in power despite the growing electoral and popular success of the rival MDC – the Movement for Democratic Change, led by a former trade union leader, Morgan Tsvangirai. After 2000, Mugabe came to believe that *'L'état, c'est moi'*. The dictator looked set to stay in power for life; without him, his generals feared chaos, exile, or a summons to the International Criminal Court.

In 1980, Mugabe inherited a potentially rich state. The war was over, sanctions were lifted, and aid flowed into the country. The small British military advisory team worked hard to forge a professional army from the highly efficient Rhodesian forces and the battle-hardened guerrilla armies loyal to both Robert Mugabe and his ally in the Patriotic Front, Joshua Nkomo. Mugabe preached reconciliation and most whites stayed. Zimbabwe appeared a model to the rest of Africa, and especially apartheid South Africa. Hope turned to despair, however, as Mugabe used his security forces to cling on to power for over thirty years, forcing millions of black and white Zimbabweans to flee. The African messiah was transformed into the ugliest archetype of an African dictator-for-life.

The Rhodesian security forces were praised the world over by military analysts for their skills in counter-insurgency. The Rhodesians fought a brilliant tactical and operational war, but they lost because their racist overall strategy, such as it was, was damned and doomed. Mugabe inherited both a competent army and air force, and the industrial base to support it. In the end he eviscerated his country and its military. How that happened, and what it means, is the subject of this book. *Mugabe's War Machine* also considers possible ways out of the current imbroglio.

Professor Paul Moorcraft spent six years in Rhodesia/Zimbabwe as a journalist and academic, during and just after the liberation war, and returned on a number of occasions, despite being banned. He also reported extensively on other wars in the region. He co-authored what has been almost universally considered as the definitive history of the 1965-1979 conflict, *The Rhodesian War,* and has written a number of other related works.

*Mugabe's War Machine* is founded on four decades of direct personal experience in Zimbabwe's wars and related regional conflicts, sometimes in the front line. Numerous interviews were conducted with a wide variety of military and intelligence personnel; I am also grateful to my academic colleagues' research. Footnotes have not been included, not least to maintain anonymity for sources. Also, I have simplified some of the traditional academic conventions, for example I have used only 'Shona' and 'Ndebele' when discussing the peoples and languages etc. I trust that this account, although likely to be controversial, is both accurate and informative.

Paul Moorcraft

Surrey Hills, UK
10 May 2011.

# Chapter 1

# Mugabe: A Revolutionary Tyrant

B efore considering the historical context of the war and his leadership of the liberation struggle before his ascendancy to political power, it is important to consider the nature of the central character in this story: Robert Gabriel Mugabe.

When leaders destroy their own countries, as Hitler and Mugabe did, it usually conjures up a bedlam of pop psychologists trying to decipher the dictators' peculiar form of madness. It is the author's contention that Mugabe is not clinically insane – a ruthlessly consistent pattern of behaviour is apparent, with its own internal logic. Perhaps the fairest psychological assessment was made by ex-Zimbabwean Heidi Holland, a white liberal who encountered Mugabe briefly during the anti-colonial war, and later managed to secure a lengthy interview for her well-known book, *Dinner with Mugabe*. She worked with a group of psychologists as well as interviewing many of Mugabe's close associates and family. Holland profiled Mugabe's lonely childhood, Catholic upbringing, and scholarly leanings. She tried to explain his paradoxical affection for certain white leaders, especially British royalty, and his policies which led to murder and mayhem in the white farming community after 2000. Mugabe's more than a decade of imprisonment under Ian Smith, and the refusal of the authorities to allow him to attend the funeral of his son, are quoted as part-causes of his anger towards whites. Yet Mugabe's offer of reconciliation to whites in 1980 was almost certainly genuine. Later, he felt betrayed by Tony Blair's Labour government in London because of its refusal to pay for white farmers' compensation; he also felt betrayed by the fact that most Rhodesian whites, and the farmers in particular, voted continuously for the opposition, especially the MDC.

Holland describes Mugabe's delusions of omnipotence thus:

He is unaware of the contradictions within himself. He can insist that he never sacrifices principle because of the way he sees it, he did not set out to murder, and the torture people suffered was of their own doing. While he may not be mad in a clinical sense, his is a mad way of being in the world: a cut-off, deluded way.

Holland also asked Mugabe, in her long-delayed interview, how the long prison years – about one-third the term of the much more magnanimous Nelson Mandela – had affected him. She asked specifically:

'When you came out of prison, were you the same person who went in?'

Mugabe paused to reflect: 'No, you came back with the sense that you had been punished for nothing, and that you must fight for that for which you have been punished – which has not come. We were released in 1974 but [Ian] Smith was still stubborn and we needed to intensify our fighting.'

Mugabe said he was not vengeful. He claimed to be 'an ordinary person'. Holland concluded her book with this final verdict:

As an ordinary man, he could have listened rather than believed he had all the answers; made mistakes and learned from them, forgiven shortcomings in others and been forgiven; made friends and been a friend; asked for help – all the things that mere mortals do. But he believed he was special, different, born for greatness.

Mugabe had very few friends. One of them was Enos Nkala. In 1963 the Zimbabwe African National Union party was founded in Nkala's home in Highfields in Harare (then Salisbury). Nkala, who had long been a faithful and fanatical ally of his leader, finally lamented that he could not stop his old colleague from blaming US presidents and UK prime ministers for all Zimbabwe's woes. Nkala said that Mugabe was now

impervious to reason. I would not want to use the word mentally sick … You do not counsel a man who is impervious to analysis and admitting mistakes, so why should I spend my time engaging in an unproductive exercise?

To those who studied his personality for years, at close hand or in the ivory tower, Mugabe appeared a mass of contradictions. His upbringing and ideology were commented on by Andrew Young, President Carter's envoy in the late 1970s: 'The trouble with Robert Mugabe is that when you've got a Jesuit education mixed with Marxist ideology, you've got a hell of a guy to deal with.' Mugabe could be extremely charming, adhering to all the slow, gentle niceties of African greeting rituals; at other times, curt and rude, even to senior statesmen. Mugabe loathed his chief rival, Joshua Nkomo, and was frequently rude to him and about him. At the time of the Lancaster House peace talks in London, Julius Nyerere, the president of Tanzania, invited both men in to his study to try to mend fences, and get them to form a united front. Nkomo, as the older man, was invited in first. When it was Mugabe's turn, he said: 'If you think I am going to sit where that fat bastard just sat, you'll have to think again.' The Tanzanian leader was utterly shocked by the remark, especially as then Nyerere was the Nelson Mandela of his era. The two rivals continued to clash, but especially when Mugabe was on the cusp of victory in Zimbabwe. He refused to fight a joint campaign with Nkomo, despite the existence of the so-called Patriotic Front. When Mugabe won by a landslide at the polls, Nkomo said: 'You give them one man, one vote and look what they do with it.' Then, showing his bitterness at having to fight the polls alone, Nkomo said almost more in sadness than in anger: 'We should have fought the election together ... Robert let me down.'

Trevor Ncube, the eminent Zimbabwean writer and editor, recently summed up Mugabe's disturbing psychological behaviour: 'Not once has Mugabe taken responsibility for his decisions and the actions of those around him. He takes no responsibility for the mess that the country is in.'

Richard Dowden, the director of the Royal African Society in London, summarized Mugabe very succinctly:

> Mugabe has not gone mad. Nor was he always bad. He is a complicated schizophrenic man. Driven by the respect for the Western mentality for logic and order and a passionate sense of injustice and rejection by whites.

As ever with Mugabe, his relationships with whites were complex and contradictory. He possessed a life-long affection for his white Catholic tutors, especially Father Jerome O'Hea. He developed an almost son-father relationship with Lord Soames, briefly the governor of Southern Rhodesia. Mugabe attended Christopher Soames's funeral in the UK in 1987, clearly out of affection, not duty. The man he should have hated, Ken Flower, the head of the Central Intelligence Organization which had tried to kill him, became a close confidant. Flower's personal diary is full of warm words about Mugabe as prime minister. Originally, Mugabe distinguished between good whites and bad ones. He accorded the unique honour for a white by sponsoring the burial, in the hallowed ground of Heroes' Acre, of the Welsh-born Guy Clutton-Brock. He had been an early supporter of the liberation struggle. Gradually, Mugabe's condemnatory rhetoric lambasted *all* whites. It was his regime's murder of white farmers after 2000 that fired up the Western media campaigns, which had largely ignored the destruction of so many Ndebele families in the 1980s.

Peter Godwin, in his recent book, *The Fear,* commented shrewdly on Mugabe's favourite parlour game – Britain-bashing:

> I've noticed that when he speaks of Britain, he subconsciously lapses in to a magniloquent sub-Churchillian cadence – betraying his agonizing Anglophilia. 'We are not an extension of Britain,' he thunders now. 'I will never stand for it, dead or alive, even my ghost will not stand for it.'

Nevertheless, Mugabe still wins much kudos in his own country and in the rest of Africa for his attacks on Western, especially British, hypocrisy, not least over the land issue, and for attempts at regime change, when it was fashionable under President George W. Bush. Tirades against Mugabe epitomized Western double standards in the eyes of many Africans. Even after Mugabe's Korean-trained Fifth Brigade had slaughtered tens of thousands of Ndebeles in the early 1980s, Queen Elizabeth awarded him an honorary knighthood. In 1994 Mugabe was appointed an Honorary Knight Grand Cross in the Order of the Bath. This entitled him to use the letters GCB after his name but not to use the title 'Sir'. It was only much later, in 2003, after the killing of a small number of white farmers, that the British prime minister was asked in parliament whether Mugabe should be stripped of his title. In June 2008, the Queen annulled the honour.

Britain, as the ex-colonial power, had to stand back from much of the power politics in the days of Mugabe's decline. The dominant player was always South Africa. And yet President Thabo Mbeki, the man tasked to try to bring a settlement to Zimbabwe, was somewhat in awe of Mugabe. Despite their arguments, Mbeki was said to be personally fond of him. Normally, Mugabe insisted on being the dominant intellect in any company, but with Mbeki there was often a meeting of minds, as fellow intellectuals. Also, Mbeki showed traditional respect for the older man, especially a liberation hero.

When the author interviewed Mugabe in late-January 1980, the initial impression was of a towering intelligence. Many of the white Rhodesian politicians were dull backwoodsmen, but Mugabe stood out not only in his own country, but in the whole continent. Bolstered by seven university degrees, most secured in prison via correspondence courses, he seemed very quick-witted. Ironically, for a man who had just come out of a savage bush war as the leader of a tough guerrilla army, now immaculately dressed he minced when he walked. And his diction was almost contrived to emulate the received pronunciation of the BBC's best Home Counties accent.

In short, Mugabe's personality was complicated, and so were his politics. This book tries to decode Mugabe, his methods and his military apparatus. It is too easy simply to label him mad. He may have surrounded himself with yes-men, like many tyrants, but his rise to power, and his skill in hanging on to it for over thirty years, need to be seen as part of Zimbabwe's often violent history.

# Chapter 2

# White Conquest of the Land: The First *Chimurenga*

T he formal conquest of what became Rhodesia was orchestrated by Cecil John Rhodes, the tycoon who inspired the name for the British colony. Rhodes's invasion of the lands north of the Limpopo, which legend depicted as the location of King Solomon's mines, was the gamble of a megalomaniac with the wealth to indulge his fantasies. Rhodes secured by deceit a mining concession from Lobengula, the Ndebele king who claimed dominion over most of the territory between the Limpopo and the Zambezi rivers. He used it as a legal basis to secure a Royal Charter from the British Crown, which empowered him to establish a settler state in Mashonaland ruled by Rhodes's British South Africa Company.

In 1890 several hundred men of the British South Africa Company's Pioneer Corps and Police, the kernel of the self-contained frontier society, defied Lobengula's threats to unleash the tens of thousands of warriors in his regiments. He had belatedly realized his folly and forbidden the settlers' entry. Outsmarted by Rhodes's multinational corporation, Lobengula was also overawed by his own fearful perceptions of the white man's military technology. He had heard reports from the frontiers of South Africa of the overwhelming firepower of white armies. The Ndebele king allowed himself to be browbeaten, and so let the columns of the Pioneers roll over the veldt to establish the Company state in Mashonaland. Its tenuous links with the outside world were guarded by a string of tiny forts, but its greatest security was Lobengula's chronic and ultimately fatal vacillation.

The settlers' dreams of finding an African Eldorado were shattered in the lean years which followed the invasion, but stories were still repeated endlessly of gold deposits – just beyond reach within the borders of the Ndebele heartland. In 1893 the Trojan horse reluctantly accepted by Lobengula into his domains - which he refused to destroy despite the demands of a hot-blooded Ndebele war party - fulfilled his worst fears. The

# THE MAJOR TRIBAL GROUPINGS IN RHODESIA WITH APPROXIMATE PERCENTAGE OF AFRICAN POPULATION (1970s)

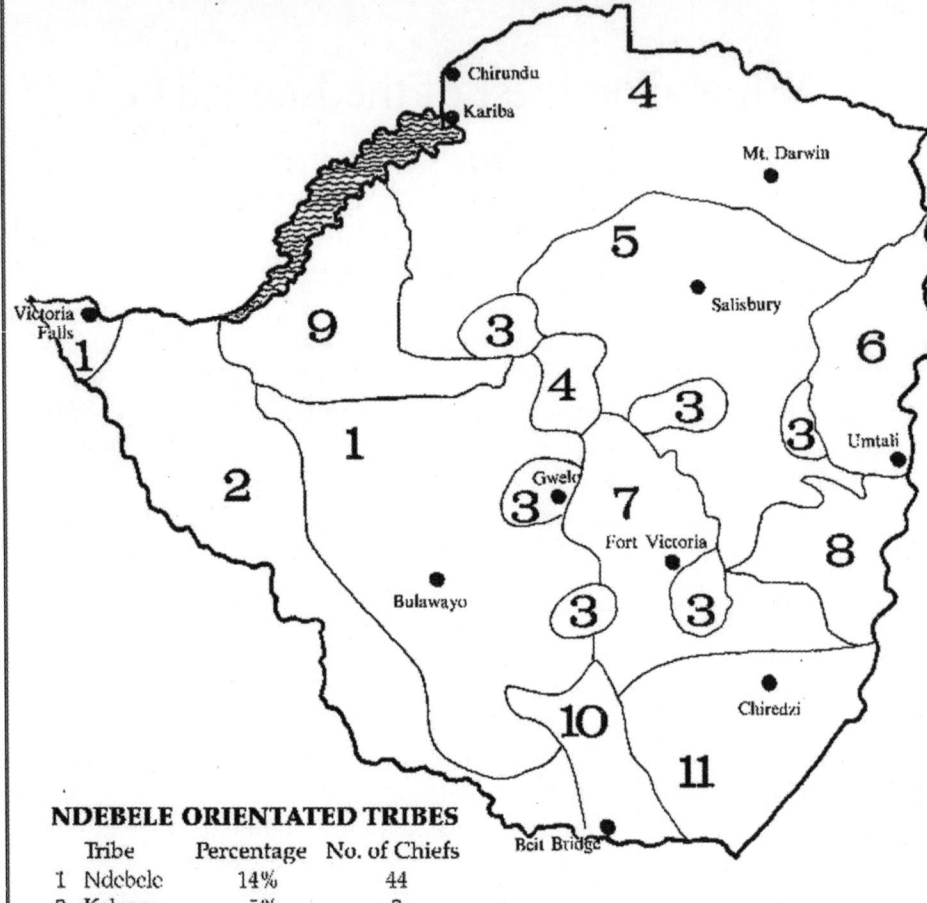

## NDEBELE ORIENTATED TRIBES

| | Tribe | Percentage | No. of Chiefs |
|---|---|---|---|
| 1 | Ndebele | 14% | 44 |
| 2 | Kalanga | 5% | 3 |

## SHONA ORIENTATED TRIBES

| | Tribe | Percentage | No. of Chiefs |
|---|---|---|---|
| 3 | Rozwi | 9% | 20 |
| 4 | Korekore | 12% | 20 |
| 5 | Zezuru | 18% | 22 |
| 6 | Manyika | 13% | 9 |
| 7 | Karanga | 22% | 35 |
| 8 | Ndau | 3% | 11 |

## OTHERS

| | Tribe | Percentage | No. of Chiefs |
|---|---|---|---|
| 9 | Tonga | 2% | 27 |
| 10 | Venda | 1% | 6 |
| 11 | Shangaan | 1% | 5 |

**NOTE**

1. The three above divisions are based on historical fact. They do not necessarily mean that a modern African from the KALANGA group, for example, automatically considers himself to be NDEBELE orientated in matters of politics, sport or any other aspect of organized life.

2. Some of the above groups have further sub-groups. The NDEBELE, for example, have 12 such sub-groups, the ZEZURU have 8, and the KARANGA have 15.

3. The SHONA language group have approximately 65 sub-groups.

Map 1 – The Major Tribal Groupings in Rhodesia

Company cleverly engineered a war in which the Ndebele were marked as the aggressors. Columns of settler volunteers, tempted with promises of farms and mining claims, converged on Gubulawayo, the Ndebele capital, and on the way fought two encounter battles with Lobengula's brave but outgunned regiments. Shortly before his capital was captured and sacked, the defeated king fled north and died in the bush beyond the grasp of pursuing settler patrols. The victors carved the defeated kingdom into farms and mines, seized and distributed the Ndebele national herd as war booty, and built a new frontier town, Bulawayo, on the site of Lobengula's razed capital.

Rhodes's successes stoked the fires of his megalomania. As well as controlling vast financial operations in Southern Africa, he was prime minister of the Cape Colony. He was concerned about the growth of Afrikaner nationalism in South Africa and sought to exploit the grievances of the English-speaking mining community in Johannesburg to engineer the overthrow of Paul Kruger's South African Republic. The new country of Rhodesia was to be used as a springboard for Rhodes's illegal conspiracy, which was planned in deep secrecy to prevent the intervention of the Imperial government.

In late 1895, BSA Company forces struck south to precipitate a coup against the Afrikaner republic in the Transvaal. But the so-called Jameson Raid was a humiliating fiasco for the Company and its soldiers. It also invited catastrophe in the colony. The Ndebele and Shona, chafing under the Company's regime of forced labour, cattle and land seizures, as well as its arrogant administration, and suffering from the natural afflictions of cattle disease and locusts, rose against the settlers while the country was denuded of its armed forces.

The Company had not completely shattered the Ndebele and Shona political systems, and these, aided by the religious systems of the two peoples, organized countrywide insurrections which decimated the settler population. Ndebele warriors dug up the rifles and assegais they had cached after the war of 1893. The Shona had never been disarmed. The resistance raged for eighteen months. The settler forces, bolstered by contingents of British troops, were hampered by poor logistics and shortage of horses. The insurgents made good use of their superior bushcraft and intelligence network, and avoided the sort of setpiece confrontations which had bloodied Lobengula's regiments in 1893. The Company forces eventually adopted scorched-earth tactics to starve out the rebels, who then retreated to hilltop strongholds and into caves from which they were systematically dynamited. Thus ended the first *Chimurenga*.

Rhodes's hubris cost him the premiership of the Cape Colony, although his influence was strong enough to save him from gaol for illegally launching the Jameson Raid. Only the British government's reluctance to administer Rhodesia prevented the abrogation of the Royal Charter to punish the Company for its abuses of power. As well as leaving the Company's powers largely intact (though more closely supervised by Imperial officials), the events of the later 1890s bequeathed a legacy of bitterness to both racial groups. The settlers suffered from a 'risings psychosis', a morbid fear of another unexpected storm of violence. Africans were characterized as treacherous and barbaric, for in the first days of the insurgency hundreds of near-defenceless homesteaders living on lonely farms were taken by surprise and brutally murdered. Africans saw their hopes of throwing off the yoke of Company rule disappear in the smoke of Maxim and Gatling guns and the blasts of dynamite. The death and destruction they suffered passed into their folklore.

Although Rhodesian forces fought alongside British and Imperial units against the white Afrikaners during the Boer War, the settlers remained mesmerized by the spectre of an African rebellion. The defence system of the first decade of the twentieth century was geared solely towards securing the settlers against the vastly more numerous black population. Imperial supervision forced the Company to develop more subtle ways of controlling the African masses. Forced labour was no longer possible, but increasing taxation compelled African men to seek work in the labour-hungry settler economy to meet their obligations to the tax-man. Registration certificates and pass laws controlled the movements of Africans, and the boundaries of their reserves were strictly defined. African peasant farmers were moved off their ancestral lands to make way for Europeans, and armed police patrols crisscrossed the territory to display the power of the Company and to nip thoughts of insurrection in the bud.

The white man's war of 1914-18 resurrected fears of an opportunistic African rising. Internal defence remained a top priority throughout the war against the Germans. Several thousand Africans enlisted in an all-volunteer force, the Rhodesia Native Regiment. The unit saw action in German East Africa. The settlers swallowed their repugnance at the thought of arming and training the possible core of some future African insurrection, and of undermining the myth of white supremacy by putting Africans into the field against white Germans.

The Twenties and the Depression years saw a widening of racial divisions in Rhodesia. The Land Apportionment Act of 1930 formally divided the country's land between the races; the whites reserved to themselves the more fertile areas with higher rainfall and 'gave' Africans the poorer, more arid areas. These soon teetered on the brink of ecological disaster as a rapidly growing African population and its expanding herds of livestock crowded on to the overtaxed land. Labour, agricultural, industrial, educational and health legislation of the late Twenties and Thirties was aimed at creating a secure and prosperous society for the whites at the expense of blacks, and largely succeeded, despite the hard times of the Depression.

Discriminatory policies were more easily introduced after the handover of power to the settlers in 1923. The referendum of 1922 delivered self-government into the hands of the settlers, and the African population's welfare with it. Although the British government retained supervisory powers, these were never effective, and the settlers were able to create the sort of economy and society they wanted. The Africans' response was slow in gathering momentum, for they were denied the vote and their tribal political systems were losing cohesion under the impact of an alien capitalist economy. While a few small political groups tried unsuccessfully to voice African needs and aspirations, the broad masses remained inarticulate and passive.

Although the settlers' defence system was still concentrated on internal security, some concessions were made to the colony's history of warfare against other whites. In 1926 compulsory service for young white males was introduced. The new defence force was organized on a regimental basis and was headed by a staff corps. This was the skeleton of the future Rhodesian army, although in the lean Thirties it remained poorly fleshed. The phenomenally high proportion of white settlers who were commissioned during the Great War disposed the Imperial military authorities to view Rhodesia as a training ground for future NCOs and officers should the Empire ever go to war again. The rearmament of Britain's forces in the face of deteriorating international relations in the 1930s brought closer liaison between the British and Rhodesian armed forces. From 1938 onwards new units, such as a reconnaissance company and a light artillery battery, were formed with the specific aim of taking part in British expeditionary forces. A fledgling air force, attached to the army, had been created in the early Thirties. For the first time, defence policy became consciously outward-looking, planning for eventualities beyond the protection of laagered white women and children against waves of assegai-wielding black insurgents.

The outbreak of war in 1939 saw the Rhodesian forces geared for a world-wide conflict. Rhodesian squadrons of the Royal Air Force served in Europe, North Africa and the Middle East. Rhodesian soldiers fought with

British and South African formations in North Africa and Italy. The high rate of casualties suffered by Rhodesian units during the Great War prompted a policy of dispersal of the colony's treasured white manpower to avoid the possibility of some latter-day Passchendaele causing a national tragedy.

Paradoxically, the largest homogeneous unit representing the colony was the Rhodesian African Rifles. Raised in 1940-1 to counter the perennial shortage of white manpower, the unit adopted the East African battle honours of its predecessor, the Rhodesia Native Regiment, and fought with Field Marshal William Slim's 'Forgotten Army' in Burma. But there was more widespread resistance to recruiting among Africans than during the Great War. African perceptions of the racial imbalance of the Rhodesian economy and the exclusivity of white society had crystallized in the 1930s. The RAR and a labour battalion, the Rhodesian Air Askari Corps, had difficulties drumming up recruits.

While African society remained largely undisturbed by the world upheaval, white society was more profoundly affected. Not only did 6,500 men (out of an estimated 30,000) serve abroad in all the major theatres of war, but 10,000 airmen were trained in the colony under the Empire Air Training Scheme, arguably Rhodesia's most effective contribution to the Allied war effort. The scope of the fighting and the influx of trainees developed Rhodesian contacts with the wider world. The Air Training Scheme provided valuable immigration publicity for the small white community. Officers and men built contacts with the British armed forces which were to be of great practical and emotional value in the future. In the 1950s and 1960s the settlers constantly played on their contributions to the British war effort to retain British sympathy in the struggle against African nationalism.

Under the stewardship of Godfrey Huggins and in the favourable conditions of the post-war world economy, the colony grew more prosperous and, according to the politicians' rosy speeches, promised to become the jewel of Africa. The armed forces were demobilized, though the RAR was almost immediately resuscitated in 1947, and the Defence Acts of the 1950s reaffirmed the principle of compulsory national service in the Cold War era. The armed forces immediately after the war comprised a permanent staff of white officers and NCOs to command and administer the Rhodesian African Rifles as the regular core, the 1st and 2nd Battalions of the Royal Rhodesian Regiment as the European reserve component, and the Royal Rhodesian Air Force.

Huggins steered Southern Rhodesia into federation with Northern

Rhodesia and Nyasaland in 1953. The southern colony's more powerful economy and larger white population were telling factors in the negotiations over the conditions of federation, and Southern Rhodesia soon dominated this regional political structure. The colony's white population had been almost doubled in the years 1945-53 by Prime Minister Huggins's strenuous efforts to promote white immigration, even at the cost of virtually bankrupting the national exchequer. The Southern Rhodesia forces tended to dominate the federal defence system in the same way as federal politics and the economy were dominated by the Southern Rhodesian political structure. This was encouraged by an undeclared reliance by the British government on Southern Rhodesia as a cornerstone of regional defence policy. Yet this period of Rhodesian history was full of paradoxes. As the defence system broadened the scope of its operations and its horizons, the threat to internal security again grew prominent. As early as the 1920s a great deal of talk about 'Bolshevik' influence percolated among Rhodesian blacks. Units of the settler defence forces had exercised against mock attacks by columns of African insurgents led by white Bolshevik agitators. In 1927 the Shamva miners' strike pointed to a new era of protracted political struggle in the territory. African nationalism had been given a boost by the service of thousands of Africans alongside whites all over the world during the Second World War and by the democratic idealism of the Atlantic Declaration. The Bulawayo general strike by Africans in 1948 firmly launched the rise of post-war African nationalism in the colony. Legislation such as the Native Land Husbandry Act of 1951, which introduced specific restrictions on African land use and compulsory destocking of overgrazed pastures, merely provided a focus for African discontent. The Federation was supposed to bring the emergence of racial 'partnership', with blacks rising to an ill-defined position of quasi-equality at some undetermined date in the future. But Africans had little faith in the Federation and its professed prescriptions for racial harmony. Huggins unintentionally parodied the whole idea with his description of partnership as that of 'horse and rider', with Africans being supervised and guided by paternalistic whites.

In common with those in other British colonies, Rhodesian blacks followed their own path, and the first modern African nationalist party, the Southern Rhodesia African National Congress, was formed in 1957 and passed into the leadership of Joshua Nkomo, who for decades claimed the title of father of the nationalist movement. Rather like the irresistible meeting the immovable, the powerful welling of African discontent clashed head-on with the intransigence of the whites, and the result was an explosion of violence. The white response was to eliminate those elements in their own political structure which favoured reform and to curb African political activity. At first the whites held the whip hand, but the mushrooming of nationalism throughout Africa and the rest of the colonized world, and in particular nationalist eruptions in Northern Rhodesia and Nyasaland, forced the whites into beleaguered isolation. British will to contain the spread of nationalist movements and the demands for decolonization had evaporated, and the nationalist parties north of the Zambezi called for the dismemberment of the Federation as part of their own demands for independence.

Faced with a looming internal and external crisis, the white response was to resort to greater coercion and to expand the armed forces. Counter-insurgency (COIN) training had already begun in the early 1950s when members of the Far East Volunteer Unit returned home after their combat tour in Malaya. More emphasis was placed on internal security training for all units. The emphasis on COIN training continued to grow in the late Fifties. Sir Roy Welensky, the federal prime minister, commissioned a federal government study in late 1958 to survey the strategic situation south of the Sahara. Welensky drew apocalyptic conclusions from the report. He pointed to 'the stark fact that the battle for Africa was already on', and that 'a vast power vacuum was created, which the communists were only too willing to fill'. His alarm at 'the communist menace' was to be the keynote of white Rhodesian perceptions of African nationalism for the next two decades.

The Royal Rhodesian Air Force acquired more sophisticated aircraft: Canberra light bombers were delivered in 1959 and Hawker Hunter fighters and Alouette III helicopters in 1962-4. Three additional European Territorial battalions were formed. In 1961 all European males aged eighteen to fifty were registered for emergency call-up into the Territorial Force if necessary. The political and financial neglect of the armed forces of the 1950s was swept away by the winds of change in Africa, and rearmament was stepped up to a feverish pace.

A symbol of the nature of the conflict was the creation in 1961 of an all-white component of the regular forces 'to strike the balance between the European and African units'. In an era of African nationalism the white settlers were no longer prepared to entrust their security to black (and conceivably disloyal) regular troops and a weak white Territorial force. Recruits into 'No. 1 Training Unit' were formed into the Rhodesian Light Infantry, a squadron of the Special Air Service and an armoured car unit. Rhodesian units continued their close links with the British armed forces, but the final parting of the ways with Britain was coming. In a portent of future political alignments, elements of the Royal Rhodesian Air Force (RRAF) exercised with the South African Air Force in the Republic of South Africa in 1962. The Sharpeville massacre of 1960 and the growing apparatus of apartheid had made South Africa an international pariah. Rhodesia was on its way to joining it.

Nkomo's ANC survived repeated bannings to re-emerge under different names (as the National Democratic Party, and later as the Zimbabwe African People's Union and People's Caretaker Council), and the collapse of the Federation would clearly not be far behind the imminent achievement of independence by Nyasaland (as Malawi) and Northern Rhodesia (as Zambia). The rejection by African nationalists of the proposed 1961 constitution, which for the first time offered a significant degree of African participation in national politics, was followed by further bannings and eruptions of violence in Southern Rhodesia's urban areas. Africans called the outbreaks *Zhii,* an emotive word implying desperate and frustrated violence. But the victims were mainly blacks, and the European response was to stiffen their own resistance to political reform.

Legislation like the Law and Order Maintenance Act (1960), which gave the government sweeping powers for the control of political opposition and laid down draconian penalties for politically motivated crimes, and the election of the Rhodesian Front - which was committed to white supremacy - in Southern Rhodesia in December 1962, symbolized white determination to resist African political aspirations. The Congo debacle and the flood of traumatized Belgian refugees further stiffened white resolve.

When the Federation was dissolved at the close of 1963 and Zambia joined Malawi as independent majority-ruled nations, the federal defence structure was also demolished. African nationalists tried to persuade Britain to take command of the Southern Rhodesian forces to deprive the settlers of the means of resisting a possible Whitehall imposition of majority rule in the country. But Britain allowed the Rhodesian armed forces to become autonomous once again. Most of the Royal Rhodesian Air Force remained in Southern Rhodesian hands, and much other military equipment was grabbed by them.

Rhodesian whites entered 1964 in an isolated and defiant mood, beleaguered from within, their confidence shaken by the dissolution of the Federation and the depletion of their armed forces and population by emigration. The election in Britain of a Labour government, determined to complete the process of decolonization of Central Africa with the achievement of majority rule in Rhodesia, exacerbated the tensions. The independence of Malawi and Zambia were powerful spurs to African nationalism. A Unilateral Declaration of Independence, contemplated as early as 1961, seemed inevitable. White intransigence and African determination created the conditions for a major racial confrontation in southern Africa.

In 1964 the African nationalist parties, in the tradition of fission in African politics, split into two factions: the Zimbabwe African National Union (led by the Reverend Ndabaningi Sithole) and the Zimbabwe African People's Union (led by Nkomo). Both took the fateful decision to go into exile and to wage a campaign of violence against the whites. Extra-constitutional means had been considered as early as 1960, when a small number of Africans had gone abroad for training in guerrilla warfare. But it was in 1964 that both races felt they had reached the end of the constitutional path to political change. The African nationalists sought their salvation in mobilizing world opinion and fomenting armed insurrection against the white-dominated state. The Europeans sought theirs in a declaration of independence from Britain which would supposedly leave them free to deal as they saw fit with what they felt were their own internal affairs.

In the days before the declaration of UDI on 11 November 1965, units of the Rhodesian army and the Royal Rhodesian Air Force were placed on alert and deployed against a possible internal insurrection. The willingness of the Rhodesian forces to resist a possible British invasion was less clear cut. But Harold Wilson, egged on by the African nationalist parties and a large bloc in the United Nations, might have countenanced such a scenario. Although the Rhodesian forces prepared to face it, most senior officers hoped that their oaths of loyalty to the Crown would not be tested. In late 1964 the General Officer Commanding the army, Major General J. Anderson, had spoken out against talk of the 'unconstitutional' act of UDI. He had been 'retired' on the grounds of age. In 1965 only the Commissioner of Police was strongly for UDI; senior officers of the army and air force opposed the idea of resisting an armed British intervention. Rhodesian intelligence reported that only some middle-ranking officers of the RLI could be relied on to resist the British and that their (mainly South African) troops would follow suit. UDI was a gigantic bluff. While there is no doubt that an African rising would have been crushed, an invading British expeditionary force could have brought the swift collapse of the rebellion.

In the event, the British government rejected the option of an invasion. Ian Smith's Rhodesian Front government had deliberately set the date for

11 November 1965, Armistice Day, to rally the ghosts of Rhodesia's past war efforts for the crisis. And in that no British invasion ensued, the ploy worked. But the Unilateral Declaration of Independence was more than an attempt by the Smith government to grasp an illusory freedom of political action - it was an unintentional declaration of civil war.

*Chapter 3*

# The 'Second *Chimurenga*' – Internal and International Dynamics

The very nature of the act of rebellion against the Crown – UDI, the unilateral or, to its critics, the illegal, declaration of independence in 1965 – is still debated. For the white Rhodesians, it was, in retrospect, a colossal blunder. The self-governing British colony of Southern Rhodesia was practically independent in all but name. That had been the case since 1923. Provided the right kind of constitutional verbiage could have been conjured up, both Labour and Conservative administrations in London would have been happy to remove that colonial albatross from their neck. If Ian Smith, the Rhodesian prime minister, had been half as cynical as some of the British politicians he dealt with, he could have agreed to any legal wording, secured Rhodesian independence and then torn up the agreement. But his Rhodesian Front Party wanted more than a legalization of the status quo; it was committed to achieving full sovereignty so as to turn the clock back.

Whatever the moral and political arguments, Britain did not use force to crush the rebellion. There is little doubt now that after a few resignations here and there, the Army, the Royal Navy and even the Royal Air Force (supposedly the most disaffected service) would have carried out any orders to subdue the first national treason against the Crown since the American War of Independence. On the Rhodesian side, UDI was a military bluff. The bluff, though, was never called. That master tactician, Prime Minister Harold Wilson, threw away his best cards by renouncing force at the outset. He opted for sanctions instead. Threatening 'to throw the book' at the Rhodesian Front, he simply flicked a few pages ... one at a time. Sanctions were a gesture, never a concerted policy. Until 1974 they boosted rather than undermined the rebel colony. Sanctions failed to end the war in 'weeks rather than months', as Wilson had promised, for a number of reasons. Above all, they were applied slowly, halfheartedly and cynically. Britain, for one, kept on supplying oil (indirectly) to the rebels. Washington made a point of trading in strategic materials, especially chrome. The Soviet bloc accounted for more than half of Rhodesia's illicit deals, as Ken Flower, the

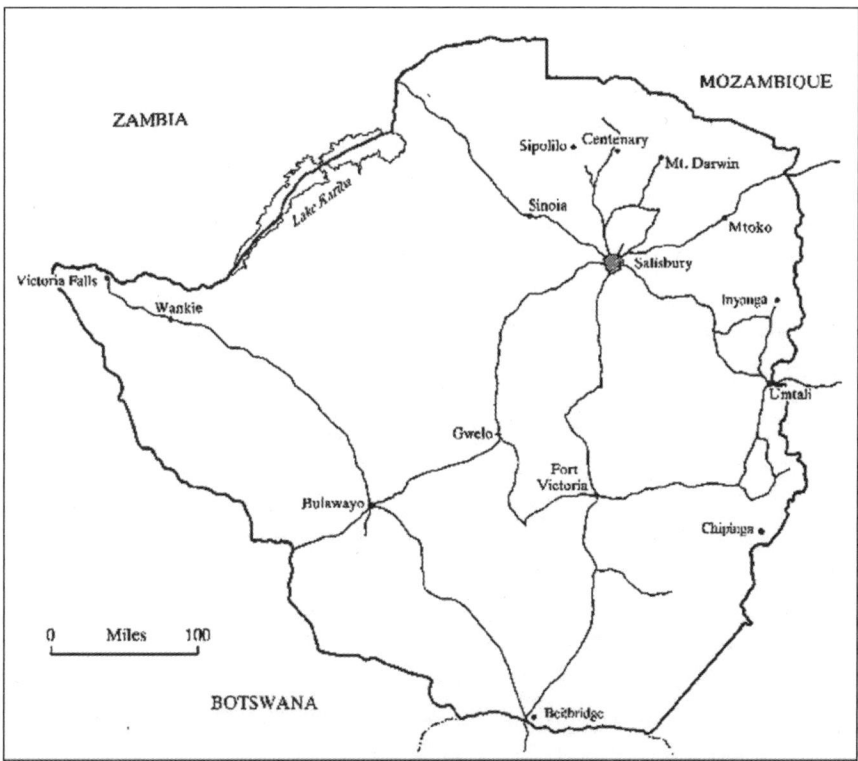

Map 2 – Rhodesia

head of Rhodesia's Central Intelligence Organization (CIO), made clear in his memoirs. Many of these transactions were arranged through pliant companies in Austria, West Germany, Switzerland and Belgium. Heavy machinery came from the East, usually in shipments brought by Yugoslavs who had no qualms about flying to Salisbury, as long as their passports were not stamped. As one Rhodesian Special Branch officer involved with these deals noted: 'Slavs were popular with [Rhodesian] immigration officers because they inevitably brought gifts of plum brandy and offered around cigarettes of heavily scented tobacco.'

The most important sanctions-breakers, however, were the South Africans. This led to the greatest paradox of the Rhodesian war. Rhodesia broke away from Britain to avoid black rule and then, with the onset of the guerrilla war, became completely dependent upon a South African regime which was even more determined than Britain to establish a black leader in Salisbury. Above all, the South African government dreaded the possibility of a victorious Marxist army marching through the streets of Salisbury, a precedent which it feared might be repeated in Pretoria. Rhodesia transformed itself from a self-governing British colony into an occasionally truculent, but inevitably subservient, sector of Afrikaner imperium. Pretoria selfishly manipulated its Rhodesian satrapy (while making a huge profit on sanctions-breaking to the captive rebel market) by providing just enough military support to allow Smith time to reach the elusive 'settlement' with black 'moderates'. This policy totally backfired and merely served to lengthen the savage war.

Until 1973 Britain tried hard to settle with Salisbury. In each settlement proposal London offered more concessions. In his administrations in the 1960s and 1970s, Harold Wilson was torn by what he termed his four 'constituencies': the Conservatives, the Commonwealth, the United Nations and South Africa. The inevitable compromises that ensued gave Wilson's policies 'that madcap flair', in the words of the American ambassador to Zambia. The end result was an impasse: no force, no confrontation with South Africa and no 'sell-out'. The inherent contradictions meant more leaky sanctions and growing white Rhodesian intransigence. Thus ensued the long diplomatic melodrama punctuated by angry encounters on ships, foolish estimates and silly superlatives. These negotiations gave Smith credibility at home and some respectability abroad. Meanwhile, Pretoria played a subtle game until 1978, when the Prime Minister, P. W. Botha, risked nearly all to back the so-called 'internal settlement', with Bishop Abel Muzorewa playing the role of 'useful idiot', to use a Marxist phrase.

In 1965, few of the key players in the Rhodesian saga foresaw the main elements of the unfolding Greek tragedy. Not only was black rule inevitable, but it was almost inevitable that, once they were allowed to get away with UDI, Rhodesian whites were unlikely to accept that fate without a considerable struggle. That struggle was bound to be prolonged, if, firstly, the black nationalist movement were to become divided, and, secondly, international pressures, especially sanctions, were not comprehensively applied. Black nationalists spent as much time arguing or even fighting each other as combating Smith's troops, and Pretoria made a political point of circumventing sanctions to show that an even larger possible set of sanctions against apartheid would not work. In the 1970s comprehensive sanctions against South Africa in addition to those on Rhodesia were not on the main political agenda.

And so the Rhodesian saga was to be decided largely on the battlefield. The war can be divided into three stages: from UDI to 1972, the small Rhodesian security forces were engaged in a conflict they could have won decisively in military terms; from 1972 to 1976, it could be described as 'no-win' war; and from 1976 to 1980 the Rhodesians were sucked into a war they were manifestly losing. If the Lancaster House talks had not intervened, military defeat hovered around the corner for white Rhodesia.

The military reasons for white Rhodesia's long survival were essentially threefold: nationalist divisions, the operational efficiency of the Rhodesian forces and massive South African support, particularly in the last phase of the fighting. The South Africans first intervened in 1967, when they sent approximately 2,000 members of the South African Police (SAP) to help guard the northern border with Zambia. Policemen were sent for two reasons. Salisbury always insisted that it was counteracting a criminal conspiracy by external communist-inspired agitators, not an internal civil war against racial injustice, and, secondly, Pretoria did not initially contribute army units as this could have been construed as a military intervention in a British colony.

Rhodesia's senior commanders were hostile to this intercession, but they were firmly told by Smith that the South Africans were needed for political as much as military reasons. Often ill-trained, overconfident and bored, many of these policemen performed abysmally. Until a number of them were killed by the guerrillas, their operations assumed 'a holiday ramp atmosphere', according to Rhodesian observers. Their reluctant allies used to call the South African Police contingents 'clumpies' because of their poor bushcraft. Eventually the Rhodesians were issued with explicit orders not to call their allies by disparaging names. (Presumably an order ignored as much as the later official instructions to the Rhodesian Special Air Service to desist from referring to their own Combined Operations HQ as the 'Muppet Show'.)

The South Africans rapidly learnt, however, for they were in Rhodesia to improve their own counter-insurgency skills as much as 'to pull their neighbour's chestnuts out of the fire', as their prime minister, John Vorster, put it. Vorster used this force as a political lever. In 1975 he recalled the police (but left his pilots and helicopters on loan), as a part of his detente exercise with black nationalist leaders such as Kenneth Kaunda. Then, in 1976, during the American peace initiative led by Henry Kissinger, Vorster played a major role in bringing Smith to heel. Tying Smith down, confessed Vorster, was 'like trying to nail jelly to a wall'. But the Afrikaner did just that when he cut off nearly all military shipments to Smith. Rhodesian troops in the field were sometimes reduced to a few days' supplies of ammunition. In this sense, Vorster did as much as Robert Mugabe to break the Rhodesian fighting spirit. Pretoria feared that an escalation of the war would prompt direct Cuban and Russian involvement, just as happened later in the Angolan war.

So Smith was compelled to utter the unsayable and accept majority rule (though he never defined the term). White morale slumped. But the ensuing conference in Geneva collapsed and Vorster resumed military aid. More pilots and equipment were loaned, particularly aircraft such as Alouettes and Canberras which, because they were in both Rhodesian and South African arsenals, could be passed off as Rhodesian weapons. One of the most vital forms of assistance was the loan of army signallers, who formed 'V Troop'. This unit eavesdropped on nearly all the guerrilla and host states' intelligence and military communications. P. W. Botha, as the South African defence minister, had always tried to back Ian Smith to the hilt, but Vorster and particularly his *eminence grise*, the intelligence chief Hendrik van den Bergh, spiked some of Botha's more adventurous plans to intervene in Rhodesia, as well as in Angola and Mozambique. When Botha became prime minister in September 1978, South African equipment and troops (often in Rhodesian uniform) poured in. Large South African helicopters (the French-supplied Pumas) and the crack Reconnaissance Commandos took part in Rhodesian cross-border raids ('externals' in Rhodesian parlance), especially against guerrilla bases in Mozambique. In raids elsewhere, against Zambia and Angola, South African Air Force Mirage fighters stood in reserve should Russian- or Cuban-piloted MiGs have intervened. Numerous South African agents also infiltrated Rhodesia, and the local Special Branch was hard-pressed to keep these supposedly allied spies under surveillance. Pretoria also recruited widely to establish an extensive spy network for the time when Zimbabwe became independent.

The stage was now set for a rapid increase in the tempo of the war. The Cubans had indeed prepared a conventional invasion plan for Russia's protégés, Joshua Nkomo's army, based in Zambia. Nkomo's better-trained troops formed, with Mugabe's guerrillas, the Patriotic Front alliance which was dedicated to destroying white minority rule.

By mid-1979, 95 per cent of Rhodesia was under martial law. In effect, the senior generals, led by Lieutenant General Peter Walls, who had served in the Black Watch, and the CIO's Ken Flower, a genial Cornishman, were running the country behind the facade of the new prime minister, Bishop Muzorewa. The bishop had emerged victorious from the elections of April 1979, which had been boycotted by the Patriotic Front. Ian Smith, however, was still in the cabinet, as minister without portfolio, or 'Minister with all the Portfolios', as Nkomo dubbed him. Hardliners in the Rhodesian Front still insisted that the war could be won militarily; under Muzorewa the raids on the neighbouring states were intensified, but already large swathes of the country could only be entered by the security forces in strength.

No formal liberated areas existed inside Rhodesia, but government infrastructure – schools, clinics, animal dip-tanks and local government – had been wiped out in the more isolated 'native reserves' or Tribal Trust Lands, where most of the approximately six million Africans lived. Guerrilla commissars, especially in eastern Rhodesia, along the long porous border with Mozambique, were building up rudimentary administrative systems to support Mugabe's ZANU party. The Marxist government in Mozambique fully backed Mugabe and sent in at least 500 Mozambican regular troops to assist ZANU inside Rhodesia. White power was being swamped by the sheer numbers of the guerrillas. As one member of the elite Selous Scouts put it, after a major raid into Mozambique in 1979: 'We knew then that we could never beat them. They had so much equipment and there were so many of them. They would just keep coming with more and more.'

Short of international recognition and the removal of sanctions, Muzorewa's shaky government, controlled and protected as it was by the Rhodesian security forces, could not have survived for perhaps more than another year. Only massive South African military intervention could have propped it up, but that might have prompted the kind of Eastern bloc conventional assault that so concerned Pretoria (and Washington). The South African government never recognized the Smith or Muzorewa regimes, nor did any other state. The vital factor was always British recognition. Despite the fact that a Conservative observer group officially acknowledged the fairness of the April 1979 election, the new British prime minister, Margaret Thatcher, refused to accord diplomatic recognition to Muzorewa's government. That was the bishop's death knell.

At the ensuing Lancaster House Conference Muzorewa was persuaded, despite Smith's adamant opposition, to resign. In December 1979 the well-fleshed Lord Soames took over as governor, the first time in the long imperial recessional that a white colonial official had replaced a black African president. Senior security officials such as Walls and Flower had played an important part in persuading the Rhodesian politicians that the war was lost and that only a political compromise could forestall defeat. Behind the scenes they played a vital national and international role in forging a settlement, despite the last-ditch opposition of Rhodesian Front politicians. In this paradoxical sense, military intervention was required to maintain the Clausewitzian paradigm of civilian supremacy.

Walls and Flower, despite their mutual personal antagonism, ensured that the Lancaster House Agreement remained in force throughout the difficult period of the ceasefire and, finally, Mugabe's overwhelming electoral victory. Smith was shunted aside, while Walls and Flower played at being diplomats in London, South Africa and Mozambique. Then came the final test of their politicking: the prevention of the alleged coup in March 1980. Despite the fact that many bitter Rhodesian soldiers and policemen still believe that an elaborately planned coup was aborted, in fact there was no formal *coup de main* waiting for the blue touch-paper to be lit. There were several contingency plans to prevent a pre-emptive assault by Mugabe's men and another one to annihilate the ZANU guerrillas in their ceasefire assembly points should they have refused to accept the verdict of the February 1980 elections. Such plans would have included the active support of the South Africans and the presumed passive assistance of Mugabe's ally and rival, Nkomo, whose guerrillas were not a target. But there does not appear to be any evidence that the Rhodesians deliberately planned to stage a coup to stop Mugabe from winning. The official intelligence line, despite warnings from Special Branch to the contrary, was that Mugabe would not win a majority of seats. Contingency schemes existed for bogus ballot boxes to be stuffed with pro-Muzorewa ballots and a number of semi-official assassination operations were planned or activated to kill Mugabe, including one at Lancaster House. But no elaborate coup plot emerged, for the simple reason that nearly every Rhodesian decision-maker firmly believed that Mugabe would not win, and nor would the British let him. They were convinced that London had concocted the ABM plan: 'Anybody But Mugabe'. When he did win, many Rhodesians felt utterly betrayed. They argued that the elections had been fraudulent, mainly because of the massive intimidation. Full details of such charges came a little later. Immediately after the election results, Walls stood very firm against unconstitutional action.

In April 1980 Zimbabwe became independent. A right-wing Conservative prime minister had caused, probably by accident, the first electoral triumph of a Marxist in Africa. White Rhodesians had hated Wilson in the 1960s, now their loathing was focused on Thatcher's foreign secretary, the peer who had stage-managed the Lancaster House marathon: Lord Carrington. To many Rhodesians, Lancaster House and the following elections had been a stab in the back, another Munich. They had not been defeated, but cheated. Carrington was a second Chamberlain. According to the Rhodesian assistant secretary of defence, Carrington had separately and definitively promised both Mugabe and Muzorewa that London unofficially supported each man. 'In Carrington's view,' the defence official said, 'the only way to stop the fighting was to hand over to Mugabe. It was a convenient way of getting rid of the problem. It was dishonest, immoral ... but effective.'

With hindsight, however, it could be argued that Carrington's diplomacy was astute: the main contenders in the election acquiesced in the British-supervised programme only because each man was convinced he could win. Nevertheless, it was ironic that a namesake, Major General Sir Frederick Carrington, had presided over the consolidation of white power in Rhodesia in 1896, after the first *Chimurenga*. What one Carrington gave, another took away. Or such was the judgement of white conservatives in Rhodesia. In another perspective, Lancaster House had ended the war and perhaps saved white Rhodesians from the worst excesses of their own folly.

White Rhodesia had been a well-armed suburb masquerading as a country. The whites had numbered, at their peak, just 275,000. They had spat into the winds of change and the rebellion was terminated after much bloodshed. But the Rhodesians were not defeated militarily, although they would have been, despite their operational ingenuity. The history of the Rhodesian armed forces is one of tactical brilliance and strategic ineptitude. Rarely in military chronicles have such thinly-stretched troops, hampered by chronic manpower, training, equipment and financial constraints achieved such consistent successes against enemy forces which enjoyed the tactical and strategic initiative for most of the war, and often reached numerical parity in the field. But the Rhodesian obsession with successful operational techniques created a fatal blindness to the strategic and political imperatives required to counter a protracted insurgency. The initial aim of the war was to prevent the passing of power to any black government, no matter how moderate. An admission of racism, if only within the high command and cabinet, might have produced a more coherent grand strategy, but no clear political programme – beyond a vague preservation of the status quo – was ever articulated. Rhodesian grand strategy, such as it was, was shot through with a fatal negativism. There was little faith in far-reaching reform as a war-winner. Such a recognition, of course, would have undermined the very reasons for the war ever being fought at all. White Rhodesians struggled long and hard against the only thing which could have avoided war – African participation in national politics. To change horses in midstream was extremely difficult, but the Rhodesians did try it: the war shifted from a confrontation with the principle of black majority rule to a war for the sort of black government white Rhodesians were prepared to live under: a Muzorewa-led internal settlement. But once the principle of having any kind of majority rule at all was conceded, the Rhodesians' war aims became increasingly confused and their strategy consistently weaker.

Faced with the inner weaknesses of their strategies, the Rhodesians resorted to more and more desperate measures. The policy of winning 'hearts and minds' was largely abandoned in the field just as the first moves towards a political strategy of a moderate black government were coming to fruition. Perversely, it was considered that black participation to the political process would permit tougher, war-winning operations. Martial law was extended, the punitive destruction of villages and livestock of those who were accused of aiding the guerrillas became routine and a more aggressive external strategy was adopted. As one senior officer at Combined Operations admitted: 'We relied 90 per cent on force and 10 per cent on psychology and half of that went off half-cocked. The guerrillas relied 90 per cent on psychology and only 10 per cent on force.' The insurgents had a clear vision of their purpose: to break the back of white supremacy and establish a black majority government. This gave the guerrillas remarkable stamina and their cause the strength to weather numerous political crises and almost consistent military defeat in the field. The apparent simplicity of the guerrilla objectives did, however, mask enormous confusion and conflict as to how to achieve those objectives. At times, dissension among the nationalists was far more potent than the firepower of the Rhodesians in delaying majority rule. Nevertheless, despite being clothed in the ferocious Asian garb of a people's war, the guerrillas accomplished what Marxists would term a 'bourgeois nationalist revolution'.

After the war some Rhodesians insisted that the war had been winnable. They asserted that detente in the mid-1970s had been mere appeasement, that the nationalists released from detention, especially Mugabe, should have been indefinitely imprisoned or shot, and that the guerrilla bases in the frontline states should have been obliterated in the early 1970s. 'War is war,' argued the diehards, 'so why didn't we bomb Lusaka or do a "dam-buster" on the massive Cahora Bassa dam and knock out Mozambique in one single blow?' Such an escalation depended upon the wholehearted support of Pretoria which was never forthcoming. Any successful long-term containment of the guerrillas would have been dependent upon diplomatic recognition and military aid from the West. Yet that would never have been given to a white-dominated government. If a plausible political solution – perhaps an assertive Muzorewa administration in 1976 – had been gracefully conceded by the Rhodesian Front, then Anglo-American military backing might have led to a defeat of the Patriotic Front, if the guerrillas had chosen to fight on. But, in the pattern of all colonial wars, the Rhodesians always gave too little, far too late.

Sanctions, too, played a part in the rebels' defeat, albeit a secondary one to the pressure of the guerrilla war. Initially, economic constraints were merely a nuisance: shortages of razor blades, ladies' stockings and good whisky resulted; and the Salisbury Club ran out of port for the first time since 1896. By the late 1970s sanctions were undoubtedly biting. They did contribute to winding down the morale of the whites and prompting emigration, thus draining the life-blood of white military manpower.

Most of the consequences of sanctions were unintended. While privileged whites suffered a loss of perhaps ten Rhodesian dollars per capita per annum, most of the hardships were shifted on to the poorest blacks, particularly in the Tribal Trust Lands and the neighbouring black states. Sanctions polarized the political spectrum: whites became more intransigent; but, similarly, black peasants became radicalized as they slipped deeper into poverty and into the propaganda grip of the guerrillas. The incomplete sanctions against Rhodesia generated international credibility and legitimacy for the liberation movements, created a more radicalized peasantry, and thus, in the longer term, inspired the conditions for the victory of the most revolutionary black contender for power, a far cry from making the whites bend the knee in a few months as Harold Wilson had predicted.

Pretoria, particularly in 1976, was also instrumental in forcing Smith to compromise. War, sanctions, propaganda and Pretoria overwhelmed the rebellion, but its repercussions reverberated throughout southern Africa. Mugabe's accession to power emphasized the basic tenet of pan-Africanism: that Africa could not be truly free until the whole continent was purged of white supremacy. Rhodesia's defeat accelerated Nelson Mandela's release.

## Chapter 4

# Mugabe's Liberation War

*Mugabe – the early years*

It was an inauspicious beginning for a future African leader. Robert Gabriel Mugabe was born on 24 February 1924, near Katuma Jesuit Mission in the Zvimba district, about sixty miles northwest of what was then Salisbury, Southern Rhodesia. Both his parents were Roman Catholics: his parentage and good education were to inculcate in the young Mugabe a sense of mission, discipline and love of learning. His father was Malawian and his mother, Bona, was a Shona. (She later lived to almost reach her century, a sobering thought for those whose sole current policy is to wait for Mugabe to die in office.) He was the third of six children. One of his older brothers, Michael, was very popular in the village, whereas young Gabriel Mugabe was a bookworm and a loner. Both his older brothers died when he was young. The Malawian father abandoned his family in 1934 to go in search of work in Bulawayo. Perhaps this encouraged Robert Mugabe's solitariness and sense of self-sufficiency. Mugabe was ten when his father left, and he took on a self-perceived role as head of the family. He attended Mass every day with his mother, and twice on Sunday. His mother constantly told him he would be a special child, blessed by God. Initially she had wanted him to be a priest.

Without overplaying the psychological impact of Mugabe's childhood, it is important to understand his obvious absorption of the prime Jesuit principle – only self-discipline can allow a person to triumph over adversity. Self-discipline was a constant feature of Mugabe until late in life when absolute power turned his original virtue into utter self-indulgence.

Mugabe studied in Marist Brothers and Jesuit schools, including Katuma College, which had a fine local record for scholarship. There the priests, particularly an Irishman, Father Jerome O'Hea, took a keen interest in the bright young boy. Despite his teachers' encouragement, he continued to prefer his own company. His surviving brother, Donato, later admitted that his brother's only friends were books (though occasionally the young scholar did enjoy playing tennis). In 1945 he left St Francis College, Katuma, having

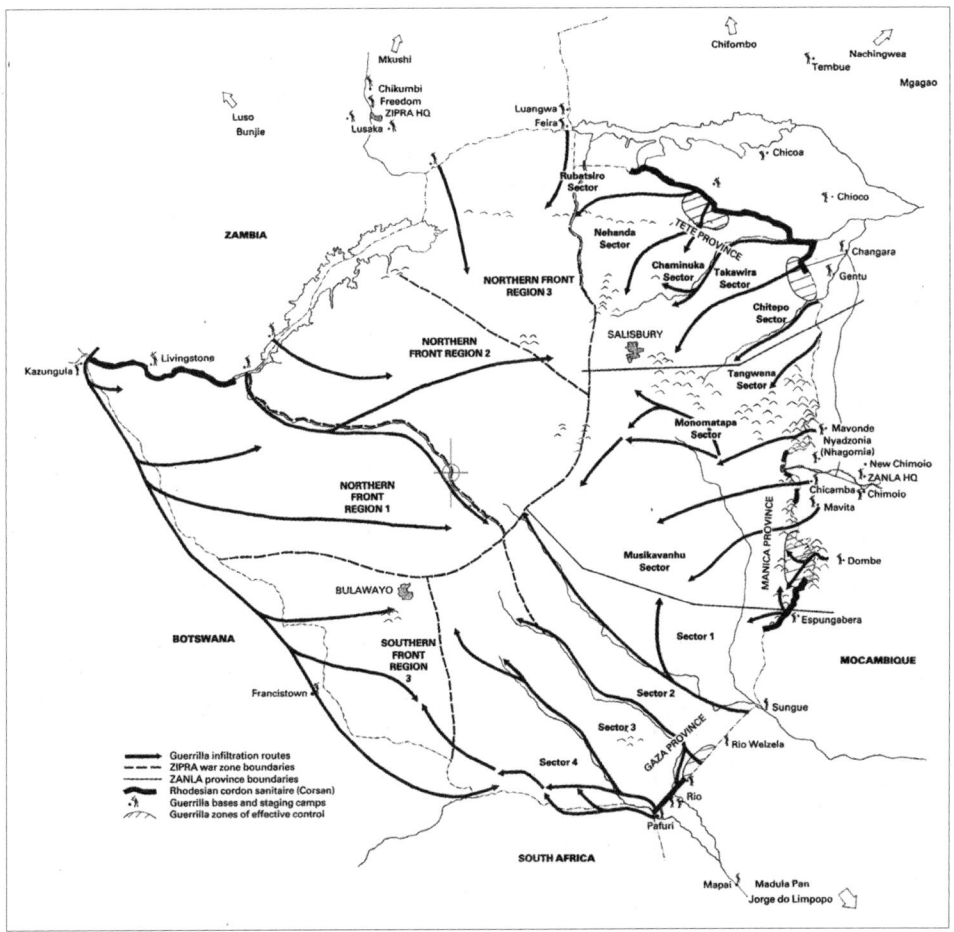

Map 3 – Guerrilla Infiltration Routes

qualified as a teacher. In 1949, he secured a scholarship to study at the University College of Fort Hare in South Africa. There he got to know, or know of, future leaders such as Julius Nyerere, Herbert Chitepo and Kenneth Kaunda. He graduated with his first degree in 1951. He studied further and taught in Southern Rhodesia, Tanzania and Zambia. Mugabe spent most of 1958-1960 in Ghana, teaching at a secondary school. He was influenced by Ghana's fiery, idealistic and hopelessly utopian prime minister, Kwame Nkrumah. Mugabe was also influenced by the charming and much more down-to-earth Sally Hayfron, who became Mrs Mugabe in 1961. Many of Mugabe's close associates maintain that it was Sally who kept him grounded – she was always prepared to speak her mind in private to her husband. She was also said by one biographer to have put 'iron in his soul'. Her death from liver failure in 1992 removed a powerful source of commonsense from the leader's coterie of place-men.

In 1960, almost by chance, Mugabe gave his first political speech while he was on holiday in Southern Rhodesia. He joined the National Democratic Party, then headed by Nkomo. Mugabe's intellectual and rhetorical gifts led to his promotion as the NDP's publicity secretary. In 1961, the NDP was banned and ZAPU (the Zimbabwe African People's Union) took its place. Because of police pressure, ethic distinctions and the traditional pattern of splits in early African national movements, as well as ideological disparities, Mugabe left ZAPU to join ZANU (the Zimbabwe African National Union) in 1963. The leading light in ZANU then was the Reverend Ndabaningi Sithole, destined to be Mugabe's bitter rival in later years. Sithole nominated Mugabe as the party's general secretary.

Later, especially during the war against the white government, ZAPU and ZANU were characterized by ethnic rivalries between Ndebele and Shona. This was exaggerated by Rhodesian Front propaganda, but there was certainly more than an important element of truth in the claims. Sufficient numbers of cross-cutting tribal allegiances in the parties' leadership emerged to dilute stark ethnic labels, especially in the early days. Arguably, clan politics *within* the broad definition of Shona people were as influential as the somewhat simplistic descriptions of Shona-Ndebele splits.

ZANU was influenced by the Africanist ideals of men like Nkrumah and parties such as the Pan-Africanist Congress in South Africa. Maoism was also attractive, as an ideology, and later China was a practical source of training and weapons' supplies. In contrast, ZAPU developed more orthodox communist ties with the USSR, Cuba and the African National Congress in South Africa. The differing ideologies and foreign patronage were soon to have a major impact on both the politics and the military structures of the two main Zimbabwean nationalist parties.

In 1964 Mugabe was detained for a so-called 'subversive speech'. He was to spend the next eleven years in prison. He was moved from Salisbury prison, then to Wha Wha near Gwelo and then Sikombela. Mugabe's leadership credentials were tested and honed in prison. He studied hard for further degrees by correspondence, including a law degree from London and a bachelor of administration from the University of South Africa. In 1966 Mugabe's three-year-old son, Nhamo, died of encephalitis in Ghana; Mugabe was denied permission to attend the funeral.

Mugabe was understandably distraught. His own father had left him to fend for himself, and now his political ambitions had recreated the same conditions: he had spent only a few days with his own child. After a period of intense depression, Mugabe returned to his role of perpetual student, and teacher. In prison he acted as a headmaster to help teach his fellow prisoners to improve their literacy and general education.

The prison conditions, both in the capital Salisbury and in an isolated prison in the Rhodesian Midlands, and the refusal of the authorities to allow him to attend his son's funeral, despite his friend Edgar Tekere's solemn written endorsement that Mugabe's moral principles as a nationalist leader would prompt his return to prison, inspired a deep anger beneath the mask of composure demanded by his iron self-discipline. Mugabe rarely showed how raw were his wounds inflicted by the racism of white rule. In 2005, in a rare admission of his private thoughts, he told the *New African* magazine that 'Memories do pile up, but the most remote ones, especially those which saw us suffer and the times when we were under bondage, under colonial rule, those can never fade away, they remain for ever'.

In 1974, while still in prison, Mugabe was elected to replace the rather shifty and vacillating Ndabaningi Sithole. Mugabe's powerful right-hand man was Edgar Tekere. In the no-confidence vote against Sithole, engineered by Tekere, Mugabe himself abstained from voting. Then, in a strange twist of fate, the apartheid leaders in Pretoria instructed Ian Smith to release some imprisoned nationalist leaders, including Mugabe, in November 1974. This was a time of South Africa's new policy of détente. The freed nationalists travelled to Zambia, where the President, Kaunda, chose to ignore Mugabe, regarded by some nationalists as someone who had arrogantly and illegally upstaged Ndabaningi Sithole.

Mugabe returned to Southern Rhodesia and went underground. In April 1975 Mugabe and Edgar Tekere trekked on foot out of the country to seek refuge in Mozambique. Samora Machel, the new revolutionary leader, was not entirely sure of the status of his new guests; they were placed in 'protective custody' – comfortable but restricted. It was still unclear who was the real leader of Zimbabwean resistance or who was in effective charge of ZANU. In 1975 the charismatic Herbert Chitepo, long the ZANU leader in exile, was assassinated (by Rhodesian agents, although this is much disputed by historians). At the time, Kaunda assumed it was a result of party infighting. Innocent ZANU leaders in Zambia were taken into custody and given a brief though rough ride in prison. Lots of smiling faces, however, adorned Milton Buildings, the home of Rhodesia's powerful Central Intelligence Organization.

It took Mugabe two years in Mozambique to persuade, firstly, President Samora Machel – a former hospital orderly who had taken part in the long insurgency against the Portuguese – that the softly spoken Shona intellectual could head an unruly guerrilla army, even though Mugabe had received no formal military training. Mugabe disliked wearing army fatigues and was patently awkward in the company of his own military commanders. More daunting was the task to persuade the military commanders in ZANLA, the Zimbabwe African National Liberation Army, ZANU's military wing. Ndabaningi Sithole had been sidelined as 'a sell-out', as he moved closer to a deal with Ian Smith and 'internal' nationalist leaders such as Bishop Abel Muzorewa. And Chitepo was dead. Despite some vociferous opposition inside ZANLA, by 1977 Mugabe was not just secretary general of the party, but also de facto commander in chief. Now it was his job to win the war against an increasingly desperate and more aggressive white regime in Salisbury.

*Leading the second Chimurenga*

Mugabe was lucky in that he seized command in 1977 when ZANLA was in the ascendancy, relative to both the white Rhodesian forces and the guerrillas loyal to Nkomo, the Zimbabwe People's Revolutionary Army (ZIPRA). It is vital to understand Mugabe's methods and mindset in the crucial years 1977-80, for they became portents of his role as Zimbabwe's leader after 1980. In particular two points bear emphasis.

Firstly, Mugabe continued to rule independent Zimbabwe as though he were still in command of a politburo which was running a revolutionary army. His security forces remained an instrument of party power.

Secondly, the war was obviously a black national insurgency against white rule, but it was simultaneously a civil war among black Zimbabweans, especially ZANU and ZAPU. This pattern was repeated in the 1980s and after 2000, albeit the later challenge came largely from the Movement for Democratic Change.

It is useful to consider Mugabe's leadership and direction of ZANLA in some detail because it provides a means of making sense of post-independence policies. Mugabe's position in 1977 was that of a man who felt destined to lead, and win. But just a few years before, ZANU and ZANLA had been in dire straits. In the opening round of the insurgency, from 1965 to 1972, the guerrillas had been pounded by the conventional Rhodesian army. In April 1966, for example, a group of twenty-one ZANLA infiltrated from Zambia. Their aim was to attack white farms and cut power lines. One element, seven men who had adopted the inauspicious name of Armageddon group, was surrounded by police on Hunyani farm, near Sinoia. (Rhodesian names will be used in describing events prior to independence in 1980.) Although some of the seven men had been trained at Nanking Military

Academy in China, the unit was wiped out by Rhodesian forces in the first real 'contact' of the war. The so-called 'Battle of Sinoia' now occupies pride of place in the nationalist hagiography and the date 28 April is commemorated as '*Chimurenga* Day'. As it happened, the guerrillas were being fed and co-ordinated by Rhodesian intelligence, so their killing was something of an own goal. And the Rhodesian operation, especially air support, was completely ham-fisted. One Rhodesian officer involved in Sinoia described their involvement as a 'shambles'. He said the guerrilla response was even worse.

Racially arrogant, Rhodesians usually overplayed guerrilla incompetence, terming it disparagingly the 'K factor' ('kaffir' factor). Indeed, the military performance of the guerrillas, particularly in the early stages of the war, was appalling. Both sides learned from their mistakes, however. In the end Rhodesian forces met with fierce resistance and came to repent of their initial under-estimation of the enemy. At Sinoia, however, both sides displayed high levels of military incompetence. Yet the fact that conventional military tactics triumphed over ill-organized guerrilla incursions epitomized the first stage of the war. In short, the insurgents were completely out-gunned. They were also out-maneuvered by far superior military planning and organization.

In August 1967, a combined force of seventy guerrillas from ZIPRA and the South African ANC's *Umkhonto we Sizwe* (MK*)* entered Rhodesia near Victoria Falls. They were on a suicide mission. Told they would be welcomed by the locals, instead their presence was reported immediately to the authorities by local tribesmen. Forty-seven insurgents were killed and twenty captured; the wounded survivors struggled into Botswana, where they were arrested. The ANC involvement prompted more South African support for the white regime in Salisbury. Large-scale conventional incursions were bound to prove futile against highly-trained, mobile troops, backed by total air supremacy. The ZIPRA failures prompted ZANU to condemn the alliance with the ANC as counter-productive, which it surely was. ZAPU responded darkly by hinting that ZANU had tipped off Rhodesian intelligence. This row helped to deepen the divide which led to ZANLA focusing on classic Maoist slow-burn tactics, while ZIPRA remained more committed to the Soviet orthodoxy of preparing for a major conventional assault to seize territory, and later even Rhodesian towns. ZANLA was preparing a long-term campaign to politicize the peasantry and refused to hand the tactical advantage to the Rhodesian security forces, as ZIPRA had done. And the best way to do this was to beef up the training by Chinese instructors.

*Training*

A few ZANU people had received training in China as far back as 1963, and a handful later went to Cuba. But the serious training began in 1969 in Itumbi in southern Tanzania. Later the majority were trained in Mozambique and finally, in the last years of the struggle, basic training was conducted in Rhodesia itself. Training consisted of two phases. The first consisted of physical instruction, political indoctrination and work on basic infantry weapons; the second phase comprised tactics (ambushes, patrol formations etc). Further specialized training followed for the more able recruits.

Administration improved in April 1969, when exiled ZANU members in Lusaka set up an eight-member war council, the *Dare re Chimurenga*. Kaunda was often very frustrated with his guests, especially when ZANLA or ZIPRA press-ganged Zambian citizens or indulged in bar-room punch-ups or even the occasional pitched battles. James Chikerema, a veteran ZAPU leader and Mugabe's cousin, described the ZIPRA camps in Zambia in 1970 as representing 'the depth and height of decay, corruption, nepotism, tribalism, selfishness and gross irresponsibility on the part of the military administration from top to bottom'. In March 1972 Kaunda and other Organization of African Union (OAU) leaders compelled ZANU and ZAPU to unite under the banner of a 'Joint Military Command'. Like most shot-gun weddings, the union was brief and acrimonious. A comment by one senior ZANLA official summed up the divisions with ZAPU: 'We needed rifles; they wanted tanks.'

One of the main weaknesses in ZANU's *Dare re Chimurenga* was the lack of military expertise. Sometimes military commanders in the field were ordered to conduct operations which perhaps made political sense, but were militarily disastrous. What was needed was a thorough strategy to lay the foundations for a classic Maoist protracted war. In 1973, the able ZANLA commander, Josiah Tongogara, joined the *Dare* and injected a stiff dose of military pragmatism. Tongogara was a rising star, whose family had grown up on Ian Smith's farm (he later admitted that the Smiths had treated him well). Yet he also empathized strongly with the many young men and women who had joined the struggle:

> My grievances were based on the question of oppression which I had seen myself, from my parents or from my own people, particularly in the deprivation of land. You know our people are naturally farmers. They like soil. They know that everything is soil. And yet they are deprived of the rich soil in Zimbabwe. This and education.

Tongagara knew that the burning issue in the struggle was a suitable sanctuary. For logistical as well as tribal reasons ZANLA's operations from Zambia were very difficult; Mozambique was the more obvious choice. But the Front for the Liberation of Mozambique (FRELIMO) had long deferred to ZAPU as the senior Zimbabwean liberation movement. Moreover, FRELIMO was itself under serious military pressure from the Portuguese forces (often supported by the Rhodesians) until the Lisbon coup in 1974 suddenly ended their colonial wars in Africa. From the early 1970s, ZANLA started to build up its bases in Mozambique, with increasing support from FRELIMO.

In 1972 the war moved into its second stage. ZANLA troops had built up a widespread underground infrastructure in the north-east of Rhodesia: the local spirit mediums had been won over and the peasants politicized, or intimidated. On 21 December an isolated white farmstead, called Altena, in the Centenary district was attacked. Rex Nhongo was then a commander in the region, called the Nehanda sector by ZANLA. He was later to reach the top of the Zimbabwean military hierarchy. Other farm attacks followed, and the blowing up of security force vehicles by landmines. This was the start of the real shooting war. Salisbury established Operation HURRICANE to repulse the guerrilla drive, which had caught the Rhodesian Front politicians by surprise. Cattle were confiscated by the government as collective fines. Facilities such as clinics and schools were closed in affected areas. Even more counter-productive in psychological terms was the erection of Vietnam-style 'protected villages'. Free-fire zones were also introduced along the Mozambique border. As curfews were extended, the inevitable increase in innocent civilian deaths – the official parlance was 'civilians caught in cross-fire' – made guerrilla recruitment easier.

The harsh government measures did have a short-term military impact. By the end of 1974, Rhodesian intelligence estimated that only seventy to a hundred hardcore guerrillas remained inside the country. But then international events intruded. Portuguese rule collapsed in Mozambique – the whole eastern border of Rhodesia was now vulnerable. And South Africa enforced a (brief) ceasefire as part of its détente policy. Mugabe and other leaders were released from prison to take part in negotiations sponsored by Kaunda and Pretoria. They failed, but the nationalists won a PR triumph – they depicted the Rhodesian ceasefire as a prelude to surrender by the whites.

The nationalists were unable to capitalize on their diplomatic progress; 1975 was a bad year for attempts to unify the struggle. Nationalists became constantly embroiled in what they termed 'the struggles within the struggle'. In December 1974 the Nhari rebellion had erupted within ZANLA. Thomas

Nhari, a senior member of the general staff, kidnapped senior ZANU men in Lusaka, as well as taking over the Chifombo camp on the Mozambique-Zambian border. The mutiny was caused by complaints about lack of sophisticated weapons reaching ZANLA, shortage of supplies and poor administration. About sixty ZANLA personnel were killed in the mutiny, including the ringleader who was executed. In March 1975 Chitepo had been assassinated in Lusaka, by two former British SAS men, working for the Rhodesian CIO. But Kaunda, now utterly enraged by his Zimbabwean guests, especially ZANLA, blamed in-fighting. This led to ZANLA permanently relocating to Mozambique. ZANU was also short of money; ZIPRA was getting nearly all the OAU funding, as well as Zambian and Russian support. Samora Machel, the new Mozambican president, still distrusted Mugabe, regarding his party as a fractious offshoot of the senior party, ZAPU. Kept in loose house arrest, Mugabe gradually won over Machel by his commitment to the armed struggle and his growing support among the fighting cadres.

Gaining the complete backing of FRELIMO was just one of Mugabe's challenges. The idea of a unified ZIPRA-ZANLA was still active. Rex Nhongo of ZANLA and Alfred 'Nikita' Mangena of ZIPRA forged the Zimbabwe People's Army (ZIPA) as a 'third force' in January 1976. ZIPA included volunteers from ZANLA and ZIPRA and was led by an eighteen-member military committee composed of representatives from both forces. From the start, ZIPA was plagued by internecine factionalism; the frontline states wanted it to establish joint, integrated forces, but both Nhongo and Mangena made it clear that ZANLA and ZIPRA would field separate forces albeit under a nominal banner of unity. ZIPA did launch a few offensives into eastern Rhodesia, but the attacks were plagued by mutual mistrust and a failure to coordinate strategy between the two forces. In addition, rumours that the ZIPA High Command were meddling in ZANLA politics prompted Samora Machel to detain a number of ZIPA personnel in August 1976. Mugabe then sent Josiah Tongogara to take charge of the situation. In the ensuing purge in Mozambique, dozens of ZIPA combatants were arrested by FRELIMO and ZANLA; a number were executed for 'putchism' and most of the ZIPRA contingent returned to their home bases in Zambia, occasionally fighting ZANLA detachments along the way. The result of the continued squabbling was a decline in support for ZIPA from the OAU and frontline states as they realized that the two guerrilla armies simply could not work together.

Ian Smith tried to take advantage of the nationalists' disunity by discussing a private deal with Nkomo, though this broke down in March

1976. Mugabe reflected Stalin's Second World War paranoia of his allies conducting a separate peace – he came to loathe Nkomo and not just because of attempts at a 'sell-out' to Smith.

Pretoria's support for Smith began to wane, as South African forces were halted in Angola by Cuban military intervention. Then Smith's clumsy manoeuvres prompted the border closure with Mozambique, compounding his mistake when he closed the Zambian frontier posts in 1973. In August 1976 Smith's forces, expecting a major series of ZANLA offensives from Mozambique, ordered his special forces to attack the Nyadzonya camp, the first of what were later dubbed 'externals'. ZANLA was totally surprised – 1,028 of its personnel were killed, without a single Rhodesian casualty. ZANLA later claimed this attack as the worst atrocity of the war; they insisted it was a civilian refugee camp. From captured documents, it appeared that nearly all the personnel in the camp were indeed unarmed, but many were trained guerrillas or undergoing instruction. Pretoria was incensed by the raid, and cut back on its military support. Salisbury, after the closure of the Mozambican border, was now totally dependent on South Africa for its access to the sea. Pretoria also strong-armed Smith into attending the doomed Geneva conference. Various African nationalist parties attended, including a ZANU-Sithole party as well as Mugabe's ZANU. Mugabe, for the conference, reluctantly formed an alliance with Nkomo under the banner of a 'Patriotic Front'. The best newspaper headline of the time was about Canaan Banana's defection from the UANC, to join Mugabe – BANANA SPLITS. Banana was later rewarded by Mugabe: he became the first president of Zimbabwe (though they later fell out and the president was jailed, *inter alia*, for sodomy and male rape; Mugabe was later to display extreme hostility to homosexuals).

The failure of the Geneva talks led to the final and most bitter stage of Mugabe's war – the final round covering the years from 1977 to the end of 1979. Despite his lack of military skills, Mugabe set about firing up an army which was in disarray and to lead it to victory.

## Structure of ZANLA

In mid-1977 ZANLA had 3,000 guerrillas operating in Rhodesia and ZIPRA not many more than 100 to 200. A year later, ZANLA had 10,000, and at the ceasefire in December 1979, 17,000 of Mugabe's guerrillas reported to assembly points (and many, often the commissars, stayed out). By that stage ZIPRA guerrillas numbered about 20,000, according to ZIPRA intelligence sources disclosed after the war, though many were still scattered for training all over the world. As late as June 1981, 900 ZIPRA cadres were still in

Libya. At the final ceasefire, the two armies had split the country roughly into two equal areas of control, though ZIPRA claimed they had done this with half the number of insurgents under Mugabe's control; ZIPRA areas of operations were, however, more sparsely populated.

The guerrilla armies were in effect far larger than the figures above indicate. The *mujiba* system, which was crucial to the survival of combat guerrillas, encompassed tens of thousands of young people throughout the country. *Mujibas* (the females were called *chimbwidos*) acted as intelligence scouts and messengers for the guerrillas, and in some areas as enforcers of guerrilla discipline meted out to civilians. Towards the end of the war their organization was highly developed. ZANLA *mujibas* boasted a hierarchy which paralleled that of the ZANU parent party (with the president and the treasurer the most important officials) in most villages in eastern Rhodesia. ZANLA claimed 50,000 *mujibas* by 1979, and this was not an unrealistic figure. That number could probably be multiplied several times if the men, women and children who gave occasional but vital assistance to the guerrillas are counted for their contribution to the guerrillas' military effort.

Guerrilla armies are usually young armies. Certainly the unmarried youth welcomed the chance to challenge not only white rule, but also their village elders. Despite official rules stating that fighters, as distinct from *mujibas,* had to be over eighteen, ZANLA records for the post-1980 demobilization and Zimbabwe National Army (ZNA) integration showed that the majority of combatants were in the 16-21 age bracket. Most of these guerrillas were of peasant stock, which fitted the Maoist philosophy of the movement. ZIPRA attracted a much higher percentage of volunteers from a more urban background. Over half of ZIPRA had been employed before joining the insurgents.

ZIPRA training was dominated by the revolutionary theories of the Soviet Union and its satellites. It was the Russians who supplied – with some reservations about its use – ZIPRA's conventional war capability. Rex Nhongo, who became ZANLA's senior commander on the death of Josiah Tongogara in December 1979, had originally trained under ZAPU auspices. In an interview with a British journalist, David Martin, he contrasted his training in the Soviet Union with that under Chinese instructors: 'In the Soviet Union they had told us that the decisive factor of the war is weapons. When I got to Itumbi, where there were Chinese instructors, I was told that the decisive factor was the people.' It is interesting to note how the Soviets had become mesmerized by weapons technology, even in guerrilla warfare, rather like the Americans in Vietnam (and now Afghanistan).

Nevertheless, ZIPRA did wage a guerrilla campaign in western Rhodesia which was not dissimilar to the 'people's war' fought by Mugabe's army. One difference which did stand out was the use of terror in mobilizing mass support; ZIPRA tended to be more selective in its targets and used far fewer of the spectacular disciplinary massacres that ZANLA carried out in the eastern part of the country. ZIPRA did not practise the mass politicization and night-time *pungwes* (indoctrination sessions) because it claimed that it had sufficient local support, nourished by the more extensive branch structure of the older ZAPU organization, although much of it had been driven underground.

ZANLA training emphasized the political indoctrination of recruits. This was not only to entrench their commitment to ZANU but also to equip them for politicizing the African populations among whom they were to operate. In the beginning of the war some units comprised more political commissars than combat cadres. Thereafter the political content of training fluctuated with the conditions of the war. When ZANLA was trying to push large numbers of guerrillas into Rhodesia for specific offensives, training was shortened and political education had to be skimped.

The Marxist orientation of the guerrilla armies was the subject of considerable debate during the war years. The white Rhodesians were unequivocal - to them the guerrillas were either 'communist terrorists' or, at the very least, 'communist-trained terrorists'. Western observers sympathetic to the guerrillas tended to see them as Marxists only for the purpose of gaining from the Eastern bloc the military and other assistance denied by Western governments. The guerrillas themselves added to the confusion in their practice of revolutionary warfare by the addition of elements of their traditional culture.

The works of Marx, Lenin and Mao were the staple fare of guerrilla political education. Nkomo's insurgents paid little attention to Maoist doctrine, but did in practice use some Chinese revolutionary tactics. The Soviet connection meant that Castro's Cuban experience was more important to them. But ZIPRA training throughout the war tended to remain more diverse than ZANLA's, and its theory of guerrilla warfare less precisely formulated. ZANLA doctrine was dominated by Chinese theory and FRELIMO practice. As early as 1970, ZANLA guerrillas fought alongside FRELIMO troops in Mozambique to temper the theoretical training given at Itumbi. By 1978 the works of Mao were ZANLA's bible of guerrilla warfare.

If the Marxist basis of the guerrillas' struggle was sometimes little more than skin-deep, nationalist objectives tended to dominate all political thinking. ZANLA recruits were educated in the 'National Grievances'.

Issues such as land alienation, education, health and welfare discrimination, political oppression, low wages and social inequalities were the staples of the recruits' political diet. ZANLA guerrillas also learnt of their ancestors' risings of 1896-7. A ZANLA document of 1976, which outlined the overall war aims of the guerrillas, claimed that 'the principal objective of our revolution is the seizure of power by means of destruction of the racist political-military machine and its replacement by the people in arms in order to change the existing economic and social order'. Significantly, it made no specific reference to socialist objectives.

While much guerrilla propaganda was heavily larded with the jargon of 'scientific socialism' and spoke of the 'inner contradictions' of the capitalist system in white-ruled Rhodesia, some bizarre contradictions in the guerrillas' organization and thinking were evident. Multi-coloured *'Chimurenga* cloth' was worn by ZANLA guerrillas as scarves. The red in it signified blood, the black was to make the guerrillas invisible to government forces, and the white was to intensify the guerrillas' vision so that they could more easily evade enemy patrols. Items of clothing of these colours were worn for the same purposes. The constant linking of the first *Chimurenga* of the 1890s and the second of the 1970s was somewhat bogus in that the risings and resistance of the early colonial period were backward-looking reactions, not progressive movements for social reform. Nevertheless, the rhetoric of the *Chimurenga* was to run consistently through Mugabe's speeches for the next three decades.

The most glaring contradiction was the embracing of traditional religion by the guerrillas. A spirit medium, Mbuya Nehanda, became a heroine of the guerrillas' struggle. In the early stages of the 'people's war', launched by ZANLA in 1972, she was consulted on a wide range of military and political matters. The names used by spirit mediums could be confusing, especially when rival mediums claimed to be the reincarnation of the same traditional Shona spirits. In 1898, a young woman, Chari, who was reputed to be the medium for the Shona spirit known as Nehanda, was executed by the settlers for incitement to murder during the 1896-7 troubles. Her death, and stoic refusal to convert to Christianity before dying, turned Chari into a martyr of the first *Chimurenga*; hence the significance of her reputed reincarnation for the second *Chimurenga*. While Marx exposed religion as 'the opium of the people', the ZANLA guerrillas saw it not only as an important functional factor in their struggle but personally believed in it. Josiah Tungamirai, who became ZANLA's chief political commissar, the very guardian of the army's political education, was a staunch believer in the powers of mediums. He said: 'Personally I didn't believe in that because I was brought up in the church.' But in time he changed his beliefs and he reported: 'When we wanted to go and open a new operational zone we would have to approach the mediums first.'

These contradictions were exposed by some radical party elements and left-wing critics of the guerrillas' politics. International Trotskyites criticized the *petit bourgeois* origins and attitudes of many of ZANU's leaders, including Mugabe. In 1977, adherents of more radical, socialist ideologies in ZANU attempted a coup against the party leadership. They were branded as 'ultra-leftists' - a Marxist code-word for Trotskyites - by the ZANU leadership.

The early history of the ZANU regime established in April 1980 provided few clues as to the real convictions of the guerrillas and their political leaders. The radical socialist Edgar Tekere was purged from his cabinet post as an embarrassment to the party and Mugabe's government. The capitalist economic system and much of its social infrastructure remained intact. Initially, Mugabe seemed intent on creating a Western-style social welfare state rather than a typical communist economy. By and large it seems that Marxist doctrine had a strong emotional attraction for the guerrillas, that it offered them a straightforward explanation of what had happened historically in Southern Rhodesia, and provided a model for a solution to their struggle. But the guerrillas' adherence to anti-capitalist, anti-Western dogma was pragmatic; they were forced to look to the communist bloc states for guiding principles in the same way as they were compelled to look to them for arms.

## ZANLA strategy

Guerrilla military strategy was in a constant state of flux until the late 1970s. The nationalist politicians and their military wings wrestled with the problems of translating their fluid political ideas, even within the framework of a clear war aim, into a military strategy that would bring about the defeat of the well-armed and motivated government armed forces. The disastrous first phase of conventional, commando-type operations of both ZAPU and ZANU was important in the evolution of the guerrilla strategy which eventually threatened the defeat of the white-led security forces in the field. The 'Battle of Sinoia' was nothing more than a minor skirmish in 1966. It was to be some years before the guerrillas absorbed the lessons of 1966, and similar incursions took place in 1967 and through 1970. The victorious guerrillas later emphasized the symbolic importance of Sinoia for their armed struggle, but they did expect military gains at the same time. Some nationalists later tried to deny this. One commented: 'In purely military terms it must be seen for what it was - a defeat ... That particular battle could in any case not have been won by as small a group of guerrillas surprised and subjected to superior ground and air bombardment.'

What then did the guerrillas hope to achieve? Was this a stage in which the nationalist politicians deliberately sent in suicide squads of guerrillas merely to raise the political temperature of the conflict? It appears that they did not make this sort of cool deliberation and that the group killed near Sinoia was instructed (before being subverted by the CIO) to seize the town and precipitate an insurrection against the government. This was consistent with the diplomacy of the nationalist political exiles who at that time sought to force a British military intervention in the rebel colony. It was also attuned to the dominant influences in the guerrillas' training. The emphasis in Soviet satellites was on the coup type of revolution and on the subsequent consolidation of power. In the 1950s and early 1960s this was bolstered by the success of Castro's revolution.

The conventional strategy of the 1960s has been dismissed by observers of the war, and by the guerrillas themselves, as impractical and futile in the face of Rhodesian conventional superiority. But had the ten years following the debacles of 1966-8 been spent in building up a conventional army equipped with more of the weapons the guerrilla armies deployed in 1978-9 (automatic anti-aircraft weapons, SAM-7 missiles, tanks and field artillery), there might have been a chance of a conventional victory. ZIPRA and the Soviets clearly believed that a time could come when conventional weapons would be vital in the armed struggle and built up a conventional brigade for that decisive stage. (And the Rhodesians, aware of this threat, also trained for conventional war.)

Looked at historically, the guerrillas were probably right in opting for the guerrilla/revolutionary war strategy, but the myth and mystique of the guerrilla should not obscure the alternatives. When it is remembered that North Vietnam conquered South Vietnam only through the conventional invasion of 1975, guerrilla warfare is placed in its proper perspective. And if the Lancaster House settlement had not intervened, would ZANLA or ZIPRA have won power through military means in 1980-1?

There was, however, a strong drift towards 'revolutionary war' among the guerrillas, particularly in ZANLA. In the aftermath of the Geneva conference in 1976, the concept of protracted war became more than a way of reconciling the militarily weaker guerrillas to a long haul. At that time the guerrillas did not want a swift handover of power by the whites. Not only did they need to set their own houses in order and build their armies, but they hoped that a protracted war would sweep away rival nationalist groups which relied on internal political support in Rhodesia. A swift white collapse at that time would have caught the guerrillas unprepared to take control of the whole country or win an election.

From the opening of the guerrilla offensive in the north-east in December 1972 their presence inside Rhodesia was continuous until the ceasefire seven years later. This marked the transition from the earlier commando war of externally-based incursions to guerrilla, revolutionary warfare. The ZANLA objective was to carry out at first as many military actions as possible without jeopardizing the continuity of their presence in the remote region. A year's supply of munitions had been cached in the months preceding the offensive, and nearly all this was consumed before large-scale resupply became possible again in late 1973.

A new cycle of violence emerged. The guerrillas reinforced surviving cadres inside Rhodesia or mounted new offensives at the height of the rainy season (December to February), when covering foliage was at its lushest and water supplies plentiful. Thereafter conditions for guerrilla operations deteriorated, and this was reflected in mounting casualties inflicted by Rhodesian forces. September and October were murderous months for the guerrillas because of the lack of cover and scarcity of water. It was also a highly dangerous period at guerrilla bases outside Rhodesia, for then the guerrilla forces had to be concentrated for the offensives to be mounted with the coming of the rains, and they presented vulnerable targets for enemy raids.

The guerrillas used an 'oil-patch' approach to their campaigns. From 1972 the fringes of ZANLA political influence and organization spread slowly through the TTLs of the north-east, filtering towards the capital. Once safe havens had been established among co-operative civilians, military operations were launched against the government infrastructure in the TTLs or against neighbouring white farmlands. But the potential of the north-east for the guerrillas was limited. The area was remote from the heartland of white power. Whites spoke initially of the war 'on the border' or in 'the Zambezi valley'. As FRELIMO worked southwards inside Mozambique so the invasion front widened, but the security forces were able to seal off the north-east with Operation HURRICANE. A three-year stalemate developed, with the guerrillas unable to break out from the arc of TTLs in the north-east and the Rhodesians unable to eradicate the guerrillas and their political network.

In 1974, Herbert Chitepo, one of the major forces behind ZANLA's adoption of a 'people's war' strategy, wrote:

The strategical [sic] aim ... is to attenuate the enemy forces by causing their deployment over the whole country. The subsequent mobilization of a large number of civilians from industry, business and agriculture would cause serious economic problems. This would have a psychologically devastating effect on the morale of the Whites...

But while the guerrillas were confined to the north-east by the containment strategy of the Rhodesian security forces, ZANLA's capacity to stretch the white economy to breaking point was illusory. The collapse of Portuguese power in Mozambique instantly revolutionized the strategic positions of the opposing armies in the Rhodesian war. The ripping open of the entire eastern flank with the withdrawal of the screen of Portuguese troops was made more catastrophic by the renewal of ZIPRA operations against the country through Botswana. Rarely has the strategic initiative passed so swiftly and so decisively to guerrilla forces.

In early 1976 attacks were launched all along the eastern border. There were minor differences of emphasis in the different parts of the guerrilla front, but the overall strategy was to suck the white government into overstretching their resources to the point where they could no longer hold the entire country. Economic targets and communications links were priorities for attack. Where no permanent interdiction of routes was possible there would be attacks to create a climate of psychological isolation in the white community. The rail line to Beira was a target until the border closure in March 1976. The main road to the south, from Salisbury to Beit Bridge, was ambushed, forcing the government to mount convoys.

Throughout the country 'mobilization of the masses' went on ceaselessly, encompassing more and more districts. Once the initial preparatory phase had been completed, the guerrillas were able to develop more sophisticated strategic concepts. ZANLA worked out a rolling strategic plan - 1977 was the 'Year of the Party', during which ZANU's house was set in order and unity achieved – much of this depended on Mugabe's firmer leadership. And 1978 was the 'Year of the People', in which the party was to become strongly entrenched among the African population; 1979 was the 'Year of the People's Storm', during which the white state and its African allies would become engulfed by the revolutionary struggle; and 1980 would be the 'Year of the People's Power', bringing the collapse of the white-led resistance, the strategic capstone.

In 1978 ZANLA emphasized economic targets, in particular white farmlands and communications links. As the guerrillas became more entrenched within the African population, and government control of rural areas began to break down, so the opportunity to seal off the urban areas presented itself. One guerrilla leader commented: 'Our purpose was to isolate the cities and cut them off, not to attack them. A few well-planned strikes to frighten the white population.' For ZANLA it was the classic Maoist strategy. ZIPRA, because of its Russian influence, paid greater attention to the role of the cities, and in late 1978 announced an urban guerrilla campaign. It was ZANLA, however, which scored the most spectacular urban successes with the blasting of a Woolworth's store in Salisbury and the destruction of the fuel depot in the city's industrial sites.

The urban guerrillas were generally sent in from outside the cities, and their inability to survive the government's informer networks and intelligence work was a constant problem for the development of a sustained urban campaign. The two teachers who planted the Woolworth's bomb were able to escape to Mozambique, but the guerrillas who planted letter bombs in Salisbury post-boxes were captured at a roadblock on the road to Umtali and hanged under martial law. The guerrillas who destroyed the Salisbury oil depot were killed by Rhodesian forces in the Mtoko area. On the whole, urban guerrilla warfare was of greater psychological value than military or economic. As one security force officer said: 'Salisbury was the safest place in the country, but ironically it was the biggest morale headache we had during the war.'

*Propaganda*

The guerrillas waged a far more effective psychological and propaganda war than the white Rhodesians. While the Rhodesians viewed these vital elements of guerrilla warfare as adjuncts to the more important business of killing guerrillas, the nationalists placed a major emphasis on them. The propaganda effort was crucial to, and a natural outgrowth of, the struggle for the political allegiance of the African population. Guerrilla propaganda was simple but effective. White Rhodesians were generally contemptuous of African culture and, although there were training courses on 'African customs' for most soldiers and policemen, an unbridgeable gulf of misunderstanding persisted.

The guerrillas were in close touch with the aspirations of Africans, and their closeness was skilfully exploited in spreading their propaganda throughout the population. Although they disseminated printed material, including dramatic 'Socialist Realist' posters, the major medium of information was the spoken word. This had one overwhelming advantage over the advertising executives who supervised the government propaganda campaign - the insurgents usually came from and knew the people to whom they spoke. The typical ZANLA fighter was unsophisticated, but the impoverished peasants among whom he operated were usually illiterate and even more unsophisticated. They would never know that the photographs of 'Rhodesian Mirages' in guerrilla propaganda magazines were really shots of Boeing 737 civil airliners, or that guerrilla claims to have shot down an average of three Rhodesian aircraft a month throughout the war, or to have destroyed the town of Kariba, were ridiculous. While such strong emotional and kinship ties connected the guerrillas with their 'sea' such propaganda was highly effective,

On the international propaganda front the guerrillas were in an even more privileged position. The entire Eastern bloc, and virtually all Third World nations and their propaganda machines, strongly supported the guerrillas' cause. In the West the media, with a few exceptions, was strongly sympathetic to the guerrillas' struggle against the discriminatory white regime, though it had reservations about some of the guerrilla tactics and links with the Eastern bloc. The Western liberal tradition precluded broad sympathy for the white Rhodesians. For the influential liberal and radical chic sections of Western opinion the guerrillas had a romantic, Che Guevara mystique far removed from the dirty little war in the bush. The guerrillas managed to create the impression that atrocities, especially against 'refugee camps', were a Rhodesian monopoly. Another propaganda ploy was the treatment of white captives. Given the conditions in which the guerrillas themselves lived and fought, they were treated well, and the freed captives testified to this. But not many observers asked why there were so few live captives in guerrilla hands and what had happened to those prisoners who never reached Mozambique or Zambia. But while the Rhodesians pressed on with mass hangings of captured guerrillas after secret criminal proceedings, the guerrillas were able to appear more humane in the eyes of the world.

Ultimately it was on the propaganda fronts, both internal and international, that the guerrillas created the conditions of their victory. At the crucial point of their struggle, in mid-1979, no nation, not even South Africa, was able to recognize the Muzorewa government. The Conservative Thatcher government in Britain could not bring itself to fulfil its promise to recognize an arguably legitimate black government in Rhodesia. The way was clear for a guerrilla triumph.

### Strategic achievements

Mugabe set himself ambitious strategic tasks for 1979. These included the creation of true 'liberated zones', some of them to be defended by a 'people's militia', the establishment of more areas with a low level of security force activity as potential 'liberated zones', to intensify attacks on government forces, and to continue to tear apart the social and economic bases of white power. And, crucially for events decades later, Mugabe's specific objective was to drive as many white farmers off the land as possible and to establish complexes of *povo* (people's) villages on the abandoned estates. There was an added dimension to the politicization programme for 1978-79, for the guerrillas had to discredit those nationalists who had joined the internal settlement. ZIPRA held back the bulk of its forces, but recruiting went on at a feverish pace in 1979, and their guerrilla operations seeped eastwards. One of ZIPRA's objectives was to establish a presence over as wide an area as possible, given expectations of some sort of imminent collapse of white resistance and a more confused and open political situation in the aftermath. As early as 1977, Rhodesian intelligence reported that ZIPRA was establishing in western Rhodesia arms caches which were earmarked for a post-war political struggle with ZANLA. The seeds of civil war had been long sown, but no one in the 1970s foretold the ethnic cleansing which was to come.

The guerrilla programme was impressive, but it had been only partly achieved by the time of the ceasefire. The internal nationalists were discredited, principally because they could not stop the war, and, indeed, had intensified it. The Patriotic Front parties had a political network, which could be backed with force, right across the face of Rhodesia. There were more numerous, and more ferocious, attacks on the security forces, civilians, economic and communications targets. No true 'liberated zones' had been achieved, although there were areas, like Headlands and Mtoko, in which highly developed systems of *povo* camps had been established. Some areas of Rhodesia were a no man's land. Guerrilla bands and security forces' patrols roamed across an empty landscape. The guerrillas also hoped to cut the road to Beit Bridge from Salisbury continuously. This was to be done by intensive sowing of landmines, but the supply of these was inadequate to achieve this strategic task. Guerrilla groups were firmly established in the Chinamora TTL near the northern suburbs of Salisbury and had worked west through the Wedza area and into the Seki TTL south of Salisbury, but the capital was isolated only in a psychological sense and not in effective military terms.

### Military organization

ZANLA's military organization was far more highly developed and sophisticated than ZIPRA's. ZANU initially organized its war effort into 'war zones'. The first was the Zambia-Zimbabwe Zone along the northern border of Rhodesia. The north-east front, opened in 1972, was designated the Mozambique-Zimbabwe Zone (MZZ) and there was another, the Botswana-Zimbabwe Zone (BZZ) which was never really operational. Once the entire border with Mozambique was available to the guerrillas for infiltration into Rhodesia, ZANLA theatre organization was based on Mozambique's administrative structure. The ZANLA operational areas were simply extensions of Mozambique's provinces. 'Tete Province', for example, covered the old MMZ theatre and extended it southwards to the Inyanga North area. While these 'provinces' theoretically extended right across Rhodesia to its western border, it was only in 'Gaza Province' that ZANLA infiltrated as far as Botswana.

ZANLA divided its 'war zones' and 'provinces' into 'sectors'. In the north-east these were named after heroes and spirit mediums important in the folklore of the 1896-7 risings. The first to open up was 'Nehanda' sector, followed southwards in 1973 by the 'Chaminuka' and 'Takawira' sectors. In the other provinces, sectors were designated on a different basis. The sectors in 'Manica Province' were named after heroes of the modern nationalist struggle: 'Tangwena', after chief Rekayi Tangwena who defied government orders for his people to evacuate their ancestral homelands to make way for white farms, and 'Chitepo' after the slain Herbert Chitepo. 'Gaza Province' was divided into four sectors, starting with Sector IV in the Beit Bridge area and ranging through Sector I in the vicinity of the Fort Victoria-Birchenough Bridge road. Also within that province were two independent 'detachments', the 'Musikhavanhu detachment' and the 'Zimbabwe detachment', which was responsible for operations around the symbol of the nationalist struggle, the Zimbabwe Ruins (Great Zimbabwe).

Sectors were broken down into detachments, usually numbering 100 to 200 men operating in ten to fifteen 'sections', the smallest administrative and combat unit. The strengths and boundaries of sectors and detachments were fluid. Although boundaries would be drawn along watercourses, main roads and other prominent landmarks, a sector would often mean more in terms of specific guerrilla personnel than any geographical area.

The President of ZANU, Mugabe, was the commander-in-chief of ZANLA, rather in the way the President of the United States is the commander-in-chief of the American armed forces. He was elected by the party central committee. ZANU and ZANLA were officially linked via the *Dare re Chimurenga,* ZANU's 'war council'. Initially, none of the members had any military experience, nor were they active in field operations. Even the secretary of defence, who automatically headed the ZANLA high command, had no military background. Since the *Dare* was dominated by civilians, the decisions made were those of politicians, not soldiers. The dictates of African or international diplomacy tended to weigh more heavily in military decisions than the military situation in Rhodesia and the capabilities of the guerrilla army. The change came in 1973 when Josiah Tongogara was appointed to the *Dare* as secretary of defence, and therefore automatically to the chairmanship of the ZANLA high command. Tongogara was a military man first and foremost, and after 1973 no one without military experience sat on the ZANLA high command under his control.

The high command comprised the senior guerrilla officers responsible for translating the *Dare's* war strategy into a concrete military campaign. It was headed by Tongogara from 1973 until his death in December 1979. His deputy, the chief of operations, was Rex Nhongo, who succeeded Tongogara as ZANLA commander in 1979. Other members of the high command included the ZANLA political commissar, the chief of logistics and other departmental heads. The high command's bureaucratic instrument was the general staff, numbering several hundreds by the mid-1970s. This contained the personnel responsible for training, logistics, communications and routine administration.

Each 'province' was controlled by a 'co-ordinating committee' which, by the war's end, was in close contact with the FPLM units (FRELIMO's military wing) stationed inside Mozambique. The co-ordinating committee was linked to the provincial field operations' commander responsible for activities inside Rhodesia, whose deputy was the provincial political commissar. These commanded the sector commanders and sector political commissars, who in turn controlled detachment and section commanders and commissars. After Mugabe came to power in 1980 the term 'commander' was bandied about as a status symbol by ex-guerrillas, but it was an essentially ubiquitous label covering responsibilities equivalent to those of a sergeant in a Western army (section commander) up to Tongogara's post as commander of ZANLA. In the early 1970s an easy-going camaraderie was deliberately cultivated among the guerrillas, with no saluting or privileges of rank. While this was never completely lost, and ZANLA remained remarkably egalitarian in spirit to the end, the increasing strains of war and the size of the guerrilla army forced a closer definition of the powers and authority of 'commanders'.

## Co-ordinating the armies

The nationalists made several attempts to create organs to unify ZANLA and ZIPRA military operations. These moves were more for political reasons than for any practical military purposes. ZAPU was better plugged into the OAU Liberation Committee than ZANU, and sporadic alliances such as ZIPA provided a convenient way for ZANLA to make a claim on the committee's supply of arms to the guerrillas. Even the most concrete alliance, the Patriotic Front, forged in 1976 for the Geneva constitutional conference, produced no effective military unity. The last attempt to unify the two armies was made in early 1977 when J. Z. Moyo of ZAPU went to Maputo (shortly before his assassination) to negotiate the setting up of a 'Military Co-ordinating Committee' with ZANU. This would have given some credence to the claims of unity by the Patriotic Front political alliance. But Moyo's death brought the end of hopes of military unity. From then on ZIPRA and ZANLA fought their own battles, and in 1977 and 1978 the two armies clashed in areas where their operations overlapped.

Just as attempts at unity between the armies and the political parties failed, the political wings were also racked by internal disunity. The development of guerrilla strategy seems in retrospect to have been a straightforward, almost inevitable process - the commando incursions of the early 1960s failed, giving way to a period of re-assessment, then the emergence of a correct 'people's war' strategy. But the unfolding of this process was far from neat. Considerable internecine wrangling and violence erupted within the parties which was not resolved (and even then not completely) until 1978. The major struggle within ZANU began in the late 1960s. The problem throughout lay in the split between those who saw a place for negotiations with the Smith regime and those who argued for all-out war as *the* only solution. Ndabaningi Sithole had been the firebrand of the Sixties, but in 1969-70 he lost ground to the more radical elements in ZANU. The turning point for him was the declaration he made in the dock at his trial for allegedly plotting the assassination of Smith in 1969: 'I wish publicly to dissociate my name in word, thought or deed from any subversive activities, from any terrorist activities, and from any form of violence.' The other members of the central committee took him at his word, though the whites did not and imprisoned him, but it took the ZANU radicals until 1974 to lever Sithole from the party presidency. He clung on tenaciously, and it was only in 1977 that he lost any hope of regaining his former prominence. Control of the party passed inexorably into the hands of the more radical party members, and Mugabe emerged in late 1977-78 as the clear and publicly acknowledged leader and as commander-in-chief of ZANLA. This could not have been done without the commitment of the fighting guerrillas to armed struggle. The Mgagao Declaration of 1975, compiled by guerrillas at the training camp in Tanzania, was the clarion call of the irreconciliables. It declared:

> We therefore strongly, unreservedly, categorically and totally condemn any moves to continue talks with the Smith regime in whatever form. We the freedom fighters will do the fighting and nobody under heaven has the power to deny us the right to die for our country.

After fleeing Rhodesia, Mugabe began to reconstruct the war effort from Chimoio, and by 1978 was able to direct a far more vigorous and effective campaign than had been fought before. Ironically, it was the radical element which went to talk to Smith and Co. at the Geneva talks in 1976 and to Lancaster House in 1979. Significantly, in 1979 there were rumblings among the fighting guerrillas that negotiations with the Smith/Muzorewa government would rob them of the victory in the field which they felt was imminent. In terms of the party's ideology, the seizure of power by a true socialist party should have been impossible without a revolutionary struggle to the bitter end. But instead of winning that power out of the barrel of the gun in a Chinese-style people's war, ZANU won it through a Western-style ballot.

ZAPU did not lay itself open to such glaring inner contradictions. Nkomo, one of the great political survivors of all time, never rejected the possibility of talks with the Smith government. It was only the shooting down of the Viscounts in 1978 and 1979 by ZIPRA guerrillas which put him beyond the pale from the Rhodesians' point of view. The ideology of people's war should have precluded guerrilla participation in negotiations for a peaceful transition to majority rule. Tongogara adopted the Vietnamese approach to negotiations - the guerrillas had little to lose from them as long as the armed struggle continued unabated or even intensified. But the guerrillas were not so confident of ultimate victory that they could afford to treat negotiations lightly. Like the Rhodesians and the Muzorewa government, they felt they were in a race against time, a possible Western recognition of the internal settlement, and the lifting of economic sanctions. Time was one of the crucial three dynamics of Maoist warfare (time, space and will), but the guerrillas were not sure enough of their own will and of that of the 'sea' to refuse negotiations. By 1979 considerable war-weariness affected the guerrillas, and the African population inside Rhodesia. The huge turnout of voters in April 1979 was largely a result of Muzorewa's unachievable pledge that he could end the war. The heavy punishment inflicted by the Rhodesian forces on the guerrillas in cross-border raids in mid- and late 1979 increased the attractiveness of the negotiating table. This was particularly true of frontline hosts – Zambia and Mozambique were also economically exhausted by the constant Rhodesian raids. But even at Lancaster House, and throughout the ceasefire and election period, the guerrillas kept open the option to resume hostilities if they lost the election, by constantly exposing the duplicity of the British and the intimidation of, and subtler pressures on, voters by the Rhodesian forces and civil administration.

The history of the guerrillas' long struggle and events after the 1980 election showed that the war in Rhodesia, soon to be Zimbabwe, was not a classic Asian people's war. Certainly the tactics and much of the strategic framework were borrowed directly from the Asian experience, but the way the struggle was waged and the way the war ended placed the *Chimurenga* war very much in the tradition of Western revolutions. In reality it was what Marxists call a 'bourgeois nationalist' struggle, dressed in the ferocious garb of people's war.

## Weapons

Generals in modern armies bristling with sophisticated weaponry have often had to face the fact that the most cost-effective way to kill a man with a rifle is to use another man with a rifle. Although both sides deployed heavy weapons, the infantry rifle was the major instrument of death. The standard rifle of the security forces was the 7.62mm Fabrique Nationale (FN) self-loading rifle. The FN's adversary was the now famous symbol of revolution in the Third World, the AK-47 and its successor, the AKM. Firing the 7.62mm intermediate round, it had less hitting power than the NATO 7.62mm rifles, but it had certain overriding advantages for guerrilla armies which were largely made up of poorly-educated, ill-trained peasants. The AK family was in the tradition of Russian weapons: rugged, dependable and cheap. (Although in this case the AK47 was actually based on a German weapon, the FG42.) Instances of AKs firing more than 3,000 rounds without being cleaned or lubricated were recorded during the war. Guerrillas could bury AKs for months, and even when the wooden stocks had been eaten away by termites and the components had become rusty, they would fire on the first shot. Lighter ammunition meant that the guerrillas could carry more rounds in the distinctive 30-round 'banana' magazines. The guerrillas did not discourage ammunition wastage and favoured extravagant automatic fire, so that these larger quantities of ammunition were vital. The AKs could also take a family of rifle grenades, but their most widely used optional fixtures were bayonets. The most common were triangular-section 'pigstickers' and saw-back bayonets. These were used for the summary executions and mutilations by the guerrillas to maintain discipline and loyalty among their supporters, and to despatch their civilian opponents. The AK was supplied in a number of configurations depending on the supplier. The Soviet Union, Yugoslavia, China and Rumania all supplied different versions of the basic rifle.

The AK was supplemented by the SKS semi-automatic rifle and a number of other small arms. In early days the guerrillas were armed with a motley assortment of weapons bought in the international arms bazaar, but even as late as 1979 the security forces captured German-made MG 34 machine guns of Second World War vintage. Most weapons and ammunition were of Soviet origin or design and included the extremely light and highly accurate RPD machine gun, the PKM machine gun with the long 7.62mm round, PPShK submachine guns and Tokarev 7.62mm pistols, which were carried as the badge of authority within guerrilla detachments.

Both sides used hand and rifle grenades supplied by their respective supporters. The guerrillas used Chinese stick grenades and Soviet and Eastern European 'egg' and standard, 'pineapple'-shaped hand grenades. For heavier infantry weapons, both sides deployed 60mm mortars, which the guerrillas used for attacks on farms, security forces, camps, protected villages and other installations, as well as against security force patrols. The guerrillas also deployed 82mm mortars for attacks against static installations. The heaviest weapons normally deployed by the guerrillas were the RPG anti-tank grenade launchers, and 75mm recoilless rifles. Each section would usually carry an RPG-2 or RPG-7, but recoilless rifles were considerably less common. There were supply problems, too, and guerrillas often had a recoilless rifle and no ammunition, or vice versa.

The guerrillas excelled at land-mine warfare and they employed a great variety of Soviet-designed anti-tank and anti-personnel mines. On most days at the height of the war the guerrillas could count on damaging or destroying several security force vehicles with a variety of metal, plastic and wooden-box mines. Increasingly sophisticated anti-lift and anti-detection devices were used. At the war's end the guerrillas were using landmines which contained a photo-electric cell which detonated the explosive if the mine was exposed to daylight after the mechanism was set. Small children and non-combatant supporters (*mujibas*) often laid mines, and their blasts became one of the most serious problems for the Rhodesian forces. They in turn sowed thousands of mines along guerrilla infiltration routes into Rhodesia and inside neighbouring countries. The standard tactical mine was a locally and South African-produced Claymore mine. Towards the end of the war

Rhodesian forces operating across the border were laying mines which, in addition to normal anti-lift devices, were sensitive to the alkalis and acids in human sweat and were equipped with sensitive photo-electric cells.

The Rhodesians manufactured a large fleet of often ingenious mine-proofed vehicles. The guerrillas used trucks and utility vehicles only in their base areas in Mozambique, Zambia and Botswana, as their 'liberated zones' inside Rhodesia were tenuously held and indefensible against security force incursions. Occasionally civilian or commercial vehicles were hijacked within the country to transport guerrillas or weapons, and buses often carried guerrillas and their skilfully camouflaged weapons. In Mozambique, ZANLA forces had the periodic support of heavy equipment of FRELIMO, including BTR-152 armoured personnel carriers mounted with 12.7mm machine guns and T-34/85s. The T-55s held by FRELIMO were deployed but not committed against Rhodesian incursions.

ZIPRA had by 1979 organized and equipped a conventional warfare brigade. It was supplied with Soviet equipment, including T-34s, MTU-55 bridging equipment, BTR-152 armoured personnel carriers, recoilless rifles, field guns, heavy mortars and Soviet command cars. This equipment was not deployed against the Rhodesian security forces inside the country, and was used in only a limited capacity in defence of base camps inside Zambia. The incompetence with which the equipment was used in the attempted rising by ZIPRA dissidents in February 1981, in the first year of Zimbabwean independence, demonstrated the poor training and tactical experience of those leading this conventional force.

In the air the Rhodesian forces enjoyed supremacy, though the guerrillas' anti-aircraft defences became more sophisticated and were better handled towards the end of the war. Most observers put a great deal of emphasis on the age of the Rhodesian aircraft, but much of the equipment, especially propeller-driven aircraft and helicopters, was acquired after UDI. The guerrillas enjoyed only indirect protection from the frontline states' air forces. Mozambique's and Angola's MiGs were not used to deter or intercept Rhodesian air strikes on guerrilla bases, nor to venture into Rhodesian air space. Too much has been made of South African Air Force assistance to the Rhodesian Air Force, but the occasions on which it was deployed in support of Rhodesian operations served to warn the frontline states of the consequences of aerial intervention in support of the guerrillas.

The guerrillas' own anti-aircraft defences were formidable by the war's end. ZIPRA pulled an ace from its sleeve with the deployment of SAM-7 Strela infra-red homing missiles. ZIPRA scored a major victory against white morale when it shot down two civilian Viscount airliners. The guerrillas also deployed a large number of automatic anti-aircraft weapons. United States Air Force experience over North Vietnam had shown the devastating effectiveness of small-arms fire, forcing it to develop tactics which previously had taken account only of surface-to-air missile and large-calibre gun defences. The standard guerrilla weapons were 12.7mm DShK and 14.5mm machine guns. The accuracy of guerrilla flak was poor, but the large numbers deployed, particularly outside Rhodesia in defence of bases, and the growing determination of some gunners, posed a considerable threat to Rhodesian Air Force operations. In 1979 reports of larger and more sophisticated SAM defences in Mozambique sent the Rhodesians shopping for electronic counter-measures pods, but the threat did not materialize before the end of the war.

*Guerrilla tactics*

Guerrilla tactics were a strange mixture of fecklessness and competence. Their combat tactics were often so bad as to border on the farcical, yet the way in which they mobilized and maintained mass support was a model of the people's war. The guerrillas infiltrated into Rhodesia along a number of well-established corridors which were sometimes as much as twenty kilometres wide. The crossing of the border could be dangerous as the Rhodesian army created a *cordon sanitaire* consisting of fences and minefields, supported by periodic patrols, along much of the eastern frontier. In some areas the guerrillas were able to pass through with ease, but in others they suffered heavy casualties from 'ploughshare' mines, a large version of the Claymore.

Once across the frontier the groups, consisting of between ten and thirty guerrillas, but up to 300 on rare occasions, followed landmarks such as hills, roads, railways, fence lines and rivers. Aggressive activity was kept to a minimum and there were few incidents along infiltration routes, to avoid attracting the security forces' attention. Some of the routes were extremely long, such as the 300-kilometre route along the Lundi river valley from the south-eastern border to the Belingwe Tribal Trust Land. The guerrillas always carried heavy loads of weapons and ammunition with them as they made their way to their operational sectors. Each infiltrating group would normally carry enough for its own needs. Guerrillas or their carriers were recognizable to the security forces by the calloused marks on their shoulders where their pack straps bit into the flesh. The guerrillas put a great deal of emphasis on physical fitness in their training, for conditions on the march or in operational sectors were often gruelling.

Re-supply was a constant headache for the guerrillas. ZIPRA was more lavishly supplied by the Soviets; ZANLA, however, faced periodic logistics crises. Landmines were an unpopular burden because of their weight, and guerrillas would often plant them soon after they crossed the border rather than lug them into the interior. The guerrilla groups crossed white farming areas and game parks as rapidly as possible and made for the relative safety of the densely populated Tribal Trust Lands. They moved from kraal to kraal or along a network of base camps until they reached their area of deployment. In areas with less sympathetic inhabitants or in those where much of the population was in PVs, 'contact men' fed and aided guerrillas in their temporary encampments. In some areas guerrillas were able to move around with considerable safety and these were used for rest and regrouping. Some areas like Mudzi had almost the status of 'liberated zones' in that security forces could venture into them only in strength. Kandeya TTL in the north-east was a safe haven for guerrillas for much of the war.

The guerrillas normally operated in sections of at least ten men comprising the commander, political commissar, security officer, medical officer, logistics officer and three to five cadres. Standard section equipment was an RPG launcher or 60mm mortar, a light machine gun, with the rest armed with varied weapons depending on their supply state. Once inside Rhodesia the guerrillas began operations from base camps sited near friendly villages or *povo* camps. *Povo* is a Portuguese word used by FRELIMO to denote 'the masses' and borrowed by ZANLA. Their populations consisted of Africans freed or abducted from PVs or populations moved from established kraal sites. *Povo* camps were set up in remote areas and operations were mounted from these logistics bases. These sympathetic or captive groups grew crops to feed the guerrillas, carried out base camp chores, gathered intelligence on security forces' movements and generally acted as the guerrillas' 'tail'. Occasionally guerrillas were able to use PVs as rest and recreation and feeding points, particularly when many of these were handed over to auxiliaries under Internal Affairs control in 1978 and 1979. Many auxiliaries, initially loyal to Muzorewa or Ndabaningi Sithole, sensed a guerrilla victory in the future and came to a *modus vivendi* with local guerrilla groups.

One security forces' officer said towards the end of the war that if Africans lived in TTLs they could be automatically classified as supporters of the guerrillas. (The rural areas of Mashonaland remained largely loyal to Mugabe and ZANU for the next two decades.) Certainly the guerrillas could rely heavily on local Africans' willingness to act in concert with them. Guerrillas mounted operations from their base camps, often joining up with other sections (there were three sections to a detachment) for large operations. By 1979 guerrillas were occasionally operating in groups of seventy-five to 150. Movement usually took place at night, though there were some areas where guerrillas moved around openly during the day. In the Nyajena TTL, guerrillas knew that Rhodesian Selous Scouts posing as guerrillas were operating there because they moved through the bush and not along the open pathways. Moving up to fifty kilometres a night, the guerrillas would lay ambushes or attack farmsteads in the early morning. In the first years of the war, when the Rhodesian forces were not overtaxed, they would attack in the late afternoon so that they had all night to make good their escape. But later in the war attacks were typically launched just before sunrise.

The guerrillas took the maxim that they must live to fight another day more than seriously. Although some units fought with determination, most withdrew rapidly once fire was returned. A willingness to accept a few casualties might have shortened the war considerably. Sometimes remote farmhouses defended by a single family would hold out against twenty or thirty guerrillas equipped with mortars and rockets. Although this ultimately did not matter, in that the guerrillas achieved their war aims, their irresolute tactics prolonged the conflict by years. As one Rhodesian officer commented in 1979: 'If we had been fighting the Viet Cong, we would have lost the war a long time ago.' Ambushes were often poorly sited with an emphasis on escape routes rather than on the killing zone. The guerrilla propensity for using tracer simply pinpointed their firing positions for those attacked. But their operations did not necessarily have to be totally successful, if at all. Only half a dozen ambushes on a road, no matter what the outcome, compelled the Rhodesians to mount convoys which tied down men and materials and created a siege mentality and climate of fear. The range of guerrilla activities was enormous. Farmsteads were attacked, roads dug up, cattle dips destroyed, PVs and Rhodesian security forces' bases mortared, stores were robbed, mines laid, punitive murders carried out, buses and commercial vehicles were hijacked and robbed or burnt, convoys attacked, civil airliners shot down, tobacco barns razed, bridges blown up, irrigation pumps destroyed, and railway lines sabotaged. The entire political, economic, administrative and military structure built, maintained and protected by the Rhodesian government was attacked by guerrilla groups ranging from one or two individuals to company-sized detachments.

Once the guerrillas had disengaged from their operations they moved to a number of rendezvous points. These allowed those who became detached or scattered to rejoin the group and make their way back to their base camp. Anti-tracking techniques were used if security forces' follow-up was expected. These included walking along stream beds and busy paths in populated areas, removing or changing footwear and arranging for sympathizers to sweep the tracks with underbrush or to drive livestock across them.

In the early seventies many of the ZANLA attacks had been haphazard and designed to fulfil an external as well as internal strategic imperative; much of the funding for the liberation movements was being funnelled through the OAU Liberation Committee and a key criterion for funding was proof of activity ? actual contacts. Both ZANLA and ZIPRA thus felt compelled to scale up the quantity of their attacks rather than focusing on quality, in a bid to ensure that they continued to receive funding and recognition. By the late seventies, ZANLA had become a lot more professional in its approach. The quality of training and weaponry had improved, but also critical was more thorough pre-planning and a more serious approach to intelligence-gathering. The ZANLA provincial commands established sectoral and district intelligence structures and standard operational methods. By 1978, wherever possible, ZANLA campaigns and contacts were 'mapped out' by reconnaissance groups. These reconnaissance personnel were required to draw, to scale, sketch maps of potential target areas prior to attacks in the various sectors. The *Dare re Chimurenga* and Chief of Defence insisted on detailed information on infiltration routes. This entailed information on the shortest possible routes, including the likely time it would take for combatants to reach a specific place. Information on obstacles such as mountains, rivers and other obstacles was included as well. Where possible the recce group would profile the local population, security forces and likely security power armaments prior to an attack. This more detailed planning involved experienced ZANLA combatants at the top of the intelligence command and control structure. Below them and functioning as a complementary force were the foot-soldiers who were the *mujibas* and *chimbwidos* who relayed information about the Rhodesian forces, the local population and the local topography. This was particularly important because it was standard practice that insurgents should not operate in their home area for fear of being compromised. They were thus often unfamiliar with the local topography and needed guidance. Improved intelligence thus played a key role in elevating the insurgency from the tactical to the strategic level. The recce teams did, however, have to get their intelligence right; harsh penalties from the superiors awaited the scouts if a guerrilla attack failed because of faulty intelligence.

But most of the guerrillas' time - up to 80 per cent - was spent in 'mobilizing the masses'. The guerrillas had a number of sound starting points for politicizing the population. They were black, and – despite the intelligence rules – sometimes from the same area in which they operated, and had the avowed intention of overturning an obviously discriminatory government and securing a better life for Africans. Politicization took place on a daily basis. Living in day-to-day contact with their supporters, emotional links were built which often transcended political beliefs. While the guerrillas lived alongside their supporters, security force contact was often limited to passing patrols, punitive actions or escorting administrative officials. Even in PVs the security forces lived separately from their charges. While the guerrillas might withdraw temporarily when Rhodesian forces were active in an area, they would usually return. Casualties were covered up by claiming that guerrillas who had in fact been killed had been transferred to other sections or detachments, although the wounded were always an embarrassment.

The political commissar attached to every section had a central role to play, both within the unit and in mobilizing civilian support. Political meetings, *pungwes,* were held in villages at night. Speeches would be made by the political commissar, and almost invariably would follow the singing of *Chimurenga* songs and often beer-drinking. Summary justice might also be meted out to those who were accused of collaboration with the Rhodesian government. Great play was made of the *Chimurenga* tradition of resistance, the need for land, the brutality of the government forces and the general poverty of rural life. Hammering on a few simple themes was highly effective in convincing the rural population of the need for the armed struggle.

Government propaganda often spoke of an indiscriminate reign of terror inflicted on the African population by the guerrillas. There was indeed a deliberate reign of terror, but only against those who sympathized with or aided the Rhodesian cause. 'Collaborators' or 'sell-outs' were brutally murdered, or mutilated, and often whole households and kraals were destroyed. But the targets were normally carefully selected and the local population could usually see the point of the executions or mutilations. In many cases completely innocent people were suspected of collaboration and murdered, but, by and large, the guerrillas were careful in their policy of selective terrorism. In 1978-9 a deliberate policy of killing labourers who refused to give up their jobs on white-owned farms was adopted. The guerrillas perpetrated several large massacres of farmworkers and the tactic was highly effective in denuding farms of their labour. This was a foretaste of what was to come after 2000.

The ZANLA leadership imposed a strict code of ethics among the guerrillas to avoid alienating local supporters. Some *Chimurenga* songs spread the guerrilla code, such as this chant:

> *There are ways of Revolutionary soldiers in behaving.*
> *Obey all orders.*
> *Speak politely to the people.*
> *We must not take things from our masses.*
> *Return everything captured from the enemy.*
> *Pay fairly for what you buy.*
> *Don't take liberties with women, don't ill-treat captives of war.*
> *Don't hit people too severely.*
> *These are the words said by the people of ZANU teaching us.*
> *These are the words said by Chairman Mao when teaching us.*

Transgressions could be dealt with by corporal punishment, as were disciplinary offences. There was no set scale of punishment: some commanders punished attempted desertion with death, while others inflicted twenty-five lashes; yet others gave thirty-five lashes and assigned offenders the section's most inferior weapon for combat. Guerrillas were theoretically forbidden to procure beer (for which there was a sentence of twenty lashes) and to 'interfere' with local women, but these strictures were generally ignored. Guerrillas indiscriminately robbed buses and stores on their own initiative. Discipline and adherence to the code of ethics, usually slack, depended on the personalities of the individual commanders and commissars. ZANLA commanders and commissars kept detailed diaries about their operations, disciplinary procedures and success of politicization. These records often fell into the hands of the security forces after contacts. They provided a great deal of personal information, particularly on individual insurgents.

The Roman Catholic Commission for Justice and Peace, which tended to sympathize with the cause of African nationalism, remarked that:

> Although it is not possible to give a comprehensive picture, it appears that there are two distinct types of guerrilla groups operating in the country at present. One type is well-trained, well-disciplined and maintains the trust of the people. Another, however, is poorly trained and ill-disciplined and can only maintain the allegiance of the rural population through the use of terror tactics.

The civilian population in the rural areas was often caught between supporting the *vakomana* (guerrillas) and the *vabhunu* (Rhodesian security forces). To add to the confusion, black security force soldiers from the Rhodesia African Rifles, Guard Force or Selous Scouts often masqueraded as guerrillas to extract information from the civilians and find out who was supporting the guerrillas. Once the hapless civilian had given themselves away they would usually find themselves taken away for questioning, and probable torture at the nearest police station. The war also provided a cover for the settling of ancient scores amongst the rural population; more often than not, those accused of being *vatengesi* (sell-outs) by the guerrillas were set up by jealous neighbours who resented them. This explains why the bulk of those killed by the guerrillas during or after *pungwes* were business people, teachers, headmen etc – their wealth and social status often made them easy prey for jealous neighbours who used the guerrillas to remove the competition. By 1979, particularly in the Manica sector, the guerrillas had realized that they were killing innocent people. They thus instructed that anyone who denounced a fellow villager must do so in public, with the accused present to answer the charges, and had to be prepared to execute the accused if need be. The guerrillas' insistence that the accusers must now do the dirty work themselves led to a drastic decline in the number of *pungwe* 'denunciations' in 1979.

Nkomo's guerrillas were usually more selective in their use of brutality and terror than Mugabe's forces, whose discipline was more lax and who were less discriminating. ZANLA forces were more active than ZIPRA and covered a far larger swathe of Rhodesia, with the result that there were many more instances of ZANLA atrocities.

After spells of combat in Rhodesia, guerrillas would return to their bases in neighbouring states for re-equipment or regrouping, though some guerrillas stayed in one area for periods up to five years. Medical cases which could not be handled by the poorly trained and equipped medics attached to guerrilla units, or treated in sympathetic mission clinics and hospitals, were evacuated on foot to base camps across the borders. Messengers and political agents made frequent trips to and fro across the frontiers. On occasion disciplinary sections would cross into the country to stiffen demoralized or inactive sections or to mete out justice to offending guerrillas.

In 1976, Rhodesian Army Brigadier Derry McIntyre commented:

I doubt whether the terrorists are so well organized that they can influence their cadres in the field. I would say possibly the moon affects the terrorists more than Geneva conferences. They go mad at periods quite unrelated to world affairs.

The guerrillas, however, did stay in touch with world affairs, both through their own cadres and through listening to local or foreign stations on the portable radios which they bought or stole from stores or farmhouses. The official Mozambique station, Radio Maputo, carried a great deal of information and propaganda about the guerrillas' struggle, and was an important factor in politicizing guerrillas and civilians inside Rhodesia. The speed and thoroughness with which the guerrillas honoured the ceasefire in December 1979 gave the lie to observers who saw guerrilla control over their cadres in the field as tenuous at best. It was also a comment on the guerrilla sympathizers' statements that atrocities such as the Elim Mission massacre were perpetrated by groups acting outside the control and orders of their high commands.

While the Rhodesian forces never really developed a successful antidote to the guerrillas' mobilization of the masses, they displayed consummate skill in defeating the guerrillas in combat. Even low-calibre units such as the Police Field Reserve could easily repel guerrilla attacks, though the insurgents tended to be more aggressive against units like Guard Force and Internal Affairs. In the years 1966-72, guerrilla activity, no matter how small the group, would invite the full attention of regular units and the Rhodesian Air Force. Insurgents were rapidly followed up by helicopter-borne patrols, and if they failed to re-cross the frontier were almost invariably hunted down. But from 1972 both the size and geographical spread of guerrilla incursions rapidly expanded. From 1976 every area of the country became affected by guerrilla operations. There were simply not enough well-trained Rhodesian soldiers to cover all the ground, and as increasing reliance was put on reserves the problem of pinning down guerrillas so that they could be eliminated by superior firepower and tactics became acute.

The answer devised by the Rhodesians was Fire Force, an efficient way of stretching limited elite manpower and the helicopter fleet. A typical Fire Force comprised four Alouette IIIs. At least one was configured as a 'command car' from which the Fire Force commander directed the action. One or more of the helicopters would be a gunship. Later in the war a C-47 Dakota carrying a stick of fifteen paratroops was a standard component of Fire Forces. Strike support was given by fighter-bombers in the early days of Fire Force operations until Cessna 337G Lynxes were acquired. After this Hunters were available for particularly large or hard-fought actions.

So effective was the Fire Force concept that it seemed to be *the* solution to winning the war. But the sheer numbers of guerrillas operating in the country and guerrilla counter-measures upset this extremely cost-effective tactic. Fire Forces became more and more stretched to cope with incidents.

The guerrillas adopted evasion tactics based on lookout positions and scatter drills, and began to move about in small groups of less than five to avoid detection, concentrating only for meetings or operations. Air strikes were evaded by running at an oblique angle to the aircraft flight path. Initially the arrival of a Fire Force meant certain death or capture, but effective counter-measures had been devised by 1978-9.

The tactical successes of the Fire Force system were also blunted by guerrilla measures against observation posts. Base camps were sited away from prominent features on which security forces might keep watch on the surrounding terrain. Guerrilla operations in the flat country of south-eastern and much of western Rhodesia were already facilitated by the dearth of high hills in those areas. *Mujibas* and herd boys on apparently innocent domestic chores were sent through likely OP positions to compromise their presence and booby-traps were even laid in the more obvious sites. Guerrillas often wore two or three sets of civilian clothes to confuse watching security forces. By the later years of the war government troops were forced to move OPs well away from villages and to use telescopes with optical ranges of up to five kilometres to maintain their secrecy. The Selous Scouts pioneered new, painstaking techniques for setting up OPs and keeping them secure. Teams of pseudo-guerrillas, usually Selous Scouts or Special Branch agents, including amnestied guerrillas, gathered intelligence on the locations of guerrilla bases. The guerrillas devised counter-measures, such as placing taboos on eating certain foods by their cadres. A kraal head who was suspicious of groups asking the whereabouts of their 'comrades' could test their identity by offering them prohibited foods. The stratagem needed to be spread widely, but at the same time changed frequently, to be proof against security forces' interrogations of captured guerrillas.

The lavish provision of radios gave the Rhodesian forces the tactical flexibility they needed to cover vast areas of countryside. The guerrillas rarely operated radios (which they called 'over-overs') until the last two years of the war. In areas in which PVs had been established, security forces destroyed crops found outside areas prescribed for cultivation around the PV itself. When people were moved into a PV the guerrillas tried to spirit away as many as possible to set up *povo* camps. These were treated as military targets by the Rhodesian forces. In areas where curfews had been imposed any person moving about at night was liable to be shot by ambushes. Africans refusing to stop when challenged by security forces were shot as 'suspicious persons'.

The Rhodesians developed a range of exotic tactics beyond conventional infantry variations, such as the use of 'Q-cars' (military vehicles bristling with firepower and disguised as civilian or commercial vehicles) and booby-trapped radios. The Selous Scouts also developed a major interest in biological and chemical warfare. An organophosphate, Parathion, was used to impregnate clothing. The three most common types of clothing treated were underpants, T-shirts and denim jeans, the preferred dress code of ZANLA guerrillas. Usually sick guerrillas were left by their comrades to suffer a slow and agonizing death alone in the bush. Perhaps thousands of guerrillas were killed by this method. Such 'kills' were not mentioned in official Rhodesian communiqués, but they were frequently described in diaries recovered after contacts with guerrillas. Food was contaminated with thallium, especially canned corned beef, mealie meal, tinned jam and beers. The thallium was injected into sealed tins, through bottle tops and into packets with a micro needle. Cartons of cigarettes were impregnated with toxins. Cholera and anthrax were also spread deliberately. In February 1978 the new Commissioner of Police, Peter Allum, gave a direct order to stop all covert poisoning operations, though the manufacture and distribution by SB and the Selous Scouts continued until mid-1979.

Constant Rhodesian externals, heavy raids in Zambia and Mozambique, went on week after week in the closing two years of the war. The guerrillas often felt safer inside Rhodesia than they did in the border regions of their host states, for the marauding troops were the highly-trained and motivated elite of the Rhodesian army. Guerrilla offensives were often disrupted by timely Rhodesian spoiling attacks, and camps had to be moved back from the borders, dispersed and more heavily defended. The series of raids culminated in an attack on the massive guerrilla base at New Chimoio in September 1979. The blitzkrieg put significant pressure on the leaders of the Patriotic Front to remain at the Lancaster House conference which ended the war.

A backhanded compliment to the Rhodesian forces was paid by an official of the Mozambique government when he claimed that they had destroyed a vital bridge deep inside his country. 'It must have been the Rhodesians,' he said, 'because it was done so well.' But the 'field' in revolutionary warfare is not the same as that in conventional warfare. In a guerrilla war the battlefield is the political loyalty of the mass of the population. The Rhodesians did not develop tactics to win enough battles in that more subtle war.

### Lessons of the insurgency for ZANU

Detailed consideration of ZANLA's *Chimurenga* war is important because much of the methodology and ethos were re-applied in the first three decades of Mugabe's premiership, which are set out in the following chapters. The second *Chimurenga* led directly and consciously to the third *Chimurenga* to secure the land against the alleged revanchism of the international community, Britain in particular, and their 'stooges' inside Zimbabwe, whether they were ZIPRA survivors, recalcitrant white farmers and industrialists or organized as formal opposition such as the MDC.

The call and response of the second *Chimurenga* were fairly standard in the *pungwes*:

*Pamberi na Comrade Mugagbe!*
(Long live Comrade Mugabe)
*Povo: Pamberi na Comrade Mugabe*
*Pamberi na Comrade Samora Machel!*
(Long live Comrade Samora Machel)
*Povo* response
*Pasi na Muzorewa!*
(Down with Muzorewa)
*Pasi ne vatengesi!*
(Down with sell-outs)
*Pasi ne vasumbwagata!)*
(Down with imperialist running dogs)

These chants, accompanied by foot-stomping, could go on for hours and hours, sometimes days if punishment was part of the ritual. Attendees soon got the message. In the third *Chimuenga*, Tsvangirai or MDC were substituted for Muzorewa, but the ZANU-PF brainwashing was the same.

At the strategic level the aims were similar: deployment of the party and its armed wings to maintain victory, even if it meant permanent conflict. Despite the initial mood of reconciliation with the whites and flirtation with Western-style capitalism, in the end almost total control of the land and other means of production fell into the hands of the party and its close supporters. This was Marxism by other means. Just as in the anti-Rhodesian war, propaganda was mixed with intimidation to win over the *povo* in the Shona-speaking heartlands, and to physically eliminate opponents elsewhere who refused to flee. Mugabe had a legalistic bent: the courts would adjudicate, and parliament would meet and elections would be held, but nearly all were rigged, sometimes cleverly, but often clumsily, to maintain the permanent dominance of the party. It is impossible to understand Mugabe's civilian leadership without fully comprehending how he waged his earlier successful guerrilla war. In many senses, Mugabe remained a guerrilla leader, even though he was lionized throughout Africa as a political statesman.

The conservative tally of those killed in the war was 30,000. The number of security force members killed in action (including twenty South African policemen) was 1,047. As roughly 75-80 per cent of the security forces were black, then the casualty figures approximately were equivalent: up to 400 white servicemen and women were killed, including some foreign volunteers. Since figures were then collated in racial categories, 374 white, coloured and Asian civilians were killed, as well as 107 in the two Viscount tragedies. The Rhodesian government claimed that 7,772 black civilians were killed, of which 3,256 were killed by guerrillas and 535 by landmines. In this figure were included 183 mutinous auxiliaries, wiped out by security forces. The Rhodesian government also said that 10,506 guerrillas were killed inside Rhodesia, while an estimated 10,000 were killed in camps in Mozambique and Zambia. Church groups sometimes put the total killed of black men, women and children in and out of Rhodesia as high as 80,000.

Whether the lower figure of 30,000 or even the unlikely higher figure of 80,000 killed during the fifteen years of the liberation war is accepted, it is likely that Mugabe in his three decades of misrule directly caused the death of more of his own countrymen, especially during the ethnic slaughter in Matabeleland and the reign of terror after 2000. Both modern *Chimurengas* wiped out thousands, often with very similar methods, and with a similar goal: total power.

## Chapter 5

# Mugabe Comes to Power

Mugabe had personally wanted and expected a military victory over the white settlers. At the Lancaster House conference, he threatened to walk out on a number of occasions. He did not want to compromise. But his frontline backers kept him at the talks. In the last months of the war, the Rhodesians had launched a blitzkrieg on the economic infrastructure, especially in Mozambique. These major raids, not all militarily successful, were politically counterproductive for the Salisbury leaders. Although all 'externals' were stopped on 22 November 1979 the frontline presidents feared an escalation to all-out war in the region. A tactful lull or promised pause, declared at the outset of the Lancaster House talks, may well have prompted Mugabe to go for the unconditional surrender option and just walk out, and so force the main British negotiator, Lord Carrington, to hand the baton to Muzorewa. Thus Britain, by default, would have been forced to recognize the internal settlement.

In what the Foreign Office called 'a leap in the dark', Lord Soames travelled to Rhodesia as the new governor on 12 December. The final agreement was signed at Lancaster House on 21 December, seven years after the main guerrilla war had begun. Mugabe was resentful. He said later: 'As I signed the document I was not a happy man. I felt we had been cheated to some extent, that we had agreed to a deal which would ... rob us of the victory we had hoped we would achieve in the field.' On 28 December the ceasefire creaked uncertainly into life. By 4 January 1980 more than 18,000 guerrillas had heeded the ceasefire and entered the agreed rendezvous and assembly points inside the country. Just as the ceasefire began, one of the main architects of the Lancaster House compromise, Josiah Tongogara, the ZANLA commander, was reported killed in a motor accident in Mozambique.

Murder by car is an integral part of southern African politics and folklore. Many thought that Mugabe was ridding himself of his chief rival. Some Zimbabweans subscribed to the rumour – there was no proof – that Mugabe still laid a place at the dinner table for Tongogara to appease his *ngozi* or spirit. (This story partly inspired the play *Breakfast with Mugabe*.) The charismatic forty-one-year-old Tongogara was certainly very popular with the army he led. As one senior ZANLA man later said, 'Tongogara was the epitomé of a freedom fighter … He believed in the empowerment of his junior officers and allowed them to implement the agreed policy as they saw fit.' Another disgruntled liberation commander said recently, 'Tongagara was a true leader. The current ones are all thieves.' Precisely to avoid such a deleterious mythology, at the time ZANU went out of its way to try to prove that the incident was an accident – even to the extent of asking a white employee of a major funeral home in Salisbury to travel to Maputo to embalm the body. ZAPU intelligence believed that an 'East German specialist in road accidents' had arranged the job. Smith's intelligence people were suspicious, but Ken Flower, the CIO head, leaned towards the belief that it was a genuine accident. Later, the conspiracy theory grew in ZANU that Tongogara's willingness to compromise with ZIPRA at Lancaster House had been the cause. Whatever the truth, the removal of Mugabe's main rival continued to act as a constant reminder for the Zimbabwean security bosses whenever they were minded, in later years, to conspire against Mugabe.

As 1980 dawned Mugabe's men had more immediate problems – above all, would the ceasefire hold? Lord Soames might have been Winston Churchill's son-in-law, but he had a mere 1,300 Commonwealth troops to police the uneasy peace deal. Like the Pope, he had no divisions. Five armies roamed the devastated countryside. ZIPRA was pushing in its forces from the west; ZANLA was dominating the eastern regions – meeting in the Midlands, now they were fighting each other as much as the Rhodesian forces, who were itching to launch a final onslaught on both their old enemies. In addition, both Muzorewa and Sithole each had motley militias, called auxiliaries, or *Pfumo reVanhu* (spear of the nation), though on a number of occasions the government forces had 'culled', to use the jargon of the time, up to 180 of Sithole's rampaging and ill-trained auxiliaries. Mozambican regular troops were active on the Rhodesian side of the border, and up to 6,000 South African soldiers, with large reserves just over the Limpopo border, had entered the country. Rhodesia was one huge booby-trap for the born-again British colonists, led by Soames. Would the ceasefire hold – if it didn't, the region would be engulfed in full-scale conflict?

Despite his almost total lack of knowledge of African affairs, Soames was an excellent choice as the Empire's last pro-consul. As one Foreign Office insider said of the burly ex-Etonian and Sandhurst man, 'He's large, noisy and impossible to ignore.' His Churchillian connections appealed to the old-fashioned patriotism latent in many white Rhodesians, while his blunt patrician manner earned him the respect of the African leaders. As one of Nkomo's aides said: 'We Africans get on with old-fashioned Tories better than modern Labour politicians.' Crucially, despite some initial difficulties, Mugabe eventually developed a close relationship with Soames, even to extent of almost begging the governor to stay on in a supervisory rule after the elections.

Soames's installation prompted the removal of sanctions; he opened all the borders and put an end to secret trials and released dozens of political prisoners. But he had to rely on the Rhodesian security forces and police to maintain the ceasefire. Eventually 22,000 guerrillas were cooped up in seventeen assembly points (APs). Of these, over 16,500 were ZANLA. Mugabe had sent many of his second-tier troops – often with inferior weapons – to the APs while keeping his best men, especially the commissars, to prepare for military emergencies and to take part in 'encouraging' the voters – mass intimidation – if the elections went ahead. Both ZANLA and ZIPRA kept large reinforcements of men and equipment in Mozambique and Zambia respectively.

The Rhodesians were itching to wipe out their enemies in the APs, but Soames and the Rhodesian Commander, Peter Walls, maintained a tight leash. Despite the numerous examples of intimidation and dirty tricks, especially by ZANLA, Soames did not cancel the elections or ban ZANU in areas of egregiously aggressive thuggery. On 27 January 1980, just before his fifty-sixth birthday, Mugabe's return to the country was met by rapturous mass audiences in Mashonaland. Despite ZANU's pressure on the *povo*, it was absolutely clear that Mugabe was perceived as the Shona saviour who could bring peace, and freedom. Mugabe showed considerable bravery – he had survived a large number of Rhodesian assassination attempts, including one planned, and aborted at the last minute, by CIO agents during Lancaster House. A Welsh former 22nd SAS operative, who had also been fingered as the assassin of Herbert Chitepo, smuggled plastic explosives in cans of fruit. Contriving an explosive device hidden in a briefcase, full of ball bearings and a receiver which could be activated by an impulse transmitted via the control box of a model aircraft, he planned to blow up Mugabe in his Kensington hotel. Apparently MI5 got wind of the plot and probably managed to persuade the CIO to call off their hunter, though another version had second thoughts in Salisbury as the explanation.

As late as 2 March 1980 the Rhodesian SAS had planned to use a SAM-7 Strela missile to shoot down a plane carrying Mugabe and twenty-two members of his central committee as it came to land at Salisbury airport. Some SAS operators objected to killing the crew as well and it was cancelled by Rhodesian Combined Operations HQ, also at the last minute. Even as late as April, during the independence celebrations, an elaborate South African plan to kill Mugabe, as well as possibly his guests such as Prince Charles, was *prevented* by the Rhodesian CIO. (The CIO officer Danny Stannard, who managed to thwart the assassination, was later personally decorated by Mugabe.)

The election was held in the last three days of February. General Walls urged Soames to ban ZANU-PF, at least in certain areas, because a large ZANLA army, led by commissars, was active outside the APs and were making it abundantly clear to the Shona peasantry that they could vote for only one man. The British governor was unresponsive. Soames had already declared, with a refreshing lack of political correctness:

> You must remember this is Africa. It isn't Little Puddleton-on-the Marsh, and they [black Africans] behave differently here. They think nothing of sticking poles up each other's whatnot, and doing filthy, beastly things to each other. It does happen, I'm afraid. It's a very wild thing an [African] election.

The British military officers in the Ceasefire Commission – made up of ZANLA, ZIPRA and the Rhodesian forces – worked tirelessly to prevent break-outs from the APs and the Rhodesians over-reacting or pre-empting. As a final piece of old-fashioned security, Soames requested that 570 British policemen should stand around the polling booths. And so it was that that under the watchful eyes of British Bobbies, in the middle of African rainstorms, 2,702,275 men and women voted. No one except ZANU-PF expected any of the nine competing parties to win an overall majority of the eighty seats reserved for blacks in the new parliament. Nkomo's ZAPU won twenty seats in their Matabeleland heartland, while the victor of the 1979 internal election, Bishop Muzorewa, won only three seats. Mugabe took the other fifty-seven. Despite the accurate predictions by his own party advisors, Mugabe was personally stunned by his victory. His party had so long geared up for war that he fretted that he might not be ready for the reins of government. This explains why he asked Soames to stay on for at least six months. The British, however, were eager to get out as soon as possible.

Despite a massive display of Rhodesian troops, armoured vehicles and tanks around the main government buildings, road junctions and communications centres just before and after the results were announced on 4 March, the coup – codenamed Operation Quartz – did not materialize. General Walls told his HQ staff that Rhodesia would 'not copy the rest of Africa'. The plans, especially in Pretoria, for an anti-Mugabe coalition, comprising Nkomo and Muzorewa, could not work in the face of Mugabe's triumph. It bears repeating that despite the massive intimidation, mainly by ZANLA, Mugabe had won overwhelmingly because only he could end the war and bring peace to a war-ravaged people. In short, he hadn't needed the ZANLA thuggery to procure his victory.

As early as 1976 Mugabe had said:

> Our votes must go together with our guns. After all, any vote we shall have shall have been the product of the gun. The gun which produces the vote should remain its security officer – its guarantor. The people's votes and the people's guns are always inseparable twins.

In the beginning Mugabe's popularity was so overwhelming among the Shona majority that force was not required. As misrule undermined his electoral base and real opposition emerged, Mugabe never deviated from his original credo that guns and votes were 'inseparable twins'.

On 18 April 1980 Zimbabwe became independent with Mugabe as premier. The Rhodesian albatross had finally been removed from Britain's neck. Soames, the amiable Tory patrician, had accomplished his 'mission impossible' and handed over a British colony to a Marxist guerrilla leader. A new black leader took over a white-constructed dictatorship with a panoply of emergency powers – nearly all of which were to remain active in the new Zimbabwe. Many white Zimbabweans, shell-shocked at Mugabe's victory, prepared for the 'Beit Bridge 500', the dash to the South African border, with their carefully hoarded petrol reserves. Then Peter Walls and Mugabe appeared on television to call calmly for reconciliation. Mugabe cogently asked for understanding between the races. 'Let us deepen our sense of belonging,' he said, 'and engender a common interest that knows no race, colour or creed. Let us truly become Zimbabweans with a single loyalty.' Most whites accepted Mugabe's statesmanlike approach, while others prepared to quit Zimbabwe. Others could not, because the financial restrictions on emigration grew tighter.

Rhodesian Front propaganda had utterly demonized Mugabe as a barbarous thug, so whites were astounded by the articulate and conciliatory new leader they saw on TV. He would have the strength to enforce peace. The black Hitler had suddenly become the great white hope. Hitler was an apt comparison. Every foreign journalist visiting Rhodesia would daily hear two things. One, that the BBC threw sweets into dustbins to film allegedly starving African children scavenging for food. Two, that – like Hitler's one-ball myth in the Second World War – Mugabe had little, if any, of his penis left because of syphilis. Checking the prison records turned up one minor urinary infection during Mugabe's eleven-year-incarceration. And the fact that his second wife bore him three children suggested strongly that Mugabe was intact as far as the plumbing department was concerned.

Under the averted eyes of the British, the South African Defence Force repatriated most of the loaned equipment. The majority of the white regulars in both the armed forces and the British South Africa Police (renamed the Zimbabwe Republic Police) left their units and in many cases their country. The Selous Scouts, detested by ZANLA, were quickly disbanded without ceremony. Many of the black and white regulars left to join the South Africans. (Some of the 'turned' ex-ZANLA men in the unit suffered grisly and largely unpublicized deaths in the next few years.) The Rhodesian Light Infantry fared a little better. It disbanded with some dignity on 17 October 1980, after completing its last deployment, an anti-poaching operation. Mugabe tried very hard to persuade the last commanding officer of the SAS, Colonel Garth Barrett, to stay on to form the nucleus of a Praetorian guard. Barrett very politely refused. Some of his men joined the South African Reconnaissance Commandos based in Durban, while others went to assist the pro-apartheid forces in South West Africa. The regiment's silver was presented to their fellows in the British SAS HQ in Hereford.

Mugabe's Rhodesian inheritance for his new military was small, but crucial. A few black Selous Scouts and members of the RLI with the remnants of the Rhodesian African Rifles formed the core professional component of Mugabe's new army, the Zimbabwe National Army (ZNA). They became the nucleus of a special forces unit, 1st Parachute Battalion, led by Colonel Dudley Coventry, a former SAS officer. Most of the white officers in the BSAP quit within a year or so. But Ken Flower, who had already served three prime ministers, stayed on as head of the CIO. He remained full-time for eighteen months, before semi-retiring to work as a consultant for another five years for Mugabe. (He died in 1987, shortly after he had received from his publishers an advance copy of his memoirs, *Serving Secretly.*) Some of the key Special Branch personnel stayed on, though a number had already been subverted by the South Africans. Elements of the air force remained too, with the pilots hoping to receive modern aircraft in the post-sanctions dispensation. The former Combined Ops HQ remained the centre of military control. But the magnetic markers and arrows on the maps showing ZANLA bases in Mozambique and ZIPRA deployments in Zambia were cleared away. The new locations were of South African bases. The change of enemies was dramatic.

The prime military problem for Mugabe, besides South Africa, was merger of the tens of thousands of guerrillas who wanted to join the ZNA (as well as disbanding those who expected good jobs in civilian life). How should he unify three rival armies? In a magnanimous gesture, Mugabe asked Walls to supervise the ZNA integration. (Unfortunately for this process, Walls was soon pushed out after his undiplomatic remarks about his appeals to the British about ZANLA electoral intimidation were made public. Like many of his colleagues, he too went 'down south' to retire in South Africa.) Before he left he formed a Joint High Command (JHC) which consisted of Rex Nhongo, the ZANLA replacement for Tongogara, and the ZIPRA commander, Lookout Masuku. The former Rhodesian army commander, General Sandy Maclean joined it as well, as did Air Marshal Frank Mussell. The civilian leadership was headed by Alan Page, as the Secretary of Defence. The JHC was initially chaired by Walls, then, after his dismissal, by Alan Page or his deputy, Harry Oxley. The chairmanship then passed permanently to Emmerson Mnangagwa, a former insurgent with a high intelligence and ruthlessness to match.

Mugabe's focus was on his military pressures – to forge a unified army which could retain white expertise, without alienating his own ZANLA supporters, or ZIPRA, where rumblings of civil war were growing. South Africa was absorbing many of the skilled military personnel as well as tactical lessons from the Rhodesian war, even though Pretoria seemed to ignore the *strategic* lessons. On top of that, the guerrilla leader had a country to run. Likewise, while Mugabe needed skilled whites, how could he also satisfy the crisis of expectations of his black supporters? Land redistribution, new schools and clinics were demanded all over Zimbabwe. True, sanctions had ended, and aid and trade began to flow into the country, although South Africa, as ever, could exert a stranglehold on rail and road access to the land-locked country whenever Pretoria felt ill-disposed towards Mugabe.

Mugabe needed to transform himself from guerrilla to statesman, and quickly. His attempts to reconcile with the whites were impressive. The initial choice of Walls as military supremo was magnanimous, and wise. In the beginning Mugabe warmed to the blunt Walls. Mugabe asked him about the various attempts on his life. The General vehemently rejected the allegations, offering the most obvious evidence that any plotters were nothing to do with him: 'If they had been my men, you would have been dead.' Mugabe was incensed when Walls's private contacts with London about the elections were revealed. On Sunday 7 September 1980, Ken Flower confided in his diary that he had spent two hours alone with Mugabe talking about Peter Walls. 'There will be no recovery there. Mugabe believes that Peter betrayed him: having sworn a personal loyalty but still living in the past and not really serving him as Prime Minister, though Mugabe described how he had done everything he could to win his friendship.' Flower maintained a very cordial relationship with Mugabe, describing him as 'the best prime minister I have served'. Mugabe also developed a lasting rapport with Denis Norman, well-respected in the white farming community. Mugabe later made him minister of agriculture. David Smith, a finance expert and former Rhodesian Front minister, was also brought in to the cabinet fold. The new ZANU-PF-led government did not fit the image painted by Rhodesian Front propaganda. The all-white units of the old Rhodesian forces could disappear, so long as the life-style the whites had fought so long and so hard to preserve remained largely intact for the privileged.

The military structure of the young republic continued to be a big headache for Mugabe, however. The new government faced two simultaneous and inter-related challenges: demobilizing thousands of ex-combatants and re-integrating them into society, simultaneously melding those who stayed on in the military into a cohesive national force. Nearly 100,000 personnel would have to be encouraged and persuaded to take one or other route. Time was of the essence. In such an uncertain environment and with political tensions already rising, it was essential that structures be created as soon as possible to ensure that both processes could begin. Failure to do so would have had catastrophic consequences.

A Demobilization Directorate was created in June 1980, comprising representatives from the Rhodesian forces, ZANLA and ZIPRA. About 30,000 ex-combatants had opted for a return to civvy street. They were processed by the Directorate; temporary accommodation was found for them (often in rented urban accommodation where the demobbed ex-combatants lived as many as fifteen in a house at a time). A package of Z$200 was established for each processed ex- combatant, and many were re-settled in communal agricultural 'co-operatives'. Zimbabwe's return to the Commonwealth prompted a number of Commonwealth groups to query whether trauma counselling of the ex-combatants was part of the reintegration process; it was not, and it is likely that this failure to address the psychological legacy of violence from the second *Chimurenga* played a tragic part in Zimbabwe's continued violence over the decades. Nor was finding civilian jobs for so many male and female guerrillas an easy task. During the war, insurgent recruits had been promised that they would immediately receive the land and good jobs which the whites controlled. The reality was different, as it became clear that there would not, could not, be an immediate expropriation if the new nation's economy was to survive. Operation SEED (Soldiers Employed in Economic Development) was an attempt to literally turn the ex-combatants' AK-47s into ploughshares by engaging them in small-scale agricultural production. Operation SEED was launched with great fanfare in 1981 and had a high symbolic value as a re-integration exercise, but the actual outputs were minimal, and the operation was a failure. Few of the ex-combatants were trained farmers, and they were expecting jobs, cars and houses in the city, not to be dumped with a hoe in the bush. Inadequate accounting also caused the ZNA to lose millions of dollars in fraud to ghost soldiers who were on the books but never reported for duty yet still collected a salary. Simultaneously, many of the demobilized combatants never received their demobilization pay because of slipshod book-keeping, fraud and questions over who was supposed to administer what.

Meanwhile, there was also the challenge of integrating three mutually hostile military forces to forge a national army. Creation of the ZNA in Operation MERGER was a crucial part of nation-building. Mugabe, in his capacity as a civilian prime minister, announced that the government would create a new national army of 35,000. He micro-managed by insisting that he personally would vet all officers' promotions above the rank of lieutenant colonel. He declared publicly that the ZNA would be an integrated endeavour comprising forces from the Rhodesian army, ZANLA and ZIPRA (although ZANLA was privileged right from the start). The announcement was the easy part. Behind the scenes lay months of tough bargaining and confidence-building measures and compromises between the three forces to create a composite whole. For instance, the figure of 35,000 was a compromise figure between those who wanted a larger force of 45,000 and those who wanted a small national force of 25-30,000. The Joint High Command had laid the groundwork for the integration. Walls, the first JHC commander, was careful to be diplomatic in his on-the-record assessments of his guerrilla colleagues in the JHC, referring to them as 'excellent chaps', 'professionals' and 'colleagues'. In private, he was far less charitable in his assessment of the calibre of ZANLA recruits and leadership, although he continued to have a high regard for ZIPRA. 'If I had all ZIPRA, I could colonize all Africa,' he said privately.

The demonstration of apparent unity of purpose at the top percolated down to the ranks and was vital in creating the environment for successful integration. Just as vital was the mediation and training implemented by the British Military Advisory and Training Team. The British personnel were able to mediate many of the internal tensions between the various groups. In addition, the BMATT intervention confirmed that the new national force would be a professional force based on a conventional – Western –

command and control structure. A number of new cabinet members were calling for the new army to adopt a revolutionary command structure based on militias and nominal ranks as had been the case during the liberation war. Meanwhile, the Rhodesians, ZANLA and ZIPRA contributed three brigades each to the new force. But after an initial honeymoon period tensions within the JHC resulted in Walls' resignation in June 1980 followed by a spate of senior Rhodesian officers. At the time, the resignations spread a good deal of alarm throughout the white civilian population. These events were undoubtedly worrying, but they also had a useful effect. Many of the guerrilla commanders had resented the apparent dominance of the Rhodesians in Operation MERGER. The departure of many of the more hard-line Rhodesians reduced the racial in-fighting within the new ZNA, and forced a greater accommodation amongst those who stayed on. The rapid departure of whites caused severe administrative deficiencies in the armed forces, even allowing for the small British Army training mission's attempts to upgrade replacements. For example, inadequate control continued to cause the ZNA to lose millions of dollars in fraud, mainly due to the payment of bogus 'freedom-fighters'. The problems of housing and feeding such a large merged army were immense. A year after independence the army numbered about 65,000 including the ZNA and guerrillas awaiting integration and demobilization. Satisfying so many disgruntled male and female guerrillas had already been a thankless task. Operation SEED had largely failed. Few soldiers possessed the agricultural skills or the inclination to till the land. As 'heroes of the revolution' they had been taught to expect good jobs, houses and cars in the city, not to be dumped with a '*badza* in the *bundu*'. Attempts to integrate former insurgents into the ZRP had also produced very ragged results.

The prompt creation of the ZNA was a minor miracle, partly thanks to the British. Twenty-four of their officers involved in the monitoring force stayed on and they were augmented to bring up the numbers to 167 at its maximum. This was the start of a new role in Africa: turning guerrillas into a professional conventional force. The trick was to be repeated in South Africa in the 1990s. The British were chosen because they were in place and had performed bravely and efficiently in the ceasefire period. Mugabe had also rekindled his affection for the British, partly because of his closeness to Soames, and later a perceived amity with Prince Charles. Also, it was felt that a British presence might deter the South Africans from excessive meddling.

Mugabe granted the first BMATT commander ready access to him, and they conferred on a very regular basis. The general BMATT view was they were being kept in the dark by the three armies they were supposed to integrate. They were made to feel by ZIPRA that they were standing in the way of their coup. For ZANLA, the British were colonialists trying to prevent the new society they wanted to build. While the Rhodesian military made it clear that a civil war was imminent. The British stuck at their frustrating mission. It was frustrating because ZANLA kept short-circuiting BMATT in order to dominate the military structure. BMATT faced minor mutinies on a daily basis, particularly about the need for training. ZANLA officers felt that as they were officers they didn't need to undergo further training. Logistics and especially accounting were also difficult to teach. Health was a problem too – in some units venereal disease affected 45 per cent of the troops. BMATT also had to understand when 'spirit' ailments could be treated only by a witchdoctor. Unofficially, BMATT came to see that ZIPRA were usually better soldiers. They did have the educational advantages and many had been trained in a conventional army format. And yet BMATT had to accept that ZANLA parity, then dominance, was a political necessity.

BMATT had to deal with numerous guerrilla complaints about the glaring differences between pay and pensions for the remaining whites (race-based pay scales were removed only in 1990). Female guerrillas complained about male dominance. All complained about the rank structure and the pressure to pass educational tests. But BMATT's main challenge was the brewing civil war. The two guerrilla armies wanted their officers to do well in training so as to dominate the officer corps, but only ZANLA could win this race. Yet they also kept some of their best troops outside, firstly from the APs and then from the training centres. This was an insurance policy in case integration failed. ZIPRA concentrated its crack troops together in Gwaai River Mine. They also tried to keep some of their best soldiers together in Harare and Bulawayo. BMATT's official integration role was completed in August 1981

The ZNA order of battle was thus. The ZNA HQ was at King George VI barracks in Salisbury, while four brigade HQs were in Bulawayo, Salisbury, Umtali and Fort Victoria (although the place-names were about to change). A fifth brigade, soon to be very controversial, was being planned. Each brigade would have the following support elements: an engineering and signals squadron, maintenance, pay and medical companies, and a provost platoon. The following units were controlled directly by Army HQ:

   • armoured regiment, with one squadron of T-55s and two squadrons
   of Eland scout cars and Ferret scout cars

- Grey's Scouts, mounted infantry
- artillery regiment
- commando battalion (mainly ex-RLI)
- parachute battalion
- SAS squadron
- an anti-aircraft regiment and mechanized battalion were still being formed.

The Air Force consisted of:

- No 1 Sqn (Hunter FGA 9s)
- No 2 Sqn (Vampires)
- No 3 Sqn (transport aircraft)
- No 4 Sqn (Cessna 337G Lynxes)
- No 5 Sqn (Canberras)
- No 6 Sqn (Genet trainers)
- No 7 sqn (Alouette III, Bell 205s [Hueys of Vietnam fame])

In 1982 BMATT helped to set up the Basic Training Centre for the ZNA at Inkomo barracks – this was for officer and NCO instruction. Within a year the British had 'trained' 12,400 ZNA members. Later, the British Army improved the tank and armoured car units. They also played a constructive role in establishing the ZNA military academy in Gweru and the Staff College in Harare. Moreover, the ethos of the British suited Mugabe's determination to establish a professional conventional force, capable of internal and external roles. One key factor in the British military tradition was fudged – the need for an *apolitical* army. Commander (now promoted to Lieutenant General) Rex Nhongo called for a 'highly efficient, well-disciplined and effective *political* army'. Mnangagwa agreed with him, saying that an apolitical army would lead to 'undesirable and total confusion'. Others such as Air Marshal Tungamirai argued that apolitical structures might be desirable but only once the liberation generation of commanders had died or retired.

A conventional professional army also meant the end of conscription. Before Mugabe's victory, a very small number of blacks were conscripted in 1978-9 for political reasons associated with the internal settlement. All white males were effectively conscripted with some serving up to the age of sixty. With the end of the war and the need to reduce numbers, conscription was unnecessary. The issue was revisited in later years once the numbers in the ZNA were stabilized, but high black unemployment had always prompted a large excess of volunteers in the white-led army, and the same applied under Mugabe's rule.

The North Koreans were also brought in as instructors. They had no truck whatsoever with any Western notions of an apolitical army. The North Koreans were asked to train the Fifth Brigade. Behind the scenes the British and some Zimbabwean commanders questioned the need for North Koreans, especially as they had enjoyed no real operational experience since 1953. Also, the previous four ZNA brigades had tried to mix ZIPRA and ZANLA, but the Fifth Brigade was exclusively Shona. Mugabe's rather lame excuse was that by the time the integration reached the Fifth brigade no ZIPRA were left. More convincingly, the North Koreans came laden with free gifts: seven T-54 tanks, and also armoured personnel carriers and artillery worth a total Z\$12.5 million (when the Zimbabwean dollar was worth something).

The training and arms of the Fifth Brigade were unsurprisingly different from the brigades mentored by BMATT. It was armed with AK-47 assault rifles instead of the standard NATO rifles. The point of integration was to meld the previously distinct armies, so why now create an elite force with a very different ethos? What was Mugabe planning? In the rest of the ZNA the North Korean-trained A-team created a great deal of envy, for their special privileges, and sometimes hatred of their tribal and party arrogance.

Bearing in mind China's big contribution to the struggle, Beijing's immediate post-independence military contribution was small (though the Chinese embassy did help BMATT on a number of crucial occasions). China sold thirty-nine T-59 tanks to Harare in 1981, and China played a small part in the training of the ZNA artillery units. Pakistan helped out with air force training both in Pakistan and Zimbabwe. Nigeria offered facilities in the Nigerian staff college.

Except for the Fifth Brigade, the British approach tended to prevail. Much depended on their diplomacy in a unique transformation in which no side was a clear victor in the liberation war. Integration and the creation of a professional force from often disparate – to be polite – guerrilla movements was a major challenge. The British had dealt with Rhodesian intransigence for years and understood that, during the internal settlement of 1978-9, the Rhodesian Front absolutely refused to give up control of the forces. Now the guerrillas had to face up to skilled white Rhodesians who remained and who did the bulk of the basic training. Members of the former government forces, black and white, were allowed to keep their ranks, but nearly all the guerrillas – except for the top commanders who were promoted – had to revert to the rank of private, with obvious ramifications for the level of pay. The former insurgents were divided up into two groups – mainly depending on education – and placed in officer training or instruction for other ranks. This stage of insurgent training was aptly dubbed 'Operation Sausage Machine'. The racial and class distinction also intruded on attempts to induct would-be officers into the traditions of the officers' mess. Obviously some of the new officers imbibed more than just learning which way to pass the port, for volunteers for further officer training in the UK were abundant.

The departure of whites eased some of the tensions, but the tribal and ideological rifts between the two guerrilla movements largely remained. So did complaints about conditions. By the end of 1980, only 15,000 of the estimated 65,000 who wanted to enter the ZNA had been retrained. Many still languished in the assembly points, with their weapons. ZIPRA's gripes were double-barrelled. They complained of favouritism towards the white soldiers and ZANLA. Technically, the Lancaster House agreement stated that all serving members in all three armies should be allowed to integrate into the ZNA, if they so wished. The disbandment of the Selous Scouts was not a surprise; Mugabe could never have allowed the hated force to stay on the government payroll. But the ZIPRA intelligence wing and its air force were also peremptorily disbanded. ZIPRA pilots accepted that the Rhodesian Air Force personnel were more competent as trainers but they had wanted to take part, as equals, in the integration process, especially as ZANLA had no illusions about their own aviation during the war (though a few were trained as pilots by their communist allies).

Mugabe's commitment to a professional force overcame many of the problems, not least the severe post-war financial restraints. The JHC was dissolved in August 1981 and was replaced by a Defence Force HQ and a Defence Council. Officer training was encouraged at the new defence academy and staff college. In 1986 the ZNA set up a full command and staff course, largely on the British model. In 1984 Mugabe had sanctioned the creation of the Zimbabwe Defence Industries (ZDI) as a private limited company but owned by the government. His war machine was taking shape.

Zimbabwe needed to spend money on post-bellum reconstruction, not a big standing army. Salisbury, renamed Harare, also ordered Hawk trainer/strike jets from Britain. The trouble with possessing a large standing army and modern air force in Africa is the temptation to use it externally to channel attention from internal woes. But Mugabe, the ex-teacher, clearly wanted to spend more on civilian needs such as education. He vowed that he would not allow either the ANC or PAC to establish military bases in Zimbabwe, but he said he would provide shelter to refugees and political exiles. Mugabe did not want war with South Africa. Nor, initially, did he

The Rhodesian historical view of the first *Chumerenga*: British South Africa Company forces about to be overwhelmed by Ndebele warriors in 1893. (Author's collection)

Robert Mugabe campaigning just before he came to power. (Author's collection)

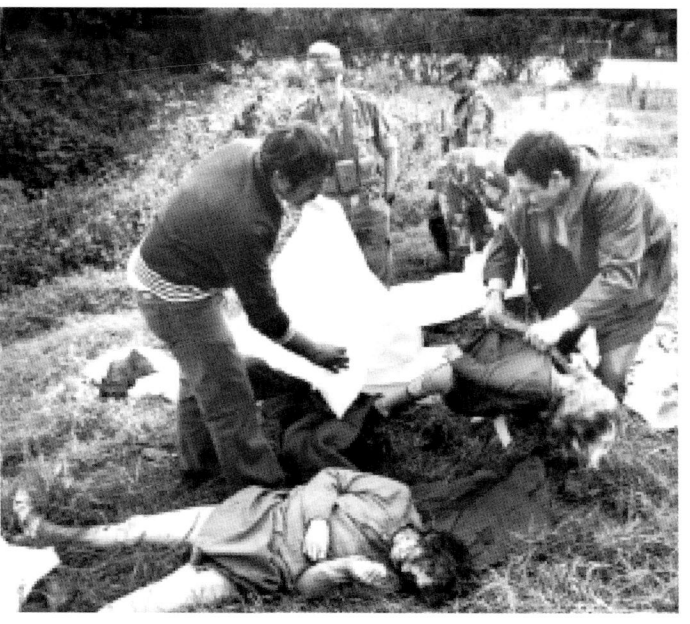

On 11 December 1978, ZANLA guerrillas fired rockets and tracers at the central oil storage depot in Salisbury. Prime Minister Ian Smith thanks the fire crew. (Rhodesian ministry of information)

Guerrilla atrocity. On 23 June 1978, twelve men, women and children were variously raped, hacked and bludgeoned to death by ZANLA regulars at Elim Pentecostal Mission, near Umtali (Mutare). (Author's collection)

ZANLA guerrillas in the bush with a fascinating array of arms: a NATO bazooka, a Second World War German machine gun, Russian RPGs, a Soviet sniper rifle and a Romanian AK-47. (Author's collection)

Chinese-produced liberation posters used by ZANLA. (Author's collection)

An early Soviet BTR-152 with a 12.7mm machine gun, used by FRELIMO. It was destroyed by elements of 2 Commando, Rhodesian Light Infantry, during Operation SNOOPY, Chimoio, Mozambique, 20 September 1978. (Author's collection)

South African troops. At the end of the liberation war, about 6,000 South African forces, some in Rhodesian uniform, were involved directly, with large reserves inside South Africa, ready to intervene. (Paul Moorcraft.)

A light ground support Impala, of the South African Air Force. The South African Air Force, especially the Mirage fighters, served as a deterrent to the air forces of the Frontline States. SAAF fighters did not intervene directly in Rhodesia, but Pretoria provided pilots and compatible aircraft (especially helicopters) for use in the country, and during 'externals'.

A ZANLA poster. *'Pamberi ne Chimurenga'* means 'Forward with the liberation struggle'.

Although ZANLA propaganda exaggerated the combat role of women, a considerable number of female guerrillas did see action.

Bishop Abel Muzorewa and his wife Maggie, just after he became the first black prime minister of the country (April 1979). His weak leadership was no match for the ruthless determination of Comrade Mugabe.

General Lookout Masuku, one of the most able ZIPRA military leaders, arriving in Salisbury just after the ceasefire (December 1979).

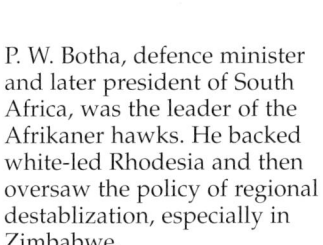

P. W. Botha, defence minister and later president of South Africa, was the leader of the Afrikaner hawks. He backed white-led Rhodesia and then oversaw the policy of regional destablization, especially in Zimbabwe.

Author with
RENAMO leader
Afonso Dhlakama,
Gorongosa base,
Mozambique, June
1986. This was perhaps
the first press
photograph of the
reclusive leader.

The RENAMO
chieftain after too
many diplomatic
lunches, on the eve
of a peace
agreement in 1992.
(Paul Moorcraft)

A RENAMO soldier in central Mozambique (1986); they were tough fighters and much better organized and motivated than their FRELIMO opponents. (Paul Moorcraft)

The British Hawk trainers played a crucial combat role in Mugabe's wars. His first fleet was wiped out by South African sabotage. Then Britain re-supplied Zimbabwe, controversially in the case of the war in the Congo. (Konflikty.pl)

Mi-35 Russian gunship. Harare bought six for use in the Congo, where Zimbabwean pilots deployed them efficiently in combat.

Honeymoon period. Mugabe on a state visit to the USA, departs from Andrews Air Force Base in September 1983. (US DoD.)

The militarization of the Zimbabwe youth. Junior cadets from 2 Brigade primary school, with toy guns, perform at ZDF day in Harare, August 2009.

Aftermath of farm invasions. Ben Freeth suffered a fractured skull. His in-laws, Mike Campbell and his wife Angela, were also tortured for nine hours after their Mount Carmel farm was attacked in June 2008. They took their case to the SADC tribunal, to little avail. The farm has reverted to African bush and Campbell died of his wounds in April 2011. (Picture courtesy of the *Zimbabwean*)

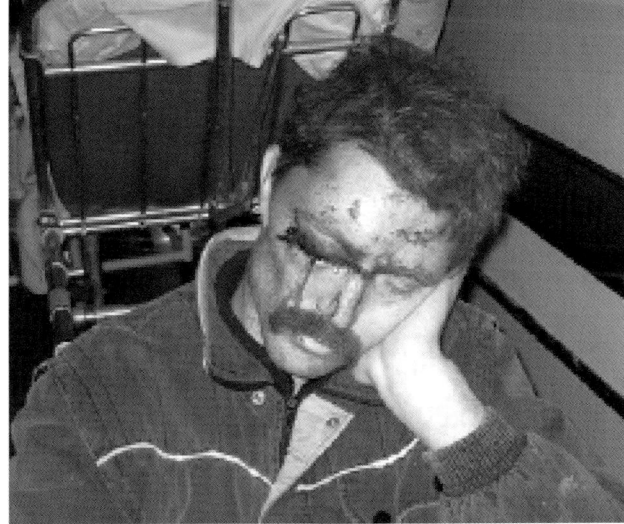

Top brass in the ZDF. From left to right: Perence Shiri, Constantine Chiwenga, Augustine Chihuri. If the military lead a formal coup, the head of the ZDF, General Constantine Chiwenga, might be the front man.

When Mugabe goes, Emmerson Mnangagwa has been a long-term contender to take over.

Power couple. Both Joice Mujuru and her husband Solomon have offered themselves as potential leaders.

Could a woman take the reins? Joice Mujuru, the vice president, often plays on her liberation credentials. Then her name was Teurai Ropa (Spill Blood) and she claimed to have knocked down a Rhodesian helicopter with an AK-47.

Another contender is Solomon Mujuru, whose *nom de guerre* was Rex Nhongo. He took over the ZANLA army when Tongogara was killed in December 1979.

Waiting for God: perhaps only the grim reaper can topple Mugabe. He is pictured here while attending the 2009 AU summit in Addis Ababa. His fellow African leaders were disinclined to criticize him, let alone organize regime change. (DoD)

Worthless money. Zimbabwe managed the second highest inflation rate in modern history. The Zimbabwe dollar had to be dumped in favour of South African and US currencies.

The two wings of the MDC. Left to right: Arthur Mutambara and Morgan Tsvangirai. (Ubuntu Hope)

Morgan Tsvangirai has suffered much at the hands of his rival, Mugabe, but does he have the skills to lead and to reconstruct a devastated country? (Ubuntu Hope)

Newspaper ad for Mugabe in the June 2008 election in which he was the only candidate. Could he win another election, even if it were massively rigged?

"I believe in your entitlement to a secure place in your God given corner of the earth; the only one you have... I believe in you; I believe in us: An empowered people, Totally free TOTALLY INDEPENDENT."

100%
TOTAL

VOTE FOR
CDE.R.G.MUGABE

PRESIDENT

want to fight an ethnic campaign in his own country. Mugabe spent long hours agonizing confidentially with his CIO chief about his concerns about splits with ZIPRA. Nevertheless, the leader who preached peace was soon to deal with a covert war with South Africa, a civil war in Matabeleland and later to send large troop contingents to Mozambique. Mugabe's hastily integrated war machine was due to see action on a large number of fronts.

## Chapter 6

# Civil War and Ethnic Cleansing

**M**ugabe's reliance on the small British military training unit was not misplaced. It was soon to play a vital part in mediating in the increasingly bitter wrangling between ZANLA and ZIPRA contingents in Operation MERGER. As 1980 progressed two military phenomena occurred simultaneously. The first was the integration of former enemies in the ZNA. Secondly, centrifugal forces of disintegration were also active: the tribal and political rivalry between ZANU-PF and ZAPU exploded into open combat between their military wings, ZANLA and ZIPRA. Although ZAPU, along with two whites, was represented in the new Zimbabwe cabinet, ZANU-PF ministers such as Enos Nkala (an Ndebele himself) were publicly contemptuous of ZAPU and its president, Nkomo. The self-styled 'Father of Zimbabwean nationalism' was nevertheless in the cabinet as minister of home affairs (this ministry controlled the police, but many of the security and paramilitary functions had been removed). ZIPRA leaders objected to the increasing dominance of ZANU-PF in the civil service, army, police and the constant stream of ZANU-PF propaganda in the tightly-controlled press, radio and TV. Initially the attacks were against ZIPRA 'dissidents', but there were also increasingly vicious media attacks on Nkomo for his 'failings' as home affairs minister. Mugabe had wanted to avoid a shooting war, but it looked more and more as if the thrust of his policy was to destroy ZAPU politically.

Mugabe said in June 1980: 'If those who have suffered defeat adopt the unfortunate and indefensible attitude that defies and rejects the verdict of the people, then reconciliation between victor and vanquished is impossible.' Firebrands in Mugabe's cabinet, especially Edgar Tekere and Enos Nkala, talked of 'a second war of liberation'. Mugabe made no attempt to dampen down the tensions which were then reflected in hostile relations between ZANLA and ZIPRA, awaiting integration or demobilization. To improve conditions and to try to curb rural banditry, large groups of insurgents were moved to both Harare, and to Bulawayo. Unfortunately, the rival urban barracks were close to each other, sited less than half a mile apart.

Map 4 – Zimbabwe

Eventually, in November 1980, ZIPRA and ZANLA skirmishes erupted into full-scale fighting in eNtumbane, a township in Bulawayo. It had started after a highly abusive tirade against ZAPU by Nkala at a political rally in Bulawayo. Soon the rival forces were exchanging small-arms fire. Within hours the eNtumbane skirmishes had triggered more tribal fighting among the mixed battalions at Connemara and Silalabuhwa camps around Bulawayo. Although the ZIPRA forces at the camps had lighter-calibre weaponry than ZANLA, they had long expected – and prepared for – a military showdown against their erstwhile ZANLA colleagues. The ZANLA forces were soon pinned down and taking casualties. Then another two ZIPRA battle groups, from Gwaai River camp (200 kilometres north-west of Bulawayo) and Esigodini (sixty-nine kilometres south), were advancing on eNtumbane in motorized columns. Faced with the very real possibility of seeing ZANLA forces in Bulawayo being annihilated by a strategic envelopment, Mugabe reluctantly called on former Rhodesian forces, particularly the armoured car unit, to take on the ZIPRA advance. For two days the see-saw battle continued and eventually it was the combination of ZANLA and Rhodesian forces, firepower and the threat of bombing by the air force which ended the ZIPRA advance. Nkomo and his two key subordinates, Lookout Masuku and Dumiso Dabengwa, crisscrossed the combat zone by helicopter appealing to all sides, especially ZIPRA, to desist. There was a high risk that they might have been shot down by their own men in the heat of the moment, but these appeals played a vital role in calming things down.

More than fifty-five people (mainly innocent civilians) were killed and more than 400 injured in the fighting which went on for two days. Air Force Hawker Hunters thundered over the battling guerrillas and new units of the national army, stiffened by the still white-officered RAR, stood by to intervene. Zimbabwe hovered on the brink of civil war. Finally, senior ZIPRA and ZANLA commanders gained some control over their troops in Bulawayo and in other centres where guerrillas were gearing up for a general conflagration.

In January 1981 Nkomo was demoted in the government. In February 1981 more than 10,000 ZNA troops were again involved in ZIPRA-ZANLA faction fighting in the Bulawayo area and at camps in the Midlands. Once more the core of the forces which quelled the mutinies was made up of RAR and the air force. Mugabe had wanted to disband the RAR but had been dissuaded by Walls and the secretary of defence. Without the RAR and its white officers, the fighting in February 1981 - which included the use of BTR-152 armoured cars and the threat of ZIPRA tanks from the Gwaai river AP - might not have been contained. The whites in Zimbabwe silently cheered on 'their' RAR as it once again went into combat against guerrillas, but this time on the orders of Robert Mugabe.

Obviously the referee role of the white-officered RAR could not last long in the new Zimbabwe. A North Korean-trained Fifth Brigade, based in Inyanga, took over the role of Praetorian Guard. Nearly all the 3,000-3,500 troops in the brigade were Shonas loyal to ZANU-PF. The formation operated totally independently of the rest of the army; not even the army commander, Lieutenant General Maclean, exercised any jurisdiction over the obsessively secretive brigade, which was soon to indulge in a murderous frenzy in Matabeleland. Mugabe had signed a secret deal with the North

Koreans in late 1980, but it wasn't until August 1981 that over 100 North Korean instructors arrived to train the Fifth Brigade. When Nkomo got wind of the North Koreans' new role, he warned that Mugabe would use the Fifth Brigade as a private army to create a one-party state – on the North Korean model.

The remaining whites in the armed forces and the 140 British instructors managed, just, to keep the ZNA together in the first demanding year of independence. Wall's initial, if brief, appointment as head of the three armies had done a great deal to prevent a white exodus. It also obviated the need to select a ZIPRA or ZANLA chief of the ZNA. But Walls's short tenure as overall commander could not prevent the clashes between the rival guerrilla forces and, to many whites, he appeared as a sell-out. Walls was disturbed that Mugabe had refused his promotion to full general. Walls had argued that he needed the extra rank to deal with the truculent ZANLA commanders such as Rex Nhongo (who were technically the equivalents of a lieutenant general). In two indiscreet TV interviews, Walls publicly criticized the government. He admitted that he had telegraphed Thatcher just after the elections to request that she should declare the results null and void because of the massive intimidation. The Zimbabwe government enacted a special law to exile Walls even though he had been born in the country. It was a sad end to an illustrious military career.

Emmerson Mnangagwa took over as the country's overall security co-ordinator. He fully understood that the transition from war to peace would be full of pitfalls. Many of the highly politicized ZANLA commanders found it difficult to adapt to low-key professional soldiering as ZANU-PF switched from guerrilla warfare to government administration. (In August 1980, for example, Mugabe's right-hand man, Edgar Tekere, shot a white farm manager, Gerald Adams, after announcing that he was 'going to fight a battle'.) The ex-ZANLA commander Mnangagwa had an intellectual equivalent in ZIPRA: Dumiso Dabengwa. Dabengwa, the urbane, Russian-trained intelligence chief of ZIPRA, had been the prime link between Nkomo and his army, as well as a useful counterweight and collocutor with the powerful Mnangagwa.

The rival guerrilla armies settled into a fitful and uneasy state of temporary truce. Even though a ZIPRA coup was rumoured to have been planned for Christmas 1980, it gradually appeared that tribal animosities would not explode into all-out war. As most of the remaining whites in the ZNA and police began to leave, ZANU-PF dominance looked like slowly penetrating all areas of administration outside Matabeleland. ZIPRA had shot its bolt and Nkomo's 'second coming' seemed remote. It had been mooted that Nkomo might have tried to repeat the experience in Katanga and declare his own UDI in Matabeleland. But this could have survived only with Pretoria's (continuing) connivance, perhaps in exchange for a promise to prevent ANC troops infiltrating through ZAPU-held territory. ZAPU officials were alleged to have approached South Africa, but it was made clear that another UNITA-type campaign was just not on. The feeling in Pretoria by the end of 1980 seemed to have been: Better the pragmatic devil [Mugabe] we know than the one [Nkomo] we don't. And in contrast to ZAPU, the South African government shared Mugabe's distrust of the Russians. (Under Mugabe's orders, the CIO went to extraordinary lengths to monitor the Russians, even when they were exhibiting at the 1983 Trade Fair in Bulawayo: all the existing furniture on the second floor of the Holiday Inn was removed and replaced with furniture containing listening devices. The Chinese were left alone.) Nevertheless, Pretoria had long favoured Nkomo over Mugabe; South African intelligence had been in touch with Nkomo for years. But the ANC/Moscow links prevented a closer relationship. After independence, Pretoria was, however, impressed by Mugabe's brief honeymoon period. The government-controlled South African Broadcasting Corporation was even allowed to air a long and flattering interview with Mugabe on the prime-time *Midweek* TV pro-gramme. The honeymoon did not last long, however.

And so the *Chimurenga* war stuttered on into a new decade. Zimbabwe in 1981 was still not free from the rattle of AKs or the crump of Chinese stick grenades. Yet a year after the election which had formally ended the struggle for black rule, the conditions for further internal military upheaval had dim-inished considerably. The threat from ZIPRA had subsided. And for the whites the anxious days immediately after the election gave way to a less hysterical tension. But Mugabe's government continued to fight a protracted war against the whites. There was no immediate confrontation, no direct assault on the citadels of white supremacy. Initially, government propaganda was careful to castigate only 'racists' and 'colonialists', naming no names or racial groups. But the position of the whites was inexorably undermined, first in one area then in another. It was a peaceful and skilfully handled phase of the long guerrilla struggle for the political, social and economic dominance of the majority. But the whites were not singled out for ethnic slaughter in the way that the Ndebele (and Kalanga) peoples soon were.

By early 1982, Mugabe felt that his new Shona-dominated ZNA was fit for co-ordinated operations; more important, the distinct Fifth Brigade was also fully trained and indoctrinated and even marching with the peculiar North Korean goosestep. Mugabe was ready to destroy ZAPU. The pretext was the 'discovery' of arms caches in Matabeleland, mostly on farms owned by ZAPU or ZAPU supporters. Many of these properties had been bought by pooling the demobilization payments of ordinary ZIPRA soldiers. The discovery of so many arms caches, including anti-aircraft weapons, was proof, said Mugabe, that Nkomo was planning a coup against him. Both ZANU and ZAPU had cached large amounts of weaponry in early 1980 and a high-level joint committee was dealing with the problem. ZIPRA commanders also insisted that the weapons were for protection, not an aggressive coup. But Mugabe was determined to crush Nkomo's perceived challenge once and for all. Mugabe's long smouldering hatred of his rival now came to an angry climax. Mugabe said: 'The only way to deal effectively with a snake is to strike and destroy its head.' Nkomo was sacked and many of the ZAPU properties seized by the state. The ZIPRA generals, Dumiso Dabengwa and Lookout Masuku, were tried for treason. Although acquitted by Mugabe's (initially) independently minded judges, they were re-arrested.

The former ZIPRA soldiers in the ZNA, after suffering increasing reprisals, left in great numbers but not in an organized exodus. Many went home to Bulawayo or to rural kraals and some turned to banditry. Stores were raided and white farmers once again resorted to wartime precautions. Six tourists were abducted and murdered. Even Mugabe's official residence was attacked by ZIPRA gunmen, at least according to the government.

Lieutenant General Rex Nhongo was totally in step with Mugabe. He was advocating 'purge' tactics to end his ZIPRA 'problem'. From 1982-83 he worked on a scheme to emulate South African moves: to invade Botswana and attack refugee camps which held ex-ZIPRA members who had fled Zimbabwe. The actual invasion was called off at a few hours' notice because of BMATT intervention.

Here South Africa took a hand, though it was a minor player in what was to come. Near civil war in its neighbour suited its purpose, especially as Pretoria started to arm some of the ZIPRA men, leavened with a handful of former black Rhodesian soldiers who had entered the SADF or taken refuge in South Africa. Mugabe called the new force 'Super-ZAPU' and grossly exaggerated its size – never more than 200 to 400 in total, including those training or taking 'R and R' (rest and recreation) in the apartheid republic. Pretoria dubbed this secret campaign 'Operation MUTE'.

Although ZAPU's minor dissidence and Mugabe's savage over-reaction was useful to Pretoria, the question of who or what triggered the 'discovery' of the arms caches has always been something of mystery. It was assumed that the CIO always knew where they were and told Mugabe who bided his time until he was ready – politically and militarily – to crush Nkomo's movement. The best explanation, however, comes from the intelligence department of MK, the military wing of the African National Congress. Mugabe had officially favoured their Chinese-backed rival, the Pan-Africanist Congress, but he had allowed MK to operate in Zimbabwe, provided it didn't 'do anything too outrageous'. The CIO, which tracked MK, would turn a blind eye, unless the South African insurgents were arrested in broad daylight with, say, a truckload of weapons on the road to the South African border, and the unwitting ZRP pulled them in for questioning. The MK was promised by ZAPU that some of their weapons caches could be used by them for the struggle against apartheid. An informant in MK had tipped off some of the locations to South African military intelligence who in turn handed on the information to a key South African 'asset', a double agent, in the CIO. He informed his nominal masters when Pretoria decided it was time to stir the pot. This, of course, was manna from heaven for Mugabe's search for a pretext to wipe out ZAPU, ZIPRA and Nkomo.

### The Gukurahundi

The eNtumbane battles were merely the prelude to a brutal military conflict in Matabeleland. More was to follow; on 23 June 1982, a botched assassination attempt on Mugabe led to the finger of blame being pointed at ZAPU and ZIPRA. On 23 July 1983, a tourist bus, headed for Bulawayo from Victoria Falls, was stopped by unknown gunmen; fifteen women and children were released by the gunmen, but six men (two Americans, two Australians and two British) were marched into the bush, where they would subsequently be murdered by the gunmen, led by a man called Sitchela. In response, the new ZNA increased its presence in Matabeleland North, establishing a task force under former Rhodesian Lieutenant Colonel Lionel Dyke. The force was mandated to protect commercial farmers, tourists and to hunt down 'bandits' in the area. Within weeks villagers were being tortured and shot as the task force, which comprised some of the most ruthless elements of the old Rhodesian army, reverted to type. But the tourists' bodies were not found until March 1985 and 'dissident' attacks in Matabeleland continued. Angered by what they saw as the failure of the task force and continued recalcitrance of the Ndebele, Mugabe and ZANU-PF decided that a different force was called for – the Fifth Brigade. It was to fight little and terrorize much, though they claimed to be 'terrorizing the terrorists'.

The Fifth Brigade was initially created as a special forces group. Trained by the North Korean army in counter-insurgency operations, it was marked by its fanatical ideological loyalty to Mugabe and its incredible brutality, which rivalled the atrocities being committed by RENAMO in neighbouring Mozambique. In December 1982, Mugabe attended the Fifth Brigade's passing-out parade. He presented the colours of the new brigade; emblazoned on it was the word *Gukurahundi*. It is a Shona word to describe 'the rain that blows away the chaff'. It was a term used previously to denote the sweeping away of the whites during the last stage of the liberation war. Now it meant sweeping away the 'rubbish' in Matabeleland. Colonel Perence Shiri, an ex-ZANLA commander, headed the new brigade. He told his men: 'From today onwards I want you to start dealing with the dissidents.' The Fifth Brigade was run from the prime minister's office and as such was answerable only to Mugabe.

According to the assessment of a senior CIO officer, 'Upon completion of their five-month training they emerged as brainwashed zombies, armed to the teeth, and with blood-lust in their eyes. All they needed was a convenient target and a venue to be set loose upon.'

From January 1983, Shiri's men conducted a long campaign of mass murders, rape, arson and theft aimed at the civilian population of Matabeleland – anyone who might be possible supporters of ZAPU. Initially, long lists of ex-ZIPRA men were targeted, then their families and finally nearby villagers. Within six weeks 2,000 were killed. In total, individual killings and group massacres amounted to probably 20,000 killed, although Ian Smith claimed it was as high as 30,000. The CIO's estimate was 18,000. CIO officers provided regular reports directly to Mugabe, but they were ignored. When a senior white CIO officer complained of the barbarity, he was told, 'This is not your war.' Curfews were imposed, the movement of transport was stopped, shops were closed. Cattle were confiscated, as triumphalist Shona soldiers reminded the Ndebele of their cattle raids against the less warlike Shona in the nineteenth century. Drought had already hit the region, now food and aid supplies were savagely curtailed. Starvation as much as murder and mayhem stalked the land of the Ndebele.

The methods of the red-bereted Fifth Brigade were deliberately cruel – far worse than anything attempted by even the toughest reprisals of the white-led security forces during the liberation war. Shiri's men, well-trained by North Korean psychopaths, would routinely round up villagers in their dozens or even hundreds, and then assemble them in a local school or other central public locations. They would be forced into lengthy *pungwes*, singing Mugabe praise-songs, and severely beaten to encourage their performances. The gatherings would usually end with a series of public executions, after the victims were forced to dig their own graves in front of their families. Sometimes the villagers were herded into their huts and then burnt alive.

A report published much later, in 1997, headed by the Catholic Commission for Justice and Peace, made it clear that Mugabe had ordered his butchers to injure, mutilate and kill in such a variety of evil ways that the terror would be indelibly etched in memories for generations to come. The report makes clear that the surviving civilian population would live with this fear for the rest of their lives, for the horror had to be so great that they would pass the fear down to subsequent generations. To quote from the report:

> In one incident at Soloboni on 23 February 1983: Five Brigade rounded up entire village at the borehole. Six people were chosen at random and were bayoneted to death and buried in one grave. Everyone was then beaten. Five people were beaten to death and one person died years later, partly as a result of this beating. Another man who wept to see his brother killed was severely beaten and died a few weeks later from his injuries. One old lady who was found in her hut was raped, and 5 Bde then set fire to a plastic bag and burned the old lady with it, setting fire to her blanket. She died three weeks later from her burns. One hut was burned.

This 1997 report was headlined *Breaking the Silence,* because Mugabe kept the press away from the massacres and, with one or two honourable exceptions, Mugabe was still treated as a media darling in the West. One of the exceptions was Donald Telford of the London *Observer* newspaper. He asked Mugabe in an interview in 1984 whether he could have tried a political solution to his perceived problems with the Ndebeles. 'The solution is a military one,' Mugabe replied. 'Their grievances are unfounded. The verdict of the voters was cast in 1980. They should have accepted defeat then. The situation in Matabeleland requires a change. The people must be reoriented.' Like Stalin, Mugabe was saying if you don't like the way a people vote, change the people, not the government – that was to be his leitmotif for the rest of his long rule. More privately Mugabe admitted, 'We eradicate them. We don't differentiate when we fight. Because we can't tell who is a dissident and who is not.'

The British largely kept silent, too. Sir Martin Evans, the ambassador to Harare, said with typical understatement: 'It wasn't pleasant and people were being killed but … I don't think anything was to be gained by protesting to

Mugabe about it … I think the advice [from London] was to steer clear of it in the interests of doing our best positively to help Zimbabwe build itself up as a nation.' Presumably, sustained massacres should not get in the way of good diplomacy or nation-building.

The local press and nearly all the international media were also silent. When the churches, including the Catholic Church, protested, they were dismissed by Mugabe as 'sanctimonious prelates' who were playing to the international gallery. Nkomo could do little – he was described as 'Public Enemy No 1'. Very narrowly escaping assassination, he fled and sought sanctuary in the land of his erstwhile oppressors: the big man rented a very small flat in London, because Tiny Rowland, the Lonrho boss, suddenly cut his long-time financial support. Nkomo said that the Mugabe government 'was led by fascists, not even comparable to Herr Hitler … We stand a cursed people. Independence has meant nothing to us.'

Some of the comparison was valid – the Fifth Brigade did act like the Gestapo in the conquered Slav lands, though any comparison with the holocaust was exaggerated. Mugabe did not plan to kill *all* Ndebeles – some of his allies, such as Enos Nkala, were Ndebele themselves. The aim was to crush ZAPU and the Ndebele as a political force, not a text-book definition of genocide. The Fifth Brigade and other elements of the ZNA concentrated on Matabeleland north in the first year of *Gukurahundi*, and then in 1984 the southern Ndebele areas. Church leaders continued to plead for Mugabe to stop, not least because of the widespread starvation. Martin Meredith in one of his authoritative books on Zimbabwe, *Our Votes, Our Guns,* quotes an officer in the Fifth Brigade in response to Church and civic leaders' pleas for mercy: 'First you will eat your chickens, then your goats, then your cattle, then your donkeys. Then you will eat your children and finally you will eat the dissidents.'

The dissidents themselves – the bandits, genuine ZIPRA resistance and South African-backed Super-ZAPU – did kill perhaps up to 700-800 civilians, including a number of white farmers and their families. ZANU officials were targeted, and twenty-two Shona civilians were massacred in Mwenezi. Their attacks on tourists and tourist centres also damaged an important element of the Zimbabwean economy. But Mugabe's response was entirely disproportionate to the threat.

Who were the 'dissidents'? Government-controlled media routinely portrayed them as insurgent groups which were organized by ZAPU with the aim of overthrowing the government. In fact, there is no strong evidence which points to direct ZAPU control. The 'dissidents' included deserters from the new ZDF and ZRP, former RAR, criminals from Bulawayo and

Lupane; there were also destabilization groups which were infiltrated from South Africa and sponsored by the South African Intelligence and SADF. Nor was there a uniform strategic objective from the insurgents. Some were little better than the Fifth Brigade which hunted them as they preyed on villagers and often executed those suspected of collaborating with the *amatsvina* (Shona) enemy. But others saw their activities as a war of liberation for Matabeleland against a largely Shona government and military which were destroying Matabeleland. The government claimed that it faced a massive insurgency in Matabeleland but it is unlikely that dissidents ever numbered more than 500 men at any one time. They established three operational zones: western region (Victoria Falls to Plumtree); northern region (around Silobela); and southern region (from Mberengwa to the Botswana border area around Plumtree). Each region was under the command of a ZNA deserter. In operational terms, the dissidents, who operated in small detachments of five-fifteen men, were never a strategic threat. They were too few, often lacked any unifying ideology and were unable to get sustained support from a local population which was being massacred by the Fifth Brigade. Tactically however, the dissidents displayed resilience and continued to operate in Matabeleland right up to the Unity Agreement of 1987.

Once Matabeleland was cowed, the Fifth Brigade was returned to barracks for re-training. As the 1985 election approached, Mugabe switched to a campaign of political intimidation. This time, instead of North Korean, or even Nazi, models, Mugabe took a leaf out of Mao's *Little Red Book.* ZANU-PF Youth Brigades, consciously inspired by the Red Guards, were sent in to 'educate the masses' in Matabeleland and in the Midlands, with its mixed population of Shona and Ndebele. Attendance at party rallies was made compulsory, and any Ndebele caught without a ZANU-PF party card could be in serous trouble. Many resorted to carrying *both* ZAPU and ZANU-PF cards, which could also result in a beating if both cards were discovered by the Youth Brigades. The odious Nkala also set up his own special unit in the ZRP which came under his ministerial control. It was called the Police Internal Security and Intelligence unit, PISI, for short. In the Ndebele language, *pisi* means hyena.

Nkomo returned from exile in London to contest the 1985 election. Much to Mugabe's chagrin, not only did Ian Smith do well in the poll for the white seats, but Nkomo's ZAPU won all the seats in Matabeleland. This was a serious tribute to the stoicism of the Ndebele after the savagery of their persecution. (This courage was to be replicated in the next generation of voters who strongly supported the MDC opposition to Mugabe, although Tsvangirai was a Shona from Manicaland.) Nevertheless, Mugabe secured his electoral majority in the country as a whole. He had successfully batted off criticism of his military cleansing against ZAPU. He had dismissed Amnesty International's 1985 report as mere lies, just as he was to ignore the more detailed indictments by the Catholic Church much later. For Mugabe, force had always worked and he became immune to internal and international criticism. He was later to boast that he had 'a degree in violence'. As ever, his psychological reaction was to see himself as the selfless father of Zimbabwe perversely rejected by some of his own wayward children. Tough love and re-education would, however, force them back into line.

Nkomo certainly had no option but to step into line. In December 1987 he signed a so-called Unity Accord, merging his party into ZANU-PF. At the same time, Mugabe declared himself executive president, thus combining the roles of head of state, head of government, and commander-in-chief of the armed forces. He gave himself the power to dissolve parliament, declare martial law and the right to run for an unlimited number of terms of office. He also talked about ZANU-PF ruling forever. Comrade Mugabe had effectively secured his one-party state and presidency for life.

In April 1988, an amnesty was offered to the remaining dissidents. (More important for Mugabe's often perverted sense of legalism, the amnesty was extended to include all atrocities committed by his own security forces during the *Gukurahundi*.) Officially, 122 dissidents surrendered in all. In June 1988, the London *Times* correspondent described how forty-three ZIPRA dissidents arrogantly surrendered in the Nkayi area. 'Some looked like extras from the film *Mad Max*: lean men with intense eyes, adorned with dreadlocks, pink scarves, necklaces, bangles, jeans and heavy military boots with puttees. Others, in overalls and floppy hats, could have been farm labourers.' The government had always portrayed the rebels as mere gangs of bandits, but the cocky interviews given to *The Times* demonstrated they had a command structure and that they were well-equipped. Moreover, they also expounded an articulate political programme of resistance.

Mugabe's sour victory set the pattern – force, political theatre, and then legal band-aids – to secure his goal of dominance. He was to pull it off again and again, most dramatically in 2008 when he imposed a merger, not of parties, but of government, on his main rivals, the two wings of the MDC. The MDC was warned that this was a repeat of Nkomo's humiliation, but once more *force majeure* had left Mugabe's rivals with few options, but exile, prison or death. In this sense the fear instilled by the *Gukurahundi* was to achieve Mugabe's goals decades later.

# Chapter 7

# Foreign Fronts

*Fighting Apartheid*

In the 1970s and 1980s, to preserve white rule, Pretoria launched a war of destabilization against nearly all its black neighbours. Smaller countries such as Lesotho and Swaziland or a placid large neighbour such as Botswana were entrenched as economic protectorates. In Angola, South Africa had sent in armies and backed large guerrilla allies, such as Jonas Savimbi's rebel troops. Russian and Cuban forces were engaged heavily in containing the pro-apartheid forces. In Mozambique, Pretoria was less active than in Angola, because the ramshackle economy and feeble revolutionary army provided fewer military challenges. In Angola and Mozambique Pretoria propped up existing insurgencies against the Marxist incumbents. In South West Africa, later Namibia, Pretoria also fought a determined counter-insurgency war to delay majority rule.

Zimbabwe was certainly part of apartheid's second front (the struggle inside the country by the ANC was considered the first). Each destabilization campaign was distinct. Zimbabwe was of special interest to Pretoria, because historically Pretoria had treated Rhodesia as almost part of the South African *reich*. Before 1923 Rhodesia was encouraged to join the southern Republic. Many military strategists in South Africa had long regarded the Zambezi, not the Limpopo, as the true border of white imperium. Mugabe's victory was a worst-case scenario for Pretoria.

Mugabe had seen firsthand what damage had been inflicted on the frontline states during his war of liberation. On taking power in Zimbabwe, Samora Machel, his former host, had warned him not only to keep white expertise but also to avoid a full-frontal war with South Africa. Mugabe cut formal diplomatic and sporting ties with the apartheid state; that was the least he could do to satisfy pressure from the Organization of African Unity (OAU); but he privately assured Pretoria that he would not allow any of the South African resistance movements to operate militarily from Zimbabwe.

Nevertheless, Pretoria soon began to apply a tourniquet to Zimbabwe's lifeblood. The Rhodesian war had locked Zimbabwe into the South African

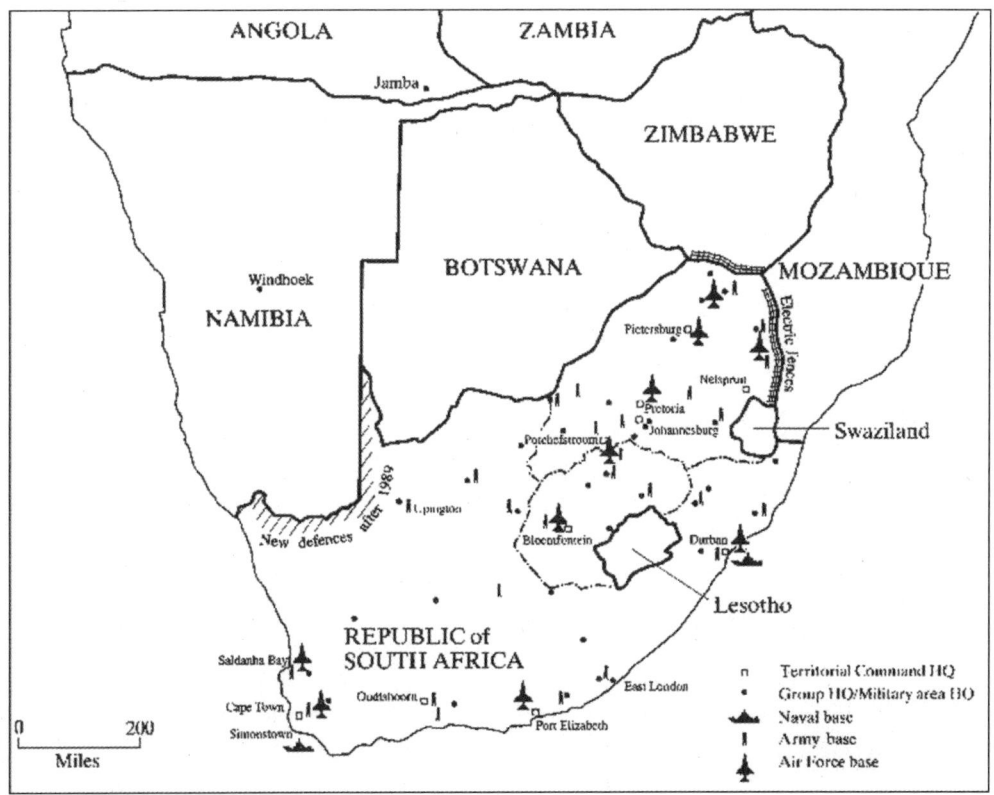

Map 5 – SADF deployment 1989. (The map does not include SADF deployment in Namibia, as the SADF was withdrawn in late 1989/early 1990 as part of the Namibian independence process. New defence structures were implemented in the northern Cape, along the southern Namibian border.

economic system. Roughly 90 per cent of its exports passed through the apartheid state. The transport nexus worked both ways: Zimbabwe was a main route for South African trade with Zaire, Zambia and Malawi. Some sort of *modus vivendi* was necessary. Mugabe initially suppressed ZANU-PF hotheads who were screaming for their *Chimurenga* to immediately march south. 'We've got to sup with the devil or starve,' said one of Mugabe's closest aides. 'But if we starve, many other African countries starve with us. And that's where South Africa knows it's got us cornered for a long time.'

Yet Pretoria was soon to serve up a varied destabilization diet: economic pressures, particularly in 1981 and 1982, support for Zimbabwean dissidents, and not just in ZAPU, selective assassinations, sabotage and anti-Mugabe propaganda. Pretoria, however, stopped short of direct and continuous military intervention. Zimbabwe was a member of the British Commonwealth where British military instructors, admittedly a small number, trained a large and battle-hardened military force. Washington might have encouraged Pretoria's legions to fight Cubans and Russians in Angola, but the US would not countenance a similar riposte in Zimbabwe. Covert, albeit deniable, dirty tricks were another matter. Pretoria had all the best cards: economic dominance, a large potential fifth column of whites inside Zimbabwe and a reservoir of revanchist whites attached to, or integrated in, the South African Defence Force.

Pretoria insisted on holding Mugabe to his promise not to harbour military active ANC insurgents. They had to be thrown out of the country. Mugabe quietly returned around 300 to Zambia. It was not enough to satisfy the South African government. In July 1980 South African railways began to withdraw its technicians and engineers lent to the *ancien régime*. 'Inexplicable' bottlenecks in the ports and on the railways followed. 'The notoriously drunken station-master in Messina' – the small railway town near Zimbabwe's main border post at Beit Bridge – became a legendary figure in this blackmail scenario.

Pretoria also took a close interest in the mutinies in the ZNA and how the white-piloted aircraft, fixed- and rotor-wing, played such a crucial role in containing them. Stirring up ZIPRA and removing the white air force component were obvious means of leverage. Although some of the Afrikaner doves praised Mugabe's reconciliation moves, the hardliners in military and intelligence circles thought that ZIPRA-ZANLA battles indicated that Mugabe was ripe for toppling. Mugabe was concerned that once again South African agents might try to assassinate him.

Pretoria withdrew more locomotives. On 16 August 1981 a mysterious explosion destroyed the armoury at Inkomo barracks near Harare. At the time it was blamed on vengeful ex-Rhodesian and South African infiltrators. Actually, it was ZNA incompetence – untrained troops had made a cooking fire near gas containers and explosives. Despite the reality, the Zimbabwean government ran with the rumour that South African saboteurs were everywhere. Many of the incidents were sabotage, not accidents, however. On 18 December 1981 a blast ripped through the new ZANU-PF HQ in Harare. One senior South African officer warned: 'If it came to a showdown, we could wring Mugabe's neck like a chicken.'

A part of the neck-wringing was being conducted in the Transvaal, not far from Zimbabwe's southern border: the SADF was training recruits for Super-ZAPU, including some genuine ZIPRA. The Entabeni camp, near Messina, could train up to sixty Super-ZAPU. Some were mere border-jumpers escaping Zimbabwe, others had been carefully recruited at Dukwe camp in Botswana. To appease their guilt at the apartheid connections, the disgruntled soldiers used to quote an old African saying: 'In order to cross a river you sometimes have to ride on the crocodile's back.' Many ZIPRA soldiers were fiercely loyal to their former commanders, especially Lookout Masuku and Dumiso Dabengwa, and less to Nkomo. The detention of the generals at Chikurubi maximum security prison in Harare prompted a major exodus from the ZNA, and a small one into the arms of the waiting South Africans.

The officer in charge of the South African military intelligence operations in Matabeleland was called 'Major Brian' or sometimes 'Mr Z'. This was in fact Major Gray Branfield, a former Rhodesian police officer, who was killed in Kut, Iraq, in 2006. Major Brian co-ordinated a wide range of operations against Mugabe's government, including assassinating ANC figures or failing to do so in the case of Jeremy Brickhill, the only white man to serve in the frontline of ZIPRA forces. Major Brian's second in command in Matabeleland was Kevin Woods, ex-BSAP and then a senior CIO officer. Woods ran a very complicated operation. His day job included monitoring ANC activity as well as Mugabe's close protection when the leader was in Matabeleland. But his work for the South Africans as a double agent entailed leaking ANC ops to Pretoria. Woods also set up a pseudo Super-ZAPU operation to infiltrate and monitor Pretoria's official destabilization plans. His double game became so complex that, in his memoirs, Woods admitted that he sometimes lost track, despite keeping a detailed ballistic log of who was using what weapons. This was important in cases where white farmers were killed, which the South Africans had expressly instructed their Super-ZAPU not to do. To add to the hall of mirrors, ZNA military intelligence ran a small pseudo unit of its own, not just to flush out ZIPRA and Super-ZAPU dissidents but also to kill off political opponents, both Shona and Ndebele, to settle old party and, occasionally, personal scores. Woods's operations became so tangled that he was caught out in a basic error of fieldcraft and ended up serving nearly twenty years in Zimbabwean jails.

So five sometimes rival groups of dissidents ranged across the vast swathes of empty Matabele bush: bandits feeding on the anarchy; genuine ZIPRA rebels held together by a disciplined command structure, with support from sanctuaries in Botswana, and perhaps only titular loyalty to Nkomo; Super-ZAPU, supplied from South Africa; and then there were the pseudo operations. Mugabe lumped them all together as disorganized bandits contaminated by the devil in Pretoria. He claimed that 5,000 dissidents were waiting to invade, in a replay of the Bay of Pigs adventure in Cuba.

In March 1983 a broadcasting station, Radio Truth, started pumping out anti-Mugabe propaganda. It said it was operating from inside Matabeleland. In fact, the radio station was a South African Broadcasting Corporation installation on the outskirts of Johannesburg. Pretoria denied any connection. The denials were unconvincing at the best of times; then on 25 November 1983 the tapes of the theme music of RENAMO's *Voz de Africa Livre* were accidentally switched with that of Super-ZAPU's Radio Truth. Mugabe had further proof that the propaganda stations were broadcasting from South Africa, not Mozambique and Matabeleland.

As the previous arms caches were used up or seized by the ZNA, Pretoria supplied weapons to both ZIPRA and Super-ZAPU. The ferment in southern Zimbabwe suited Pretoria for a number of reasons. It undermined Mugabe's policy of reconciliation and hastened the exodus of whites, especially farmers. More white farmers were now being killed than during the war that ended in 1980. This weakened the Zimbabwean agricultural economy and discouraged international investment. Attacks on foreign holiday-makers also hit the tourist industry. Secondly, the *Gukurahundi* campaign concentrated the ZNA's attention in Matabeleland and not in Mozambique, where South Africa was bolstering the anti-Marxist rebels. As a bonus, the saturation of ZNA forces in southern Matabeleland discouraged ANC penetration into the Northern Transvaal province of the white-ruled republic.

On 27 July 1982 Pretoria aimed a precise blow at Zimbabwe's military machine. A quarter of the air force was sabotaged at Thornhill base near Gweru (Gwelo). Thirteen fighters and trainers, including Hawk Mk60s recently purchased from Britain, were blown up. Six white officers, including an air vice marshal, were detained, tortured with electric shock treatment, sexually abused, acquitted, re-detained and eventually expelled from the country. The six officers were completely innocent. The airmen had cherished their shiny new British machines, so long awaited during the lean sanctions years. Their treatment caused a furore, especially in the right-wing media in the UK. The Thornhill raid was a South African special forces' operation, assisted by some former members of the Rhodesian SAS. The audacious attack virtually eliminated the jet strike capability of the Zimbabwean air force and prompted a mass exodus of the remaining white pilots and technicians.

The airmen's trial also cast a poor light on Mugabe's claims that Zimbabwe was a beacon for human rights and judicial probity in both southern Africa and the Commonwealth. John Cox, one of the officers jailed, called the trial 'one of Africa's finest examples of a comedy of errors – incompetence compounded by greater incompetence … that was to make the Goon Show look serious'. Cox, a Briton, said all this only after he had returned safely to Winterbourne, near Bristol, England.

A month after the Thornhill attack, three white soldiers from a much larger SADF raiding party were killed on the wrong side of the Zimbabwean border. The three were ex-Rhodesians who had served in the RLI and SAS. Pretoria was eventually forced into admitting that a raid had taken place, but said it was an 'unauthorized freelance operation' to rescue political prisoners in south-eastern Zimbabwe. The number of these unauthorized and freelance operations grew apace, and the diplomatic lie became laughable. Undeterred, former SAS soldiers continued to attack Zimbabwe's alternative oil supplies by hitting pipelines in Mozambique. By December 1982, the combined strangulation of South African and Mozambican sources meant that Zimbabwe was down to two weeks' supply of petrol.

American pressure on Pretoria forced a curtailment of these raids, but South Africa had made its point: the tap could be turned off whenever it suited the apartheid regime. With US mediation, South African intelligence chiefs had a series of high-level meetings in Harare to set up a liaison committee to prevent what one Zimbabwean minister termed 'nuclear war by accident'. The SADF's Major General Pieter van der Westhuizen, the head of military intelligence, travelled discreetly to Harare for talks with the ZNA chief of staff, Sheba Gava. Separately, Neil Barnard, the youthful head of the National Intelligence Service, also made a secret trip to Zimbabwe. As far as overt raids were concerned, an uneasy truce followed.

The covert intelligence war did not, however, cease. From 1980-1984 various South African intelligence agencies had run a sophisticated penetration of Zimbabwe. For example, duplicate keys of nearly every cell-block in prisons and police stations, duplicate keys of the ZRP Special Branch and CIO vehicles and the architectural plans of security installations such as army bases had been sent to Pretoria. A clever ploy but the hoard was lost by bungling spooks in Pretoria. That debacle and the unintended deaths of so many white farmers made the Afrikaner spymasters think again. Some of the farmers had been killed by genuine ZIPRA dissidents, not under Pretoria's control, although others were probably murdered by turned dissidents acting in a pseudo role under the command of the ZNA. Harare was applying the lessons learned from the Selous Scouts in the previous decade. In 1984 the peace accord with Mozambique was supposed to lead to a reduction in the tempo of the second front, including Zimbabwe. It was likely that Major General H. Roux, of South Africa's Directorate of Special

Tasks, pulled the plug on some of the dirty tricks in that year, although a number of operations continued, especially against the ANC. And of course South African military intelligence continued to monitor the communications traffic of the ZNA.

(After apartheid ended, the Truth and Reconciliation Commission investigated many of the destabilization operations which were connected to the highly secret Civil Cooperation Bureau, a means of denying state involvement in extra-judicial killings, both in South Africa and the neighbouring states. Some of the Zimbabwean operations by the 'Juliet' cell, led by Woods and commanded by Major Brian, were revealed, including actions long after Pretoria's military intelligence was supposed to have curtailed its anti-Mugabe campaign.)

The South African engagement in Matabeleland had apparently wound down before the 1985 election but it soon became clear to even the diehard strategists in Pretoria that Nkomo's chances of electoral triumph (let alone Bishop Mozerewa's) were nil. Despite continuing to vote for Ian Smith or other white conservatives, the chimera of a white-Nkomo-Mzuzorewa government had finally been interred. Pretoria had to deal with Mugabe as the undisputed leader. Pretoria shifted some of its focus to Mozambique as ZNA troops poured into the country to swamp RENAMO, Pretoria's anti-Marxist ally.

South Africa was not finished with Mugabe. In May 1986, the SADF openly attacked Harare, as part of its military assault on three Commonwealth countries in the region. The ambition was to sink the Commonwealth Eminent Persons' Group's peace drive. Air strikes were conducted against ANC facilities in Zambia and Botswana. The ground strike in Harare would be more clandestine and well-planned. The first target was 16 Angwa Street in downtown Harare. Operatives working under the general codename of Barnacle – part of the destabilization programme – had already bugged the offices, which controlled MK operations in the region. The other target was an ANC safe house in a four-bed-roomed house in Ashdown Park, a leafier northern suburb. The attack on the premises, Operation KODAK, was first allocated to 5 Reconnaissance Commando in late 1985. On the night of 18 May 1986, three Pumas flew in at a height of thirty-five metres to stay below the radar while keeping radio silence. They established a small rural communication base, with a commander and a doctor, and some indigenous help with transport. Switching from a decrepit van, they hired saloon cars, carrying their weapons in golf bags, to fit their tourist cover. They drove to Harare. Using an aluminium ladder to scale a wall, one team planted in the office three school satchels, containing 1.5kg bunker bombs. The team that hit the office was made up of three operators, two blacks and a white. The attack on the safe house, which was supposed to contain an armoury, was to be dealt with by six men, both black and white. The second team went in with all guns blazing and killed one occupant and seized documents. They escaped the same way they came in, with no problems en route, but dropping spiked caltrops to slow down any vehicle follow-ups. The one hiccup for the special forces was a severe complaint from their quartermaster that they had left behind the expensive aluminium ladder. Pretoria had made its political point – it could penetrate the very heart of Harare, hit ANC targets, and get away with it unscathed.

The government mouthpiece, the *Herald*, responded with banner headlines: 'Racists Bomb Frontline Capital'; the editorial lambasted the 'Boer Vampires'. Mugabe publicly lost his temper when he talked of 'killing Boers'. Sanctions were immediately discussed in the Zimbabwean cabinet, but the economic pragmatists won the day. Mugabe later returned to the subject of imposing sanctions on South Africa, but soon the war in Mozambique and the dramatic changes impelled by the release of Nelson Mandela were to alter Zimbabwean dynamics.

The cold war between Harare and Pretoria, sometimes interrupted by real fighting, lasted just over a decade. Nkomo's forced marriage with Mugabe and the resultant tense peace in Matabeleland, as well as the exodus (and occasional arrest) of some of Pretoria's intelligence assets in Zimbabwe had diminished the undeclared war between the two states. Occasional raids and sabotage from South Africa continued, but less frequently. The excuse was still the same: 'crazy gangs' of ex-Rhodesians were trying to rescue friends and relatives off their own bat. Yet it was strange – nearly a decade after their defeat – that ex-Rhodesians were still so bitter and so well-organized and so well-financed that they could attempt sophisticated missions without the knowledge of the generally well-informed South African intelligence system.

The SADF had fought well in the second front in Angola and Namibia, although often the Afrikaner intelligence agencies had not matched the professional skills of their combat troops. And the SADF was nuclear-armed. Those in Harare who expected the Afrikaners to fight as long and hard as the white Rhodesians were surprised when Nelson Mandela, the ANC leader, and the South African president, F. W. de Klerk, managed to negotiate a relatively peaceful transition to majority rule. The two lawyers eventually finessed a legal deal that held – just.

The electoral victory of Mandela in 1994 would transform southern

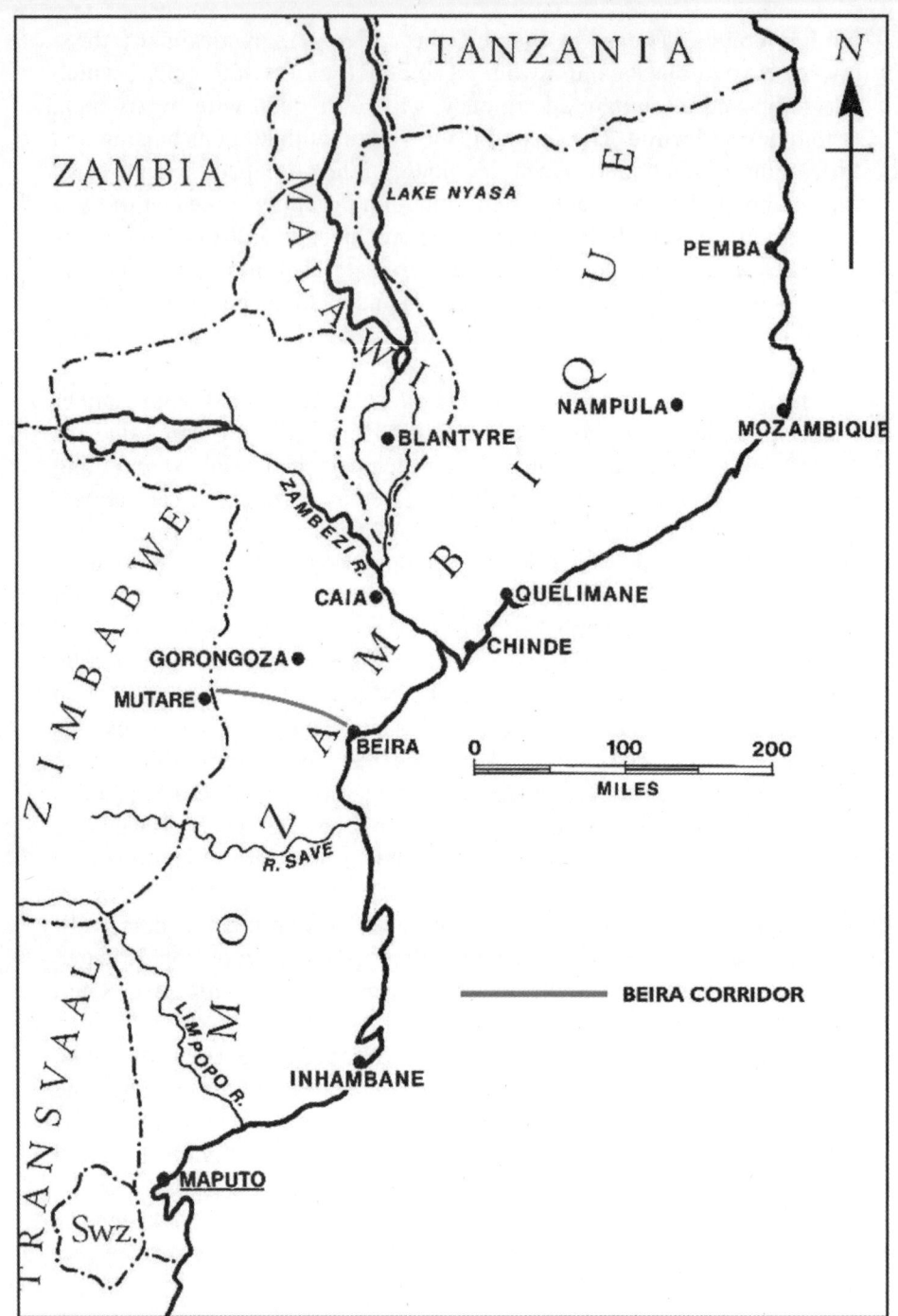

Map 6 – Mugabe's War in Mozambique

African politics. Mugabe's war with apartheid would end. The Zimbabwean leader had supported the PAC, not the ANC. The PAC's attachment to black consciousness and Maoist inclinations, plus its wariness of Moscow and trade union affiliations, had appealed to Mugabe. But it would be hard to ignore the psychological challenge as well: Mandela replaced Mugabe as the liberation hero of the region and the continent. Mandela's secular sainthood in the West was a feat Mugabe could only dream of. It became apparent from Mugabe's surliness and even public sulks at major African events – when Mandela was inevitably feted – that the Zimbabwean leader resented his relegation in the pantheon of African idols.

## Zimbabwe's war in Mozambique

FRELIMO had done much to install Mugabe as Zimbabwe's leader. Yet Mugabe's backer was constantly under fire itself. FRELIMO had to fight three wars in succession: an anti-colonial struggle against the Portuguese army, then a bitter campaign against the Rhodesians and, most savagely, after 1980, a double-barrelled war against the SADF and RENAMO (*Resistência Nacional Moçambicana*). RENAMO, the National Mozambique Resistance Movement, was born in double original sin: as the bastard child of both the Rhodesian CIO and apartheid's military intelligence. Ken Flower, the CIO director-general, had given the go-ahead in 1976-77 to set up an insurgency inside Mozambique, initially to spy on and then disrupt FRELIMO's aid to ZANLA. But it grew spontaneously, feeding on a variety of discontents such as land nationalization, the relegation of the traditional chiefs, Marxist incompetence and religious harassment of Catholics and Muslims. In late-1979 Afonso Dhlakama, a short, twenty-six-year-old bespectacled man, who looked exactly like a timid bank clerk, took over as leader of the insurgency. He was anointed by the CIO, although he told the author, during a number of wartime interviews in the bush (1986-1991), that he had been elected by his followers.

When Mugabe took over in April 1980, the CIO handed over control of Dhlakama to South African military intelligence. RENAMO said it had 2,000 insurgents at the time, though Flower insisted it was more like 1,000. It soon grew to nearly 20,000 and to operate throughout nearly the whole country. The SADF provided logistical support. RENAMO did cause lots of problems for FRELIMO in the early 1980s but the disruption of oil pipelines, railways and road bridges, especially along the crucial Beira corridor, was almost always the work of the South African Reconnaissance Commandos, often with a former Rhodesian SAS element. In intelligence circles a rule of thumb applied: if the job was botched it was RENAMO – if it was done properly, it was the work of the Recces.

Sometimes the SADF role was overt. On 23 May 1983, in retaliation for a car bomb explosion in Central Pretoria, South African jets bombed alleged ANC safe houses in the Matola and Liberdade suburbs of the Mozambican capital, Maputo. After this public humiliation of its ally, the USSR warned Pretoria directly that Soviet and Cuban troops might enter the war, as they had done in Angola. This was the time of the Reagan doctrine, when the US was prepared to support resistance against Russia's 'evil empire', from Afghanistan to Angola. Despite much lobbying in Washington, RENAMO never managed to get on Reagan's list of worthy insurgents. This was partly because of its terrible reputation for atrocities, some of it invented by FRELIMO. As Dhlakama told the author in 1986, 'Marxists are always good at two things – propaganda and the secret police.'

Supporting RENAMO was a useful policy for the hawks in Pretoria – it deterred FRELIMO's support for the ANC and it kept Zimbabwe dependent on South African transport routes. The Zimbabwean security interest focused on three main alternative routes. Firstly, the Beira Corridor – a rail, road, oil and electricity power-line linking the port of Beira to Mutare on Zimbabwe's eastern border. This 320-mile corridor became the responsibility of both ZNA and Mozambican troops. Secondly, the Tete corridor was a 150-mile stretch of road between Nyamapanda on the Zimbabwean border to Zobue town on the Mozambique/Malawi border. Protecting the Tete strategic bridge was the specific responsibility of the ZNA First Mechanized Battalion which was deployed to Tete in 1985. Finally, and of least importance, was the Limpopo corridor. This was a derelict rail link from Chicualacuala on the Zimbabwean/Mozambican border running 300 miles to Maputo. The Zimbabweans began to upgrade the railway in 1987. Disrupting these alternative routes made Harare almost totally dependent on Pretoria's borders and good will.

Pretoria's intelligence community was divided between the maximalists and the minimalists. The maximalists believed that it was the right time to overthrow FRELIMO and replace it with RENAMO. Mugabe had received a top-secret report from his own intelligence in 1982 that Pretoria was capable of toppling his main ally, Samora Machel, in forty-eight hours. The minimalists in Pretoria, headed by the feisty foreign minister, Pik Botha, wanted to draw Machel into a non-aggression pact. Botha doubted whether RENAMO 'had the capacity to run anything more than a Mercedes and a few atrocities'. Botha also complained that 'South African military intelligence was a trickier negotiating opponent than FRELIMO Marxists.'

The minimalists had their way, after the South African President, P. W. Botha, was persuaded. Machel and P. W. Botha met in a circus atmosphere alongside the Nkomati river on 16 March 1984. With cameras whirring, 1,500 guests lunched sumptuously alongside the white VIP railway carriages that had been used for the abortive Rhodesian conference on Victoria Falls bridge nine years earlier. Behind the polite, if bizarre, *coup de theatre* lay the simple truth: 'Kick out the ANC or else.' Or, as the writer Joseph Hanlon put it: 'FRELIMO was screaming, "Of course I love you, just don't hit me again".'

The Nkomati deal was simple: both sides would ditch their rebel friends, the ANC and RENAMO, although the pact did not mention either of them explicitly. The ANC reluctantly accepted that Machel 'had to hug the hyena'. It was life or death for a tottering regime in Maputo. It all depended on whether Pretoria kept its promise. RENAMO's support was scaled down but not stopped. Both Machel and Mugabe were still under the cosh.

Within a year both men realized that Pretoria was acting in bad faith, despite being aware of the conflicting opinions within Pretoria about RENAMO. Mugabe owed Machel a great deal. The two men had signed a military pact in October 1980. Since 1982 Zimbabwean troops had helped Machel with 500 troops sent to guard the Beira corridor, but the focus of the ZNA then had been on the perceived internal challenge from ZAPU. Mugabe felt by 1985 that this domestic matter had largely been resolved. Now he had to respond fully to Machel's urgent requests as FRELIMO faced an existential threat from a revived RENAMO. As one senior FRELIMO official observed, 'RENAMO was unpicking the social fabric.' The government held the crumbling cities but throughout the country RENAMO owned the night.

In contravention of Nkomati, the SADF's logistical and communications support had enabled RENAMO to expand nationwide. But the particular focus was Beira, one of the few half-functioning southern African ports not in apartheid hands. It was also Mugabe's lifeline. The leaders of Mozambique, Zimbabwe and Tanzania needed to co-ordinate militarily. They concentrated on the main trade corridors, not just Beira, but also the northern transport link, the Tete Corridor. Tanzanian and a small number of Malawian troops helped to guard the trains. In July 1985 the British granted funds to enlarge the officer training scheme in Nyanga, Zimbabwe, so as to include Mozambicans. (And, unofficially, ex-SAS troops were hired to protect Western business interests in Mozambique.) But the major rescue component was Zimbabwean. Its expeditionary force mushroomed from 1,500 in mid-1984 to 12,000 by the end of 1985. That figure soared to 18,000 during major offensives against RENAMO.

In December 1984 the ZNA deployed 800 troops, including its SAS, 3 Brigade and the Para Group, to hit the RENAMO HQ in Gorongosa. Since RENAMO was always moving its main base, and had set up various dummy HQs to confuse the enemy's air observation, the raid was not a success. Perhaps that was not a surprise as it had been code-named Operation LEMON, military slang for a screw-up. Also RENAMO had been tipped off. Zimbabwe intelligence did not know whether it was penetration of the CIO by the South Africans or a slip-up by the notoriously inept, cruel and recently purged Mozambican secret police. On 28 August 1985 Zimbabwean paratroopers, backed by Mozambican troops, stormed the real RENAMO main HQ, called Casa Banana, in the Gorongosa game reserve. RENAMO claimed that they had to flee the helicopter-led assault of 12,000 ZNA and 8,000 FRELIMO. That was their, probably exaggerated, estimate. RENAMO also claimed to have retreated in good order, and after killing two Soviet officers who had been coordinating the assault. It was certainly a major operation, dubbed Operation GRAPEFRUIT. The ZNA deployed three infantry battalions, combined with SAS and Commando groups as well as gunships using old Rhodesian Fire Force techniques.

More awkward for RENAMO was the capture of the so-called Vaz diaries. Major Joaquim Vaz was Dhlakama's secretary. FRELIMO released them with glee. They contained telling details of South African weapon supplies, SADF instructions to target Mozambican infrastructure, the SADF's construction of an air strip at Casa Banana and the regular use of their three Daphne-class submarines not only to transport RENAMO bigwigs but also to land special forces. It also contained details of the embarrassing divisions within Pretoria. South Africa was once again in the dock, and FRELIMO gained some leverage, especially in its requests for more support from Harare and also Washington and London.

The world of diplomacy was a long way from the nightmare in the bush. Despite the presence of the large ZNA army, 2,000 Tanzanians (and the promise of 5,000 Nigerians, presumably a bonus for Maputo), FRELIMO's troops in the countryside started to disintegrate. Some were FRELIMO by day, but RENAMO at night. RENAMO would send a note to FRELIMO forces saying it was planning to attack the next day. That would be enough to guarantee that the rebels would find the outpost empty. RENAMO held sway, or ran riot – depending on the political perspective – in vast swathes of territory, while government troops dug in in the cities, totally under siege from their hinterlands. Even the few major cities were more scrap-heaps than modern conurbations. Alistair Sparks, a not unsympathetic South African observer, noted in 1986 that Beira was a 'city of 300,000 people with no electricity, water, telephones, food or goods in the shops'. Adopting classic Maoist tenets, RENAMO hoped that, once the rural areas were consolidated, the cities would fall like ripe plums. Such was FRELIMO's abysmal military performance that by 1986 Mozambique could hardly be termed a state. RENAMO recaptured its Gorongosa base (though its HQ was always a very moveable feast; it was a political symbol rather than any fixed position). It also seized and held towns in key provinces.

As Dhlakama told the author at the recaptured Gorongosa base,

> We are not the *desperadoes*, it's FRELIMO that's desperate. All the aid money is being used to buy weapons to keep them in power. Not to those who are dying of hunger. ... They spend their days watching the ports along the coast, hiding and waiting in Maputo for the arrival of boats from the US bringing food.

The ZNA's protection of the Beira corridor was initially static – erecting bunkers along the road and rail line. Between 1981 and 1986 over 200 Zimbabwean railway workers were killed and 600 injured trying to run the RENAMO gauntlet. The ZNA soon moved to a forward defence, by searching out the rebels. FRELIMO never did this. The ZNA commanders, many of them experienced ZANLA officers, had little time for their old comrades. Usually, they planned operations without even telling FRELIMO, partly because their allies would often tip off their friends and relatives among the rebels. 'The only real solution for FRELIMO is to rebuild the entire army, bottom to top,' said one ZNA major. 'Right now the army is not effective. In some areas, it is just written off.'

In his fine book on Mugabe, Africanist scholar Stephen Chan recounted an incident when a Zimbabwean unit received one of the advance warnings of a RENAMO attack, but decided to hold its ground. 'RENAMO clearly thought it was a FRELIMO group it was attacking. The Zimbabweans held the attack, then countered. Then spent hours weeping over the boy soldiers they had killed.'

RENAMO did recruit or press-gang a large number of boy soldiers. The fact that teenagers could outfight most government soldiers, if not the ZNA, suggested to Mugabe's intelligence advisers that Pretoria's assessment of the rottenness of Machel's regime was accurate. Without ZNA stiffening and training, the demoralized FRELIMO soldiers would usually run from any fight. But the rebels respected the ZNA, especially their use of air power. The Zimbabwean air force's combat ability had been seriously depleted by the destruction at Thornhill, but it did use airpower, especially helicopter gunships and replacement Hawk fighters, to strike at RENAMO. The rebels did not possess effective anti-aircraft capacity; they did have a number of SAM-7s but rarely knew how to operate them. Generally, they tried to take cover if the Zimbabwe air force pressed their attacks.

In the beginning of 1986, the ZNA helped the Mozambicans to retake the strategic town of Marromeu from RENAMO. The rebels had caught the opposition napping and Operation OCTOPUS was a rushed response. One of the most famous soldiers in the ZNA was Colonel 'Flint' Magama. It was his job to coordinate with the Mozambican General Pascal Mabote. The unfamiliar terrain, persistent bad weather and lack of transport planes and gunships made the ground troops vulnerable to RENAMO counter-attack. The operation concentrated on securing the airport at Marromeu. Two Mozambican Mi-25 gunships backed the ZNA. Colonel Magama was co-ordinating the fighting from one of the choppers when it was brought down by ground fire. Such was the volume of fire the ZNA could not retrieve the body of the Colonel for three days. Eventually two Dakotas were deployed with ZNA paratroopers to seize the airport. Magama's death led to national mourning in Zimbabwe.

By this time, FRELIMO was so fragile that it was forced to beg for help from the Russians *and* from Mrs Thatcher in London. The British Army trained 480 field-grade Mozambican officers in Zimbabwe. London also supplied supposedly non-lethal equipment to the Malawians guarding the Nacala railway. London also gave the usual quiet nod to ex-SAS personnel to help train FRELIMO inside Mozambique as well as guard Lonrho investments such as the cotton plantations. At one stage even Pretoria helped FRELIMO with communications, while still supporting RENAMO. Mozambique had become a donors' republic, a Soviet surrogate state, assisted by Pretoria and right-wing British Tories, let alone a country propped up by Mugabe. Mozambique was a sorry mess.

It appeared that things could not get worse for Machel and Mugabe, but they soon did. On 19 October 1986, flying home from a frontline summit, Machel's plane – piloted by Russians – flew into a mountain, just inside South Africa. Someone had apparently moved a homing beacon. Pretoria vehemently protested its innocence, but Mugabe took the death of his friend as a clear warning of his own endangered position. As chairman of the Non-Aligned Movement, Mugabe had just hosted a summit in Harare and he had waxed lyrically to his audience about the need for sanctions against apartheid.

Mugabe's intelligence advisers noted another major South African resupply to RENAMO. Even more alarming for Harare was the information that Pretoria may have had a role in bringing together Dhlakama and

Ndabaningi Sithole, Mugabe's old rival. Dhlakama literally declared war on Mugabe and moved RENAMO troops into the Eastern Highlands of Zimbabwe. Sithole did have a tribal base in southern Manicaland among the small Ndau group, a tribe that was over-represented in the RENAMO high command. The ZNA had to resort to old-fashioned protected villages in response to RENAMO depredations. Tea plantation managers and commercial farmers on the border started hiring armed guards and redeploying the wartime farm-to-farm radios. RENAMO was operating regularly inside Zimbabwe, but it may have suited Mugabe to play up the duplicity of Sithole and his ZANU-Ndonga party. The ZNA COIN operation was called Operation *NDONGA CHIRENJE* (Remove Ndonga).

The Sithole connection had little foundation, but the RENAMO operations inside Zimbabwe were clear-cut. RENAMO launched five attacks inside Zimbabwe in August 1987, most notably at the Jersey Tea Estate, about 300 miles north-east of the capital. Four ZNA troops were killed. It was the first time that RENAMO had killed ZNA troops on their own soil. Ironically, Mugabe now faced the same problem he had posed to the Rhodesians: how could his forces (now around 47,000) defend a 600-mile border, much of it in rugged terrain? The war against Mozambique rebels was costing perhaps £300,000 a day (in 1987 prices). That was why military spending was gobbling up £270 million of the £1.8 billion national budget. Mugabe declared: 'We have decided it is wiser to fight the war now rather than later on, when the situation has grown worse and much more unfavourable to us.'

If Mugabe had turned to the Fifth Brigade to resolve his problem in Matabeleland, now the Sixth Brigade would be his answer to the Mozambique imbroglio. In September 1987 Mugabe attended the passing-out parade of the new brigade. After fifty-three weeks' training, 5,883 young men who had been selected from 77,000 applicants, stood to attention in front of their leader; and their colonel, Lionel Dyck. As his troops marched past, Dyck – standing erect alongside his wife and teenage son – tapped out the beat as the band played 'Warrior with a Silver Sword'. The former Rhodesian special forces' officer had recently honed his skills with US special forces in Fort Bragg, Georgia. Dyck said: 'These are the best soldiers I have seen since 1962. They are a pack of wild dogs looking for a fight.' Mugabe also addressed the parade: 'It is against the background of a region embroiled in South Africa-sponsored destabilization, aggression and turmoil that we have decided to form Sixth Brigade.'

RENAMO was accused of major massacres, especially the death of 400 peasants at Homoine in Inhambane province on 19 July 1987. Dhlakama cried foul and claimed that the ZNA had established, in advance, a special pseudo unit, from the brand new Sixth Brigade under the command of Dyke. The RENAMO chieftain alleged that the Zimbabweans were raping and murdering and then blaming the Mozambican resistance.

In June 1988, the defence ministers of Mozambique, Tanzania and Zimbabwe met at Quelimane to coordinate a new offensive against RENAMO. This was aimed at finally sweeping RENAMO from central Mozambique, to stop the country being divided into two halves. The rebels melted into the bush to fight another day. The Zimbabweans had planned to completely clear the Beira route, which had been de facto annexed by Harare. Cecil Rhodes had dreamed of providing Rhodesia with a corridor to the sea; hence his sponsorship of the railway to Beira in 1899. Mugabe had made the colonial dream a reality – except for rebel attacks.

Mugabe had more than repaid his debt to his dead comrade, Machel, who was replaced by the far more urbane former foreign minister, Joaquim Chissano. Mugabe had got on well with the rough-and-ready Machel, but he would now engage intellectually with Chissano. Zimbabwe had expended much blood and treasure in Mozambique. The ZDF may have suffered as many as 1,000 major casualties in Mozambique from 1982-1991; the number of fatalities was unknown because Harare imposed a news blackout on combat injuries and deaths. Unlike the Rhodesians, the ZDF did not, or could not, always reclaim their fallen comrades so the figure could be higher than even vague estimates. A major cause of death was the frequency of air crashes either because of aged equipment, such as the venerable Alouettes, poor maintenance or pilot error.

For all this cost in men and materiel, could Mugabe reap any long-term dividends, besides immediate, if disrupted, access to the sea? Indeed he could. Mugabe had larger ambitions – to bring peace to Mozambique, for national and personal reasons. Conditions were ripe in southern Africa. Collapsing Soviet power in Moscow and in Angola, the emancipation of Namibia, plus the release of Mandela, meant that peace was breaking out all over the region. Mugabe had finished off ZAPU, the war with apartheid was ending, so could he emerge as the regional peace-broker?

Chissano's economic and military position was untenable, though he still refused to negotiate directly, as equals, with Dhlakama. Mugabe ordered another offensive against RENAMO in February 1990. But it took two years of intense diplomacy to extend various ceasefires into a final peace agreement in 1992. The Catholic Church and the Italian government played a busy role at the long series of talks in Rome. In typical Italian style, the host government bought new Armani suits for RENAMO, lean men as bush fighters but now grown to be fat-cats from too many diplomatic lunches. The Italians also purchased tickets for both Mozambican sides for a World Cup football match in June. Both sides joined in cheering for the African team, Cameroon, against Argentina. The Kenyans, Malawians and, in the background, the South Africans also played a constructive role in the Rome peace agreement. The Americans were busy too, talking about 'tidying up' southern African problems in tandem with the Mandela-de Klerk process. But the cement that finally got the Mozambican antagonists to fix a permanent peace was undoubtedly Robert Gabriel Mugabe.

Malawi's Hastings Banda had originally arranged a personal meeting between Dhlakama and Mugabe. The Zimbabwean leader may have been struck by the fact that Dhlakama, especially before his fat-cat days, looked just like a young lean Mugabe. The two men soon ignored their host and talked warmly in Shona. Both Catholic-trained men struck up a rapport that lasted, even though Mugabe was said not to have liked the RENAMO chieftain. Nevertheless, Mugabe did imply publicly that he was prepared to replicate Thatcher's comment on Gorbachev – Dhlakama was a man we can do business with. During various meetings, Dhlakama managed to play it right as far as respecting the older man's intellectual and liberation credentials; in turn, Mugabe was once again the kindly teacher with a pupil whom he might occasionally concede was a little like his younger self. The Portuguese had tutored Dhlakama well in the arts of diplomacy. And Tiny Rowland was also at hand to lend advice – and private jets.

Mugabe's meetings with Dhlakama helped Chissano with his hardliners who wanted to fight on. RENAMO had 15,000-20,000 troops available at the end, while FRELIMO claimed up to 90,000 in its army. The erstwhile Marxist regime also had a huge secret service, and militias. But troop strength was a technical issue – what mattered was political equality. It became clear to Mugabe that, despite all the alleged atrocities, RENAMO had much genuine popular support among the *povo*. Mugabe patiently and cleverly engineered the personal meetings between the two Mozambican leaders in Rome in early August 1992. Once more in Rome, on 4 October 1992, the two men signed the deal, which led to peace in Mozambique after more than thirty years of conflict.

Mugabe made a formal speech. 'It is not the day of Judgement. It is the day of reconciliation. Today is not the day when we should examine who was right and who was wrong. Today is the process of peace. We cannot escape that process.' Here was Mugabe as the prince of reconciliation again – his Mozambican peace speech had strong resonances of his statesmanlike broadcast to the new Zimbabwe just after he had won the 1980 election. A well-qualified and close observer, Professor Stephen Chan, dubbed Mugabe's astute diplomacy 'a Roman triumph' and asked whether this was to be his last.

### Mugabe enters Africa's First World War

Mugabe's open war in Mozambique had a clear logic, as did the covert campaign against apartheid. Zimbabwe's costly intervention in the Congo made little sense except as an extension of ZANU-PF cronyism. Just as the '*chefs*' – the party big-wigs* – cleaned up at home, the Congo offered untold riches abroad to Mugabe's generals. The war killed hundreds of ordinary soldiers and further undermined the tottering economy, but a handful of new military millionaires laughed all the way to the bank. By African standards, Mugabe's army had performed well in Mozambique, but the ZNA was increasingly undermined, not least by the treatment of war veterans.

Not all Mugabe's officers were corrupt. Some still kept the flame of liberation idealism alive, and others had imbibed the professionalism taught by their British instructors in Zimbabwe and in defence colleges in the UK. One senior officer, Brigadier Gibson Mashingaidze, after paying out of his own money for the funeral of a veteran who had fallen on hard times, in December 1996 publicly attacked the ruling party for its treatment of ordinary veterans, while some of questionable liberation credentials benefitted from state funerals, at public expense, in the hallowed ground of Heroes' Acre, near Harare. The War Victims' Compensation Fund had been thoroughly looted by the chefs. Perence Shiri, who had commanded the murderous Fifth Brigade, was awarded a very large sum for 'mental stress disorder'. Some commented that a psychopathic disorder was a necessary precondition for leadership of his brigade. The commissioner of police, Augustine Chihuri, was paid even more for 'toe dermatitis of the right and left foot'. The president's own brother-in-law received the highest recorded payment for a scar on his left knee. Some of the ministers received nearly $400,000 for various stress conditions. It was not surprising that nothing was left to pay the pensions or genuine injuries of the rank and file.

The War Veterans Association was led by Chenjerai 'Hitler' Hunzvi. His wartime and medical credentials were extremely suspect, but as he became responsible for assessing the claims of the veterans, he was himself up to his neck in the scam (to the tune Z$45 million allegedly stolen by him). In

---

* Just as ZANU cadres in Mozambique adopted the Portuguese word *povo*, for the masses, they also used the word *chefs* to denote the bosses

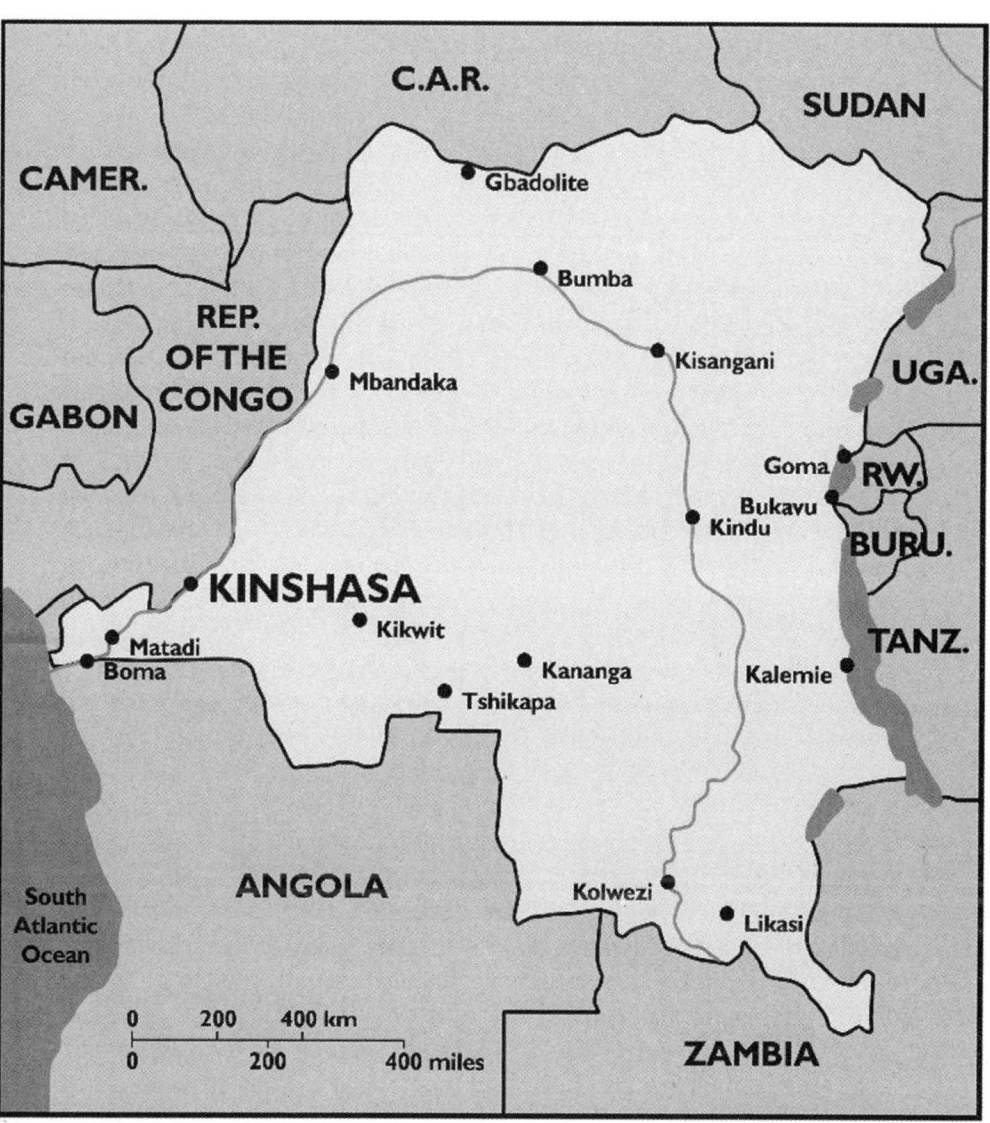

Map 7 – Congo

parliament, Margaret Dongo, a brave independent member albeit formerly a Mugabe stalwart, publicized the scandal. Led by the firebrand Hunzvi, over 50,000 veterans began to campaign for proper compensation, gratuities and pensions. Mugabe ignored them at first. The war veterans also demanded land, which helped to re-ignite the simmering issue of the white farmers who still owned much of the productive land (much of it bought with full government permission, *after* independence). Eventually Mugabe had to meet the veterans and promised to buy them off with money the state did not possess. The tens of thousands of veterans received a one-off payment of $2,500 and a continuous pension of $100 a month. In January 1998, in response to riots over price hikes in basic food stuffs, the army had to be called out into the streets of the main towns to suppress the urban violence. This was the first time that the army had to act in the streets to prop up an increasingly unpopular government. At the same time, the Zimbabwe Congress of Trade Unions, led by Morgan Tsvangirai, began to flex its industrial muscle. A wide range of civic organizations, under the umbrella of the National Constitutional Assembly, set up in 1997, also began a series of protests. The last thing the Zimbabwe economy needed was the expense of an unnecessary war in the Congo.

Mugabe was always more keen to strut on the world stage rather than address the technicalities of domestic economic governance, which appeared to bore him. With the end of the apartheid war and the traditional role of the frontline states, the Southern African Development Community (SADC) emerged as the main vehicle for regional diplomacy. In 1996 Mugabe had finagled his appointment as the chairman of the defence arm of the Community (the Organ for Politics, Defence and Security Co-operation). This was his chosen mechanism to intervene in the Congo, portraying his personal ambitions as SADC diplomacy. From June 1997 Mugabe had also held the post of the chairman of the OAU for a year. That was a useful network to intrigue with his allies in Luanda to work against what Mugabe feared would be the dominance of South Africa in the region, now that the psycho-political burden of apartheid was removed. South Africa was the regional superpower still, even if it had – uniquely – been the sole country to surrender its nuclear weapons. On a personal level the relationship had been awkward. During the South African president's first state visit to Zimbabwe he spoke on the same platform as Mugabe; it was obvious that Mandela's big-hearted speech carried a much deeper message than the shrill tirade of the Zimbabwean, even though both were couched in quasi-Marxist language. Later, in 1998, when both men were involved in mediating the latest Congo crisis, Mandela groaned to his assistant: 'Please don't tell me I have to speak Comrade Bob again.'

The politics and wars of the Democratic Republic of Congo (formerly Zaire) defy succinct analysis. In brief, however, the end of the Cold War meant that President Mobutu's position in Zaire was far less important to his main patron, Washington. Simultaneously with the surge of African optimism after the election of Mandela, Rwanda suffered the most rapid genocide in modern history. When the relieving Tutsi-dominated troops marched into Rwanda many of the Hutu perpetrators of the massacres fled into the Congo. The new Rwandan government invaded next-door Zaire to flush out the militants (the *Interahamwe*) among the two million Hutu refugees and this helped to boost the anti-Mobutu rebels; Laurent Kabila, an old adversary of Mobutu, was installed as titular leader of the anti-Mobutu forces. The 'first' Congo war was arguably a survival-inspired drive by the Rwandan government, which began in October 1996. This helped to launch Kabila's seven-month advance on the capital, Kinshasa, to oust Mobutu. The despot, in power for thirty-two years, was sick with prostrate cancer. His army began to fade away and Mobutu went into brief exile, before dying. Kabila secured victory in May 1997.

Mobutu had been detested by the southern African liberation movements because of his CIA connections in thwarting particularly the advance of the Marxist guerrillas in Angola and in Namibia. And, in 1998, Jonas Savimbi, the veteran partner of Pretoria, was still a significant military figure in Angola. When Kabila took over, South Africa's Thabo Mbeki was the first to fly to congratulate him on removing 'the man who stank' – Mobutu. Ideological payback, as well as Pan-Africanism, were parts of the pro-Kabila alliance.

Initially, Mugabe was ambiguous about Kabila. His playboy background did not please the austere Zimbabwean. But Kabila claimed an affection for Maoism, and he had once spent time with Che Guevara, when the Cubans sent a small force to the Congo. Guevara himself despised Kabila because his revolutionary rhetoric was not matched by any action outside nightclubs and brothels. Cautiously, Moven Mahachi, the Zimbabwean defence minister, promised aid. Mugabe was keen to discourage South African entrepreneurs making further inroads into the Congo honey pot. A few weeks after Kabila's victory in the first war, the Zimbabwe Defence Industries won a small supply contract of half a million US dollars. Within six months ZDI had received orders for $140 million. And negotiations about new mining concessions were conducted in earnest. Many of the deals were finessed by Billy Rautenbach, one of the few white businessmen favoured by Mugabe. Most of the legal mining companies had shut up shop because the usual chaos in the Congo had been made even worse by the anarchy following Mobutu's fall. The new concessions needed professional military protection. Rautenbach and John Bredenkamp, another veteran white Zimbabwean wheeler-dealer, paid money directly to ZNA commanders to pay for their bonuses as well as food and medicine for the soldiers. Harare seemed to care little about the noisy European lawyers disputing the Zimbabwean deals. This was a land grab almost as audacious as Cecil Rhodes's seizure of the Shona and Ndebele territories.

Kabila fell out with his old allies and ordered Rwandan and Ugandan troops to go home. This unleashed the second war, in August 1998. The Ugandan/Rwandan and Burundian invasion which followed was not a war of survival, but plunder. The invading allies would try to control the vast state, by capturing the capital; failing that, they could partition the country and hold on to rich mineral areas contiguous to their own territories. Congo was massively wealthy but totally destroyed by Mobutu's bizarrely inept rule. How else could a country of continental proportions be so easily attacked by such Lilliputian states? Kabila turned to Mugabe and friends for extra help, as invading troops were encroaching on his capital. At the eleventh hour in August 1998 Mugabe sent 600 troops, under Operation RESTORE SOVEREIGNTY. Given that the states invading Zaire – renamed the Democratic Republic of Congo – were in breach of international law and since Mugabe secured SADC authority for the mission, the Zimbabwean leader felt justified in the politically correct name for his Congo adventure. It was yet another example of Mugabe's perverse passion for superficial legalism. And an eye for the main chance: Mugabe also set up his own privately registered, state-run hybrid called Operation Sovereign Legitimacy (OSLEG) through which he intended to funnel investments and profits.

Mugabe decided to back Kabila fully, without consulting his party or cabinet, and persuaded his allies in the SADC, Angola and Namibia, to commit troops as well. The Zimbabwe Defence Forces (ZDF) component, 600 in the beginning, was soon augmented to 3,000. As in Mozambique, however, 'mission creep' grew to feed operational demands. It eventually reached 15-18,000 troops and also air force and logistical support. The war would soon cost Harare around $1 million a day, although Mugabe always publicly asserted it was a 'self-financing war'. It was in one sense, except that the taxpayers paid for the war and senior generals and a few favoured Zimbabwean businessmen took all the profits.

Mugabe and Kabila had signed a formal contract on 4 September 1998. Zimbabwe would receive a 37.5 per cent interest in Gécamines, and 30 per cent of the company's profits were supposed to pay for Harare's war effort. The company however, had over $1 billion in long-term debts. Like most of the DRC's companies it was not viable. Neither man made any money from that deal. The Zimbabwean Electricity Supply Authority also tried to cut a deal but lack of money, expertise and logistics led to a dead end. Large areas of prime land in Katanga were also given to ZANU-PF interests, but no capital was available to develop the land there, or for that matter at home in

Zimbabwe. Other state deals fell apart but some of the private military ventures did not. Nevertheless, Harare initially admitted that it was spending just $36 million a year on the Congo misadventure. Finally, Simba Makoni, the finance minister, was forced to confess that a more realistic figure was $200 million over two years. That was still a gross understatement. The World Bank put the figure at nearly $1 million per day and cut off a much-needed loan to Zimbabwe. The war costs shot up as Harare bought weapons from China ($72.3 million), MiGs from Libya and spare parts for BAe Hawks costing up to $10million. Defying Foreign Office advice, Tony Blair had insisted on allowing the British deal to go ahead. Opponents argued that the Hawks were using bombs with no guidance systems, especially cluster bombs, and it was inevitable that civilians would be killed. New Labour had come into power in 1997 with the promise of an ethical dimension to foreign policy – arming Mugabe seemed to stretch the term 'ethical'.

Mugabe also refused to listen to advice; in this case on the entangling alliance with Kabila. One Zimbabwean official observed: 'Kabila is a man who starts six fires when he's only got one fire extinguisher ... The fire fighters are the Zimbabwean army.'

Harare's financial returns were dependent on Kabila winning – otherwise the Rwandans and Ugandans would grab all the booty. And the key was Kinshasa. The capital *was* the DRC. Kabila's enemies had seized suburbs of the capital, as well as part of the international airport at Ndjili. Worse, Kabila's adversaries had taken the hydroelectric facility at the huge Inga dam, which supplied water and electricity to the capital. The strategy was to starve Kabila's forces and induce him to repeat Mobutu's flight into exile. White foreigners were evacuated by Belgian, British, French and US airlifts. Kabila's days in power appeared numbered.

ZDF strategy was to protect Kabila, save Kinshasa and then try to relieve some of the provincial towns – a big order in a country the size of Western Europe, with hardly any functioning infrastructure. Hence the need for air bridges and river transport. The Zimbabweans and Angolans would have to launch a rapid expeditionary force, with very little reliance on local military support. Mugabe ordered an immediate mobilization of a fleet of tanks (originally from North Korea), Brazilian Cascavel armoured vehicles as well as attack helicopters and fighter ground attack aircraft – from thousands of miles away. The ZDF prepared to fight well-equipped conventional forces which had dug in around urban areas. With maximum effort, Air Chief Marshal Perence Shiri personally co-ordinated the air bridge, with help later from mercenary pilots and Ukrainian and Russian transport planes.

Shiri organized a highly complex air bridge, the logistics of which might have daunted even leading NATO forces, especially the constant demands for fuel. Ilyushins with special reinforced floors were chartered to take in the armoured vehicles and tanks. But the key component was a squadron of six Mi-35 Hind gunships. Shiri chose to deal with the Russians, whose equipment was far better than the Chinese who had offered 50 per cent discounts. The US dollar purchase, maintenance and service comprised a big contract and it had to be done very quickly – all completed in three months. Rivals to the Russians offered Shiri bribes. In one case a local white businessman arrived with literally a trunk full of Zimbabwean dollars and suggested discreetly to Shiri that it could be used for 'the air force football team'. Shiri immediately summoned his aides and told them to get hold of the officer in charge of the team, which had just received a large donation. The stunned businessman left with his tail between his legs.

Zimbabwean pilots were sent to Moscow for a crash course on the Mi-35s. It was winter and despite their heavy clothing a strange rustling noise emanating from their black students made the Russian instructors curious: they soon discovered that their guests had wrapped newspapers around their bodies to provide extra warmth. In the tropical heat of the Congo, however, these pilots preformed well. Only one of the six Hinds was shot down; five survived the war, partly because of excellent maintenance support from five Russians who were paid handsomely to service the aircraft in the Congo. The Hinds' main role was as a gunship, and because of their special avionics, including FLIR (Forward Looking Infrared), they caught their opponents by surprise in raids on the enemy deep under jungle overhang, even in the dark. Other Hinds, flown by Serbian mercenaries, had suffered much grief, including one fatal crash, early in the war, but Shiri's men did their service and country proud. The ZAF Hinds flew numerous ground-attack missions but they also worked as troop carriers (maximum eight people) or as casualty evacuation (four stretchers). Shiri's air bridge also had to fly large numbers of injured troops and body bags back to Zimbabwe.

The war was fought in three phases. From August to September 1998 it became clear that the SADC troops were fighting not ill-disciplined rebels but well-organized regular Ugandan and Rwandan troops. These troops were briefly reluctant to engage forces officially sanctioned by the SADC. Also the ZDF forces benefitted from backing from the locals. The Rwandan Tutsi soldiers had committed atrocities and left the locals deeply embittered. The ZDF deployed new Land Rovers and Toyota Land Cruisers with machine-gun platforms as 'technicals' which were useful in urban fighting, but the vehicles rarely lasted more than a few weeks off the few roads outside the central parts of the city.

The invaders moved back into the forests. The capital, airport and hydroelectric facilities were secured. Then followed the second phase when the six conventional armies – three on each side – faced each other with the full might of their arsenals – including fighter aircraft, helicopter gunships, tanks, artillery and rockets as well as naval units. For six weeks the belligerents threw everything they had into the fight. Both sides faced major logistical problems in often impenetrable terrain – a stalemate ensued with Uganda, Rwanda and Angola dominating Congolese territory adjacent to their own borders, while Zimbabwe had to rely on its very expensive air bridge. Both sides lost much of their heavy equipment in this period. Prolonged stalemate led to negotiations and a peace agreement in Lusaka in July 1999. Ironically, the peace agreement led to a resumption of fighting, but between Uganda and Rwandan forces in Kisingani. In the third phase of the putative peace, the ZDF worked with DRC troops, a motley crew, to secure major cities of the central and western areas and to repulse the numerous rebel groups, which were sometimes in alliance with the Rwandan or Ugandan armies. Harare did not have the energy, men or money to push east to try to liberate the whole country – Mugabe was looking for a political exit.

The DRC had always been the richest of African states, with the poorest of inhabitants because the mineral wealth was consistently looted, by the Belgian colonists and then kleptocratic domestic governments. Now the Zimbabwean lootocracy joined in. Senior officers and politicians set up a variety of companies that had officially bought mines from Kabila, as part of the deal to give him military support. Western companies and lawyers helped to launder much of the money made so that the proceeds ended up as clean cash in Swiss bank accounts. Richard Dowden, the energetic head of Britain's Royal African Society, summed up the Congo malaise rather poetically: 'Anyone with a gun, a mobile phone and an airstrip can become a wealthy warlord. Ripped out of Africa, the loot then floats gently through the international free market system and comes to rest in the window of a jewellery shop, on the fingers of innocent lovers.'

Zimbabweans secured preferential trade deals not just for diamonds, cobalt and other minerals but for timber and other business concessions. John Bredenkamp, the aggressive former Rhodesian sanctions-buster, was a big player, but party securocrats, especially Emmerson Mnangagwa, comprised the core of the vast protection racket. General Vitalis Zvinavashe, a top ZNA commander, set up a major logistics company to supply the war. Officers and men were encouraged to do their own deals in the country and the lower ranks were given special allowances by the army for serving in the Congo.

The details of the war were kept effectively secret by Mugabe, but often casualties could not be completely hidden, nor occasional rumours of mutinies against officers who were sacrificing their men purely to defend business profits. Zimbabwean journalists who tried to report on the ill effects of the war and particularly military disaffection with Mugabe – presumably from the officers who were not making enough money from the Congo – were arrested and tortured.

Although Zimbabwean and Angolan troops saved Kabila, they often suffered major reverses. For example, in what were termed the river wars, Rwandan-led forces had trapped over 3,000 largely Zimbabwean and Namibian troops at Ikela airport. Mugabe was said to be furious that so many of his troops were besieged. Pro-Kabila troops, with heavy Zimbabwean reinforcements, launched an assault to relieve the Ikela garrison; despite use of gunships and river-borne heavy artillery, they managed to secure only a short ceasefire to allow the Zimbabwean air force to airlift its troops out. On another occasion 300 ZNA men had to seek refuge over the border in Zambia after being defeated in the DRC. On the ground, the fighting was often savage in the extreme – 'take no prisoners' was not a slogan, but a daily reality. They were usually shot out of hand. The few white pilots who survived an ejection or crash told incredible stories of endurance in the jungles, especially when white faces were so rare and hard to conceal on gruelling marches. So tough was the air war that at one stage Harare brought back 75 per cent of its aviation from the DRC, partly because of the fear of their aircraft being permanently grounded as the Harare treasury was having major problems paying for spare parts for their planes. Since none of the compensation payments promised by Kabila came through, the costs of spares, plus the enormous bills for Eastern European transport planes and gunships, had to be paid in real money – sometimes in big brown envelopes stuffed with US dollars at Zimbabwe's air bases before the mercenary pilots were prepared to take off for the Congo. This dollarization of the war further impacted upon Zimbabwe's chronic foreign-exchange problems. In expensive attempts to keep the British Hawks airworthy, as London grew increasingly reluctant to supply parts (before the military sanctions), grasping middlemen in Kenya, which also had British Hawks, filled some of the gaps.

Supply problems might partly explain the failure of a Zimbabwean fly-past requested by Kabila for a celebration in Kinshasa. Although accounts vary, the misadventure went something like this: six Chinese-built Chengdu F-7 fighters left Gweru for Kinshasa, over 1,500 miles away. One Zimbabwean wing commander had no night-flying experience and became disoriented south of Kinshasa, and ejected. He staggered out of the jungle five days later rather dehydrated. Another pilot also ejected and survived.

Another crash-landed at Lumumbashi and was killed. The three remaining fighters performed their fly-past, and managed later to get home safely. Three F-7s had been wiped out and not a sign of any combat. The planes were poor copies of the Russian MiG-21, even with the Western avionics installed in export models. They were used as ground-attack aircraft, mainly to hit enemy air bases in the Congo, although they were also deployed, unsuccessfully, to disrupt the air bridges from Uganda and Rwanda.

Combat took a heavy toll on all types of aircraft. According to Al J. Venter, the veteran South African correspondent who interviewed many of the white mercenaries in the Congo, the Zimbabwe air force lost at least four Hawks, three Cessna 337 Lynx ground-support planes, several Spanish-built CASA short-haul freighters, and five choppers including two old Alouettes and one recently acquired Mi-35. Despite the losses, the Zimbabwe air force pilots fought hard in difficult terrain. Ironically some of them were whites, including ex-South African Air Force pilots. Deploying Alouettes, sometimes allied with Russian gunships, the Zimbabwean team used classic Fire Force techniques practised in the old Rhodesian war. The transport pilots also worked minor miracles in resupplying ZNA troops deep in country. Not accidentally, the ZNA was based around the diamond-rich area of Mbuji-Mayi in Kasai province, but they also held isolated garrisons elsewhere. Except for the Hinds, pilots operated with inadequate ground support, even at the main Ndjili airport. Zimbabwean pilots and planes were ground down by poor maintenance, combat attrition and crashes caused by malfunctions or pilot errors, sometimes generated by almost zero navigation and landing assistance from control towers. More and more work was done by chartered Russian/Ukrainian Ilyushin and Antonov planes, especially when the SADC troops and remaining equipment had to be repatriated at the end of their war; South African mercenary pilots were also kept busy, including former Executive Outcomes personnel.

On Tuesday 16 January 2001, around twelve mid-day, President Kabila was sitting in his office at the Presidential Palace in Kinshasa, looking at papers and chatting to an advisor. One of his bodyguards, Rashidi Kasereka, walked up to him as though he wanted to whisper something in his ear. Instead, he fired an automatic pistol at point-blank range straight into Kabila's head. He died almost immediately. Nevertheless, his dead body was flown to Harare under the pretext of seeking medical attention. Mugabe and Co. insisted that Kabila was in hospital, although one off-message minister let the cat out of the bag. Cynics in Harare referred mockingly to the Monty Python 'dead parrot' sketch.

When Kabila's son, Joseph, took over, Mugabe maintained his largesse, despite the accelerating military and political opposition in Zimbabwe. Officially, Harare's position was that it was waiting for a suitable UN peacekeeping force to replace the SADC forces. In August 2002 just after South Africa offered to contribute 1,500 troops to the UN force, Mugabe ordered his remaining infantry out.

When the UN published its second report on looting in the Congo in 2003, the Mugabe government refused to investigate some of the prominent Zimbabwean culprits indicted in the report. 'We did a good job in the DRC and we will not respond to malicious allegations by the British masquerading as the United Nations' was the official response to UN accusations. Mugabe had long been paranoid not only about alleged British meddling in his country but he had also worried about South Africa taking over Zimbabwean business interests in both Mozambique and the DRC. At one stage, Mugabe thought that Pretoria might actually join the opposition forces to the SADC alliance in Congo. As it happened, South Africa did replace many Zimbabwean interests in both countries, as Mugabe's economy, destabilized by the pointless Congo fiasco, made it impossible for it to function at home, let alone compete with the regional economic giant.

The Second Congo War, also known as Africa's World War, began in August 1998 and officially ended in July 2003, though UN forces were still trying to keep an impossible peace as late as 2011. It was the largest war in modern African history, involving nine immediate state combatants, but many others from around Africa who stirred the pot, as well as an alphabet soup of twenty-five domestic militias. It killed an estimated 5.4 million people, mostly from disease and starvation.

Historians might use the Latin phrase *bellum se ipsum alet*: war feeds itself. Congolese warlords would agree with that sentiment. But outsiders stirred the pot and not just African dictators. Western diplomats and business magnates also played a part. Mining companies go where profits dictate and embassy officials are supposed to help their compatriots' ventures. The issue has been one of regulatory failure in Western capitals. Mining cowboys were allowed to get away with mass fraud, hiding behind companies registered in Caribbean islands; and European and American governments have not been too bothered about the ethics of their capitalists once they leave their respective borders.

The war, however, was a financial disaster for the Zimbabwean treasury. Until the beginning of the new millennium, disaffected Zimbabweans wanted an end to bad policies – and opposition to the Congo war became a focus of discontent. As Martin Rupiya, a former ZNA colonel-turned-academic, observed of the war's effect on Zimbabwe, 'On balance, the country appears to have made an enormous sacrifice for its involvement in the war, which has left it scarred, impoverished and politically divided.' After the Congo disaster, the aim was not reform of ZANU-PF and the removal of the more obvious gangsters, but rather the toppling of both Mugabe and his entire corrupted party.

# Chapter 8

# The Self-Destruction of Zimbabwe

Mugabe had deployed his war machine abroad to good effect in Mozambique and with disastrous results in the Congo. In the early 1980s he had used his security apparatus – police, intelligence and armed forces – to crush his political opponents in ZAPU's heartland of Matabeleland. After 2000, Mugabe turned his security forces against his own people – throughout the entire country. Besides the conventional security arms, Mugabe deployed militias, especially the 'war veterans' (though many were too young to have served in the liberation war) as well as party Youth Brigades. Violence, death, intimidation, false accusations, and eventually total contempt for the courts – all dissent was met by force. The violence peaked at election times. Unlike in the *Gukurahundi*, no pretence of security was made. The violence was mere repression of any dissent against a totally corrupt party elite. Any opposition was considered treason, and treated accordingly.

Anger, universally, if privately, expressed was aimed at what Zimbabweans called a 'bedroom-based personal dictatorship'. In 1996 Mugabe married his attractive long-term mistress and secretary, Grace Marufu, who was more than forty years his junior. Grace had been married, but – somewhat like King David and Bathsheba – Mugabe prompted her divorce and, while not killing Grace's husband, sent him on a long mission to China. Perhaps Mugabe was punished like David in the Bible. Grace became a millstone around Mugabe's neck, not least her incredible financial appetites. Her compulsive retail therapy led her to extremely ostentatious shopping trips abroad and palace-building at home, at a time when almost 90 per cent of Zimbabweans were unemployed, and many were starving. The air-headed Grace was loathed, though she was never quoted as saying, 'Let them eat cake.' Zimbabweans simply called her 'Amazing Grace' or, *sotto voce,* 'the First Spender'.

The whites were targeted and their farms and increasingly their businesses were looted. Nearly all the Ndebele leaders had been killed or marginalized. Then many Shona long-time supporters became disaffected, not only with the economic chaos and the foreign military adventures. Mugabe took little advice from his cabinet or party, and he had few, if any, close confidants, once his level-headed first wife, Sally, had died from kidney failure. Initially, Mugabe had ruled the state as though it were his old revolutionary politburo – though he did insist right at the start that his ministers should attend cabinet meetings dressed in formal Western suits. That was a departure from the old days in Mozambique. But power tended to be centred first on Mugabe's extended family and then Mugabe's Zezuru clan. The so-called 'Zezuru mafia' was led by Leo Mugabe, the president's nephew. He was at the centre of numerous large and fraudulent government deals. The elite ruled without much pretence of any ideology, and certainly not any socialism. The party bosses' prime concern was power, and for most of the chefs their own lifestyles were entwined with Mugabe's survival.

In the beginning the abstemious Mugabe was untouched by personal corruption. The teetotal, non-smoking leader had just one overriding vice, an addiction to power. He did very little, however, to curb corruption in the party and then in his own family. He acted only when one of the scams threatened his own position, such as the Willowgate scandal. In 1988, when some press freedom was still allowed, the Bulawayo *Chronicle* revealed a major scam involving politicians, civil servants and businessmen who took advantage of the critical shortage of vehicles in the country. The fraudsters bought up party-reserved vehicles produced in the state-owned Willowvale factory in Harare and sold them at very inflated prices. Such was the fuss that Mugabe had no choice but to call an enquiry, led by a high court judge. The enquiry investigated ministers as well as two of Mugabe's allies, Enos Nkala, then defence minister, and Maurice Nyagumbo, a veteran nationalist who had special responsibility for administering the party's leadership code. Senior army chiefs were also investigated. Nkala's first response was to send in the ZNA to arrest the editor of the *Chronicle*. When the enquiry published its report in April 1989 some ministers, including Nyagumbo, were found guilty and forced to resign. Uniquely, the avuncular nationalist recognized his guilt and humiliation, and fell on his own sword by committing suicide. Willowgate came at the beginning of Mugabe's reign of terror. He would soon dispense with all criticism and legal niceties. By 2000, the party leaders could literally do what they wanted in Zimbabwe, provided they paid lip-service to Mugabe's ascendancy. Public loyalty was the only price they had to pay in exchange for looting the state.

Meanwhile, the *povo* paid a massive price in unemployment, starvation, and a 50 per cent cut in their life expectancy, which became the lowest in the world. Mugabe may have built new schools, clinics and hospitals during his honeymoon period, but those same hospitals, now totally rundown, were full of victims of his party's brutal excesses. Mugabe claimed that he fought to return land to the peasants but much of the land seized from whites and a few black political opponents went to party cronies, who had no interest in or aptitude for modern farming. The revolution had atrophied into the worst caricature of African despotism. Richard Dowden, one of Britain's leading Africanists, observed:

> Gradually the party leaders became like the pigs in *Animal Farm*, an elite above the law, in total political control and living the lifestyle of the world's richest. They awarded themselves huge salaries and grotesque allowances, using their political position to gain contracts and take over businesses. They became as far removed from the lives of their fellow black Zimbabweans as any white Rhodesian had ever been.

Mugabe enjoyed defying the Americans and the British, espousing a particular hatred for the 'gay gangsters' in Tony Blair's government. Mugabe was especially aggrieved when Clare Short, then international development secretary, sent a letter outlining her own (Irish) colonized past and refusing to be responsible for alleged land compensation promises of a previous Tory government. Mugabe was said to regard Blair as a rather patronizing and self-righteous headmaster: 'Hold nice elections and nice teacher will give you a nice development handout.' Mugabe had poured scorn on London, and he had cowed the Ndebele, but any attacks from the left within his own party were of more concern to him. Hence his decision to buy off and then absorb the war veteran movement into his own growing campaign against the remnants of white power. Additionally, an erstwhile Mugabe admirer, Morgan Tsvangirai, had the effrontery to form a rival political party in 1999, the MDC. The Zimbabwean president decided he needed to consolidate even more power. He planned a new constitution and held a referendum in February 2000. As he controlled nearly all the seats in parliament, Mugabe assumed the results of the referendum would be a formality. So he was shocked and enraged when he lost. It was rumoured at the time that he considered standing down, but apparently he was dissuaded by party and military bosses.

Mugabe's 2000 humiliation over his first defeat was a watershed in the country's history, and it also marked the definitive step in the militarization of Zimbabwe's domestic polity. Publicly, he blamed the MDC and its small number of white financial backers. Mugabe would defeat them even if it meant destroying what was left of the economy. The way to do that was to remove a source of white money – land. Mugabe had been persuaded to back-pedal on the land issue during the sensitive transition to majority rule in South Africa. Harare had not even used up all the money allocated by the British to purchase unused prime land on a willing-seller basis. Now the land would be taken without compensation. That the British were responsible was Mugabe's line – if they didn't cough up, why should we? Mugabe diverted the disaffection surrounding the war veterans – originally aimed at him – and focused it instead on white farmers and their 'puppets' – the MDC. This was the 'Third *Chimurenga*'.

The reaction was swift. Operation *TSURO* (Rabbit) was launched. This involved 1,500 war veterans – now largely recruited from the unemployed and led by 300 CIO officers. Over 1,000 soldiers from the Fifth Brigade joined around 6,000 ZANU-PF volunteers including Youth Brigades. The operation was targeted at white farmers and the MDC, almost identical villains in the ZANU-PF mind-set. The police were not instant converts to this operation. Initially some police units protected the farmers from the invasions. In the so-called 'Battle of Murwi', on 26 May 2000, one war veteran was killed and thirteen injured after a police station was besieged by militias. The ZRP was soon whipped into line. The very few white senior officers left were quickly retired and it was decided that no more whites could join (not that they were queuing to enlist); some of the more professional black officers were also kicked out or beaten into submission or otherwise victimized. And the ZRP was promised some of the confiscated land. The police became little more than a ZANU-PF militia.

Now uncontrolled, the invaders swept on to farms, killing animals and destroying crops and burning buildings. Farmers and their families were beaten up and often humiliated; for example, after severe assaults, their heads might be shaved in police stations, their families could be forced to dance and sing in *pungwes* and the women were threatened with rape. Sometimes they were killed with guns and machetes, often with the police doing nothing, and occasionally participating in the attacks. Over 700 farmers were terrorized into leaving their properties and 135 MDC supporters were killed. Many others were brutalized or maimed. The lessons of the *Gukurahundi* were re-applied. The trick in voter intimidation was not necessarily to kill people. As Stephen Chan noted succinctly, 'A dead person has less "multiplier effect" than living ones with tales of horror.' Much of the seized land ended up with senior members of the army and police. The invasions were officially portrayed as the spontaneous combustion of land-hungry peasants, but they were nearly always carefully organized. One of the leading conspirators was once more Perence Shiri, the former Fifth Brigade commander, later head of the air force.

The land invasions were cranked up after the defeat over the constitution and before the run-up to the next parliamentary elections. Nevertheless, in the June 2000 parliamentary elections, despite massive intimidation, the MDC polled well. That was another example of both popular resistance and bravery exhibited by Mugabe's opponents in a police state. The MDC slogan was '*Chinja maitiro*' – 'Change the way you are doing things.'

The original 6,000 white-owned farms at the end of Smith's rule had been ground down to a few hundred. Some of the exceptions were arbitrary but more often they belonged to the few white business magnates who had cosied up to the dictator. Farms which were designated for fast-track expropriation faced disaster. They included the nation's major tobacco, horticultural and food producers. The Commercial Farmers' Union, worn down by endless attempts to defend their property rights in the courts, and demoralized by murders and emigration, warned of major food shortages and then starvation. Many farmers, driven off their land, sought refuge in the cities or in South Africa. But perhaps as many as 400,000 black Zimbabweans who worked on their farms, plus their families, would add up to two million people made destitute. Departing farmers did what they could; most were not the cartoon 'Boer bastards' – the farms were usually well-run for all concerned, including shops, schools and clinics for their workers. The new owners knew nothing of farming and soon wastelands replaced the once prosperous countryside. Zimbabwe had been the breadbasket of the region, now it became a basket-case. Proud independence had brought humiliating dependence on foreign food aid, much of it from the despised Western imperialists. Soon, more Zimbabweans were relying on international food aid than famine-struck Ethiopia.

Roughly 90 per cent of the nearly 200 officers from the rank of major to lieutenant general in the ZNA were granted farms in the most fertile parts of the country. This was replicated in the other security organs. Almost 14 million hectares (12.5 million acres) were seized from white farmers, reducing their numbers from 4,000 to 400 in ten years. The new farm-owning elite, from the party, military and also judges, numbered around 2,200 who took over 40 per cent of the stolen fertile lands. Mr and Mrs Robert Mugabe owned sixteen farms, although the president was always reluctant to permit a formal and accurate land audit of the whole country. Mugabe had never been a farmer, nor had his father. A man who was rhetorically obsessed with land had never used a plough in his life. Mugabe had historically made much of taking back the land of his fathers and of the spirits of his ancestors, but the land had been developed by the whites to sell to the supermarkets, and smokers, of the world. It seemed unlikely that the modern destruction of the whole agro-industrial sector would appease the ghosts of the past.

Agricultural output slumped by 60 per cent after the first land invasions, and the figures kept dropping. Dean Theron, the president of the Commercial Farmers' Union, said in 2010:

> We know the colonial history and are not opposed to land reform, but we feel sad at the way it has taken place. The beneficiaries are not the intended ones. The farms have been dished out to people with connections.

Peter Hain, the former anti-apartheid campaigner from South Africa, then young Liberal activist and later a Labour MP for Neath, and finally a minister in Blair's government, raised the temperature by saying that Zimbabwe was close to collapse and talked openly about contingency plans to rescue the estimated 20,000 remaining British passport holders in the country. Certainly, the UK Ministry of Defence dusted off its various military contingency plans, but they were concerned with evacuation, not regime change. Mugabe, however, used Hain's statements as further proof that London was trying to get rid of him. The Labour government, frequently insulted by Mugabe, did want to get rid of the truculent dictator but they were not about to launch one of their wars of humanitarian intervention to remove him. 'Hitler' Hunzvi entered the fray with a declaration that people with British passports should go back to Britain. 'They should go to the airport. If they don't, they will go into the ground.' Mugabe's propagandists made no real distinction between whites who had lived in the country for three generations and those who had settled recently. Likewise they conflated any opposition to ZANU-PF misrule, especially the MDC, as lackeys of 'the Rhodesian network' and its agents in London and Washington. Soon Mugabe included the churches, the media and the judiciary in this vast conspiracy to dethrone him.

The country was utterly bankrupted already by the Congo war, and universal misgovernment. Agriculture was almost derelict. Manufacturing companies – clothing, textiles, engineering – as well as mining – were all contracting. Constant threats of 'indigenization', and other means of forced black empowerment, discouraged businesses at home, let alone investment from abroad. Tourism was almost dead; even the tourist mainstay, Victoria Falls, had become deserted. Foreign exchange dried up, as did the supplies of drugs in the hospitals, now totally unable to counter the AIDS pandemic.

Retrained by the army, and officered by the police or CIO, the war veterans were also tasked to invade urban white-owned businesses – factories, offices and clinics – to redress workers' alleged grievances, some going back years, even when they were genuine. In 2001 the National Youth Service was set up for all young Zimbabweans, aged ten to thirty. They often wore green fatigues and hence earned the nickname 'green bombers'. (Although the term was also applied to 'flies which hang around shit'.) The training camps were generally – though not always – very poorly run, and rife with sexual abuse of both girls and boys. The education was mainly ZANU-PF propaganda focusing on the rants of not only Mugabe but also the ludicrous Hitler Hunzvi, who was given a hero's burial in 2001.

The professionalism of the Zimbabwe Defence Forces was rapidly degraded after 2000 by the nationwide mobilization against all the many perceived enemies of Mugabe. The addition of so-called shock-troops – the war veterans and the green bombers – hastened the crisis in the security forces, many of whom in the lower ranks now secretly, very secretly, looked to the MDC for national salvation. A large number remained loyal to Mugabe, especially in the senior officer corps. One former army captain, Francis Zimuto, took on the *nom de guerre* of 'Black Jesus' as he was the messiah who would liberate his people from the continuing white conspiracy. Black Jesus was a suitably dangerously eccentric replacement for the recently departed Hitler. Bizarrely, Zimuto later asked for asylum in Britain for himself and his family, claiming persecution by white Zimbabweans.

Occasionally, sunbursts of honesty escaped from the government, for the national tragedy desperately needed to be acknowledged officially. In July 2001, Finance Minister Simba Makoni admitted that foreign reserves had run out, and warned of serious food shortages. Some of the ZANU-PF faithful hoped that the articulate and well-educated Makoni might be a possible successor to the ageing dictator. For that reason he was sidelined, although he did stand later as an independent reformer. Meanwhile, most Western donors, including the World Bank and the IMF, cut aid, partly because of the self-destructive land seizures. In February 2002, new laws were passed to further strangle surviving media freedoms. The European Union finally imposed very limited sanctions, mainly on the main ZANU-PF chefs. So-called 'smart sanctions' included a travel ban and a freeze on the *chefs'* assets in Europe. Washington followed suit. The EU also pulled out their observers for the March 2002 presidential elections. These elections were so severely flawed that even the Commonwealth noticed and Zimbabwe was suspended for a year. Elections could satisfy Mugabe's curious sense of surface-deep legality, but they could not prevent the food shortages that soon became famine. As in Matabeleland in the 1980s, Mugabe used food as a weapon – giving food aid only to his card-carrying supporters. This was politics of the belly.

The 2002 presidential elections were also run as a military operation. A national command centre was set up at the Sheraton Hotel in Harare, but later relocated to Manyame air base. Besides, the usual thuggery, the military made sure the Electoral Supervisory Commission was staffed with retired or serving officers. Retired Colonel Sobusa Gula-Ndebele was put in charge. And, according to the MDC, 146 militia camps, coordinated by the CIO, were set up. By the time of the elections over 20,000 young people had gone through youth brigade training in the five camps established nationally. During the election the war veterans acted as the party's shock troops, while the green bombers acted as auxiliaries. The army provided logistics and the CIO gathered intelligence. After all this intimidation, Mugabe won a narrow victory.

In the campaigns for elections in particular and suppression in general, Mugabe regressed even more to the rhetoric of his liberation war. He told his party that it had to move 'like a military machine'. The ZDF commander, General Vitalis Zvinavashe, went along with the metaphor which was made real. He said publicly that he would not recognize any election that Mugabe lost. 'We will not accept, let alone support or salute, anyone with a different agenda.' Mugabe's paranoia seemed to infect many of his henchmen who were apparently passionate in their belief that the party could do no wrong. Drought and sanctions were now blamed for all the country's ills. They started repeating the deluded slogans of Pol Pot's Khmer Rouge – of going back to Year Zero before rebuilding the party's socialist paradise. Mugabe retreated into even more palatial splendour, allowing his wife to build ever larger and more ornate mansions. Right from the start of his reign, his fast-moving, and heavily armed, motor cavalcade would force pedestrians and cars right off the roads. Now the de facto president-for-life made a new law making it a criminal offence for anyone to brandish an insulting gesture or statement within range of his motorcade. Presumably, ending up in an overturned car in a ditch or massive pot-hole offered no mitigation for a two-fingered salute.

The Shona have a reputation for stoical resilience, yet many of the minority who actually had a job were sufficiently enraged to come out in a general strike in March 2003. Inevitably, Mugabe's party-cum-military machine responded with widespread arrests and beatings. In June of that year Tsvangirai was arrested twice in one week on charges of treason, adding to existing indictments about an alleged plot to kill Mugabe. Things were getting really bad, because the Commonwealth finally took some action over its once-favoured son: Zimbabwe was suspended indefinitely (and then Mugabe flounced out of the old imperial club). By 2004 more than three million of the population had fled, most struggling to find menial jobs in South Africa, but they were increasingly met by xenophobia and occasionally anti-migrant riots and pogroms. Many of the better-educated Zimbabweans, particularly in the medical profession, were allowed to settle in the UK, especially London, which Zimbabweans dubbed 'Harare North'.

A curious coup attempt fanned the fires of Mugabe's paranoia about Britain. In March 2004 a group of mercenaries, on the way to overthrow an even nastier dictatorship in Equatorial Guinea, was intercepted while landing at Harare airport. The coup leader was the ex-SAS officer Simon Mann. He was sentenced to seven years in jail. His alleged co-conspirator was Lady Thatcher's son, Mark. The hapless Thatcher scion denied any involvement in what the press dubbed the 'Wonga coup'. If Mark Thatcher had been on the plane – an unlikely event – Mugabe may well have pulled his punches. The president had a peculiar soft spot for the Tory leader, and visited her officially or privately on his regular trips to London, before he was blackballed. They would sit and chat for hours in Margaret Thatcher's private study; she would sip at her whisky and Mugabe would stick always to bottled water.

At the beginning of 2005, Washington labelled Zimbabwe as one of the world's 'six outposts of tyranny'. Mugabe was presumably safe from the Bush doctrine of intervention as he had no oil, a very tiny Muslim population and certainly no decent weapons for the ZDF, let alone WMD. Nevertheless, the tyranny was utterly pernicious, not least for the MDC. Arguably, in the 2005 election, the opposition suffered less overt violence and intimidation than previously, but Mugabe improved his party's performance by straightforward rigging of the results. Elated by the fix, Mugabe promised that he would stay in office until he was 100 years old. The MDC, however, maintained its support base in the main towns.

Mugabe was concerned not only about opposition support in the cities and towns, but also that the massive growth in slum population, caused not least by the destruction of so many farming jobs, could generate an urban insurrection. Under the pretext of redevelopment, the *Murambatsvina* military campaign was launched. Literally, it means 'cleaning out the rubbish'. No warning was given. Starting with Harare in May 2005 over 700,000 people were made homeless. Locals described it as Zimbabwe's tsunami. Informal businesses such as street vendors' flower stalls or second-hand clothes racks were also bulldozed or otherwise destroyed. Losing their jobs and houses, some were dumped in scrub areas outside the towns, in winter, without any means of survival. True, some 2,000 homes were built as a part of the official reconstruction, but most of them went to the army or police or relatives of party loyalists. The housing project, supervised by the military (Operation *GARIKAI*) was a national scandal but now there were almost too many to chronicle. Large numbers of the *Murambatsvina* victims fled south where some of them lost their shanties again in xenophobic pogroms in the South African townships. Mugabe had just alienated another few hundreds of thousands of voters with his heartless evictions; he would have to rely on his security apparatus even more to stay in power. The problem was his waning power of patronage – money and white-owned land were almost exhausted. All that remained in plentiful supply was brute force.

The UN humanitarian chief Jan Egeland described the country as 'in meltdown'. The government responded by printing banknotes – soon creating one of the most rapid inflations in modern history. By June 2008 a packet of cigarettes could cost 2.5 billion Zimbabwe dollars one evening, and the next morning they had gone up to 22.5 billion. The money was soon pointless as brick-sized currency wads gave way almost to Weimar-style wheelbarrow loads. Despite government attempts to fix prices, shops were almost entirely empty. Shopkeepers or bus operators could not last for long by selling goods or tickets at government-fixed prices and a big loss. Barter was the only solution until, finally, US dollars or South African rand replaced the Zimbabwe dollar entirely. ZANU-PF's solution to almost everything was another rigged election, but no amount of rigging or violence could now guarantee a victory. The party suggested delaying the 2008 polls by two years. But some members of the security elite demurred, especially Solomon Mujuru and his wife, Joice. Mujuru, originally Rex Nhongo, the former army commander, was now one of the country's richest men. They owned at least twenty-five farms, totalling 105,000 hectares. The power couple started to look at other leadership options. Joice Mujuru had been the country's vice president since 2004, often playing on her liberation credentials. As 'Teurai Ropa' ('Spill Blood'), her *nom de guerre*, she had allegedly shot down a Rhodesian helicopter with an AK. The succession debate was hot, but it was mostly kept under wraps inside the party. Mugabe never appointed a formal successor and deployed a guessing game about possible inheritors as a means of divide and rule. It was time for a change – that was obvious even to party loyalists, but how could it be done, cleanly, and without undermining their own privileges?

Rallies and demonstrations were banned for three months in February

2007, and then the ban was extended. In March Tsvangirai was badly beaten by police and hospitalized while trying to hold a rally. In May the country was told to expect power cuts of up to twenty hours a day. Set against hyperinflation in the economy, street protests, including one by the army, something had to be done, decided Pretoria. The crisis in Zimbabwe was infecting the whole region. ZANU-PF and the MDC started direct talks in private, courtesy of the ANC government, but under the aegis of the fifteen-state SADC.

South Africa held all the cards, just as during the Smith years when the apartheid rulers forced the Rhodesian Front to negotiate with their black opponents or face their supplies being choked off. Thabo Mbeki, the South African successor to Mandela, never tried force. He believed in 'quiet diplomacy'. It was estimated that the Zimbabwean crisis was costing his own country some \$2.6 billion a year; worse for the proud and stubborn Mbeki was the rampaging Zimbabwean dictator's damage to Pretoria's African Renaissance project, which involved a vision of sound leadership throughout the continent. NEPAD (New Partnership for Africa's Development) and a revived African Union (the former OAU) were all part of 'African solutions to African problems'. But if Mbeki could not resolve a disaster on his own doorstep, how could he save the rest of Africa?

The talks to reconcile the MDC and ZANU-PF went on and on. Tsvangirai was always overshadowed by Mugabe's intellectual bullying, though they rarely talked directly. Tsvangirai's courage was never doubted – he had suffered much – but his decision-making skills and constant vacillation, encouraged by Mugabe, led to a split in the MDC. Even Tsvangirai's sympathizers regarded him as something of a bull who would charge at any gate, after taking on board whatever expert had last advised him. Another African mediator in the Zimbabwe imbroglio was Nigerian President Olusegun Obasanjo. The former general was famously blunt, and showed his dislike for Mugabe; but he also said of Tsvangirai, 'I wouldn't have that man as a junior minister.' One of Tsvangirai's most egregious errors was his courtship of the white-led Democratic Alliance in South Africa. Yes, the ANC initially gave him the absolute run-around and refused to speak to him, but friendly conversations with a white and business-dominated opposition party fuelled the allegations that the MDC was merely a front for revanchist imperialists.

In 2005, the MDC had fractured into two main wings, the offshoot led by the able Oxford-educated Arthur Mutambara. But ZANU-PF had also begun to fracture – Simba Makoni made a run as an independent presidential candidate, though he had support within in his old ZANU-PF party.

Originally, Mugabe had taken to the young Makoni, but now he called him a 'political prostitute'. Some South African officials hoped – without much confidence – that, despite their divisions, the MDC might just be able to pull off an electoral victory, given Mugabe's shambolic economy. Setting aside the violence and a pro-Mugabe bias in the number of seats in the parliament, the voting system was heavily loaded in the dictator's favour. Except for diplomats, the more than three million people in the diaspora could not vote. People from the rural areas who worked in cities had to register and then later vote in their village homes, if they could find and afford a bus to make two separate return trips. Restrictions had been placed on parentage if not Zimbabwean. Many Zimbabweans' grandparents and parents, for example, came from Malawi, (including Comrade Mugabe's). Millions of likely MDC supporters were thus disenfranchised at the outset, before numerous other registration problems. ZANU-PF concentrated on rural areas in Mashonaland, Mugabe's stronghold, where suitably cowed village headmen would tell their villagers to vote appropriately. But the toughest obstacle was the state of the voters' rolls. Nearly a third of the 5.5 million voters were dead and many others were aged up to 120 (in a country with the world's lowest life expectancy) and, strangely, many of these latter-day Methuselahs all had the same birthday and were born in the same electorally significant district. Presumably these zombie voters or sprightly centenarians would vote early and often. While the Zimbabwe Electoral Commission was in the firm hands of military men fanatically loyal to Mugabe, MDC demands to reform the 'shambles 'of the 'ghost voters' would not be met.

In March 2008 Zimbabwe went to the polls again in local, parliamentary and presidential elections. The MDC won the parliamentary elections, but the country had to wait for five weeks for the presidential result. Mugabe had lost, but the ruling party needed time to massage the results and prepare for the fall-out. Eventually the rigged figure was 47.9 per cent for Tsvangirai and 43.2 for Mugabe. Because the MDC leader had not reached the minimum 50 per cent demanded by the constitution, a run-off would ensue.

Despite being banned, the author flew into Harare during the dangerous interim period. He visited Milton Buildings to meet the CIO Director General, Happyton Bonyongwe. The offices were run down compared with the last visit, but the lifts worked. The author was greeted warmly and the DG, an ex-brigadier, reminisced fondly about his military courses in the UK. After an amiable chat over tea and biscuits, the author asked him directly:

'Did you rig the March elections?'

'Hardly, our man lost,' he replied with a grin. 'But His Excellency Robert Mugabe will win next time.'

That was a certain bet, the author thought but did not say.

This interview, which took place before Tsvangirai withdrew from the second round, was a chilling example of Mugabe's reliance on his security apparatus. And yet the head of the most feared organization in Zimbabwe was reaching out to Britain. Not trusting, or liking, the embassy in Harare, he asked the author – God knows why – to pass on a diplomatic message directly to the FCO in London. The JOC was hoping that Britain might go along with the forthcoming one-man, one-vote, one-candidate ploy, as part of a new rapprochement with London. That was not totally absurd; London had many friends, not least in the Arab world, where dictators for life didn't even bother with elections at all. It was at this time that the love Libya campaign was at its height for British business, political and educational elites who were only too eager to embrace Gaddafi, or rather his wealth. It was a satisfying twist that those hallowed institutions, such as the London School of Economics, which were always the most preachy on human rights in Africa, should succumb most to the financial temptations.

Back in Zimbabwe, and so safely protected from the leftist elite in London, Mugabe handed over the run-off campaign to the Joint Operations Command. The military would now make sure Mugabe won. The Operation was dubbed *MAKAVOTERA PAPI?*– Who did you vote for? MDC activists were rounded up and beaten with clubs wrapped in barbed wire. Homes were burnt. Torture camps were established where the MDC 'traitors' were publicly tortured and killed. The techniques included *falanga* (beating the soles of the feet), electric shocks and the 'submarine' (not dissimilar to the American version of 'water-boarding'). After eighty murders and tens of thousands of beatings, Tsvangirai – who had direct experience of these assaults, including a CIO attempt to teach him flying lessons from a ten-storey office window – called off his campaign. He took refuge in the Netherlands embassy and urged the AU, UN and SADC to intervene. The ZANU-PF mouthpiece, the *Herald,* poked fun: 'His [Tsvangirai's] constituency is in Europe and he will be elected as the best Euro-American puppet of the country while having tea and Dutch cheese in the Dutch embassy in Harare.'

Since he was the only candidate, Mugabe won the second round on 27 June 2008. The day after he was sworn in as president, Mugabe indulged his second passion, after power, and that was globetrotting. He attended an

African Union summit in Egypt. It was the first test of the new commitment to continental democracy. With a few exceptions, Mugabe was hailed by the assembly. So much for Mbeki's dreams.

Washington, however, widened sanctions against Mugabe. And Mbeki doggedly struggled on bringing the two main Zimbabwean leaders together. For Mbeki, time was running out – he was about to face a fatal presidential challenge from his arch ANC rival, Jacob Zuma. Tsvangirai was in a political corner. He was also brow-beaten psychologically. Unlike Mandela, Mugabe and Zuma, Tsvangirai had not spent years in prison. Unlike Mbeki, he had not served a long exile. The MDC leader was ill-educated, nor had he fought in the liberation war. He was also younger and that counted in African councils. Mbeki always leaned towards, even deferred to, Mugabe. Mugabe made a fool of both men, outclassing them in negotiations, even though Tsvangirai had been a tough union negotiator. The son of a bricklayer, he rose from humble roots as a sweeper in a textile factory to become plant foreman of the Trojan nickel mine, while also pursuing a trade union career that eventually led to his election as general secretary of the Zimbabwe Congress of Trade Unions in 1988.

The military continued the pressure on the MDC and the white farmers, and even added an eccentric variant of state repression. The army and police launched operation *DZIKISAI MADISHI* ('Remove your dishes'): Harare residents were forced to remove their satellite dishes because Mugabe considered them to be purveyors of 'anti-Zimbabwean Western propaganda'.

In September 2008 Mugabe and the two wings of the MDC signed the outline of a power-sharing agreement – Mugabe was now in the driving seat again. They squabbled for months, however, about who was going to get the key ministerial portfolios – Mugabe, like Smith in the late 1970s, would not give up control of his security apparatus. While the politicians haggled, the disintegration of their country continued unabated. In December 2008, Zimbabwe declared a national state of emergency over a cholera epidemic and the final collapse of the health system. The only good news was the replacement of the worthless Zimbabwe dollar with US and South African currencies. That brought food to the shops in the main towns, although only the middle class had enough foreign currency to buy the goods.

Eventually, on 13 February 2009, the politicians reached a deal to form a government of national unity. Tsvangirai was sworn in as prime minister. To many, this new coalition was another shot-gun marriage, a replay of Nkomo's humiliation over twenty years before. The parallel was not exact, because the MDC, unlike ZAPU, was a national movement and now

Mugabe was discredited, unlike 1987. Short of setting up a provisional government in exile, probably in Botswana, the MDC leader had few choices. Armed insurrection was not an option, especially as Mugabe kept effective control of the army, police and intelligence, as well as the informal party militias. Soon after signing the agreement, Tsvangirai's wife, Susan, was killed in a road accident, which also injured the MDC leader. Mugabe and Grace (a distant relative of Susan Tsvangirai) attended his hospital bedside to discourage intense speculation that the party was 'doing a Tongogara' again. Tsvangirai recovered, but the loss of his wife, his most constant supporter, was a severe blow.

Tsvangirai's role, as far as Mugabe was concerned, was to act as a publicly acceptable face of the regime, to weaken sanctions and to get foreign aid flowing again. Targeted sanctions remained, but some IMF money trickled through. Tsvangirai kept up his campaign at home and abroad to say that sanctions should be lifted as a reward and incentive to the GNU – the government of national unity. South African pressure eased temporarily on Mugabe, once Mbeki was replaced by the colourful Zulu polygamist, Jacob Zuma, as South African president. Nor did the SADC do much to police the Harare government. ZANU-PF had found a new source of income in the military's control of the lucrative Marange diamond field. The military were alleged to have killed over 300 civilians in securing control of the so-called 'blood diamonds'. Zimbabwe was threatened with exclusion from the Kimberley Process, the international body that certifies the sources of traded diamonds to ensure diamonds do not fund violence, but none of the three main Zimbabwean parties wanted this crucial money supply cut off. By March 2010, Mugabe was trying to enforce new rules which compelled foreign-owned businesses to sell a majority stake to black Zimbabweans. Then the rump of the Commercial Farmers' Union complained of a fresh wave of attacks on farms.

The Western media focussed on the case of Mike Campbell, a white farmer who challenged Mugabe in the courts – and won, albeit in a pyrrhic victory. A documentary film was made called *Mugabe and the White African*, by British film-makers Lucy Bailey and Andrew Thompson. Campbell, with his son-in-law Ben Freeth, had owned Mount Carmel farm in Chegutu district since 1974 and then bought a neighbouring farm after Zimbabwean independence. They planted mangoes, citrus trees, maize, tobacco and sunflowers, while also setting up a herd of Mashona/Sussex cattle. In addition, they established a wild-life reserve with giraffe, impala and other animals. Their safari lodge was popular with tourists. By all accounts Campbell was a model farmer both in terms of efficiency as a foreign-exchange earner and as an employer to the 500 Africans who lived and worked on his lands. In 1999, the farm was registered with a 'certificate of no interest' from the Mugabe government. In short, they had permission to stay on the lands they had bought and farmed so well.

Mugabe's defeat in 2000 changed everything for the Mount Carmel farm. A small band of war veterans arrived in that year. Campbell resisted the intimidation so the veterans moved onto adjoining land owned by Campbell's son Bruce. The veterans started to poach the wild life, cattle were slaughtered and the tourist lodge was burned down. After getting no redress from the local courts, Mike Campbell made legal history in 2007 by appealing to the SADC tribunal in Windhoek, Namibia. In November 2008 the tribunal ruled in the white farmer's favour, declaring that the land seizures were racist and theft on a grand scale. Campbell and his family could keep their farms. But before the November judgement, on 29 June, 2008, two days after the presidential run-off, Campbell, his wife and his son-in-law, Ben, were abducted and taken to a remote militia camp, where they were tortured for nine hours. Mike Campbell suffered head wounds, broken ribs and damage to his lower limbs caused by the infamous *falanga* torture. His wife Angela was also tortured into signing a piece of paper promising they would not sustain their court battle. Ben Freeth was also badly beaten. Campbell was too ill to attend the tribunal's final hearing, but Freeth, whose skull was fractured, attended in a wheelchair.

Despite the Namibian SADC legal judgement, attacks on the farm continued. Campbell and Freeth returned to the tribunal in 2009 to obtain a contempt order against the Mugabe government. In April 2009, the Campbells and the Freeths were finally driven off their farm by a rampaging mob led by Nathan Shamuyarira, a veteran member of the ZANU-PF politburo. The farmhouse was burned down, along with the homes of sixty workers and a small linen factory which Angela Campbell had set up to provide employment for the wives of the farm workers. The Campbells, aged seventy-six and sixty-eight, were now penniless and homeless. On 6 April 2011, Mike Campbell finally succumbed to the injuries sustained during his torture. His farm is derelict. The SADC heads of state decided to suspend the legal tribunal's operation in a move which was widely seen as an act of regional solidarity for Mugabe's treatment of a stubborn, brave and battered farmer, a man who regarded himself as 'a white African' – an endangered species.

Tsvangirai had also suffered regular beatings and stubbornly resisted Mugabe. But the MDC leader's position was undermined daily by Mugabe's intransigence towards a man he believed almost beneath his contempt. Some of the MDC ministers were as incompetent and corrupt as their ZANU-PF counterparts. Those who weren't were kept away from real decision-making. Zimbabwe needed security sector reform, a new constitution, fair elections and, above all, the departure of Mugabe. Tsvangirai could do little about change so long as the military backed Mugabe. It was often said that a military coup was impossible in Harare, because it had already happened – but in slow incremental steps. If change did depend on the military, it is important to understand the nature of the ZDF and, above all, its politics.

# Chapter 9

# Days of the Generals

Zimbabwe had never enjoyed the classic Clausewitzian separation of military and state. The party and army were frequently fused in the war of liberation, when Mugabe was head of party and commander in chief. From independence, the senior military were regularly given top jobs in the civilian structure and received much of the land seized from white farmers. Nominal military subservience was paid to party and parliament until 2000. Mugabe's first electoral defeat, however, spread panic among the securocrats. During the undeclared civil war of 2000-2008 and then the political armistice of the national unity government, it could be argued that Mugabe became more a convenient figurehead as top cover for the generals. Members of the ruling elite were constantly concerned that loss of power would lead to prosecution, especially after President Omar al-Bashir of Sudan became the first sitting head of state to be indicted by the International Criminal Court for alleged crimes in Darfur. If Mugabe were ever dragged to The Hague, some of his generals might have to accompany him. At the very least, domestic retribution might force them into exile. The indictment of Bashir was likely to entrench the Sudanese president's position – the longer he stayed in power, the less likely he would end up in The Hague. The same could be said of the ICC threat to Colonel Gaddafi in 2011. Although Mugabe was never formally indicted, the perceived danger was one the many reasons he chose to hang on, by any means. Amnesty was an important part of the discussions to set up the ZANU-PF co-habitation with the two elements of the MDC.

*The military structure*

*Command and control*

The Joint Operations Command was the main vehicle for military control for a decade after 2000. Inherited from the Rhodesian system, it was the prime means of co-ordinating the civil war in the early 1980s and the operations abroad in Mozambique and the Congo. Initially, chaired weekly by Mugabe, it was theoretically subservient to the party. After the series of military operations to contain the domestic population, especially during elections, it came first to be a parallel government, then, by 2008, the dominant council in the land. The core element was called the 'gang of six' but the elite changed, partly caused by death or retirement. When the military reached the zenith of their power in 2008, the key power-brokers were: Brigadier General Constantine Chiwenga (head of the ZDF); General Philip Sibanda (ZNA commander) Air Marshal Perence Shiri (head of the air force); Commissioner of Police, Augustine Chihuri; Major General (rtd) Paradzai Zimondi, head of the prison service; the CIO DG, Brigadier (rtd) Happyton Bonyongwe; and *primus inter pares*, Emmerson Mnangagwa, the minister of defence. Technical advisers supported the group, including Gideon Gono, the head of the Reserve Bank, who acted as paymaster. Others might join in for specific meetings such as John Sibanda, in charge of war veterans, and other party chefs.

It would be incorrect to interpret the military as a monolith; various tribal, generational and policy disputes caused fissures. But at the top, in the JOC, the arguments usually produced a survival consensus. Collective memory of the liberation war, comradeship in more recent battles, a fear of collective punishment and a desire to hold on to their wealth all coalesced to produce unity, despite the friction about a replacement for Mugabe. In the beginning Mugabe held the prime role, followed by the commander of the ZDF, with the others accepting a secondary parity. Most had long service, often long enough to remember the internal ZANU purges of their liberation struggle, encouraged by the divide-and-rule tactics of Smith's intelligence operatives, as well as meddling by the frontline states and Pretoria. All had experience as the CEOs of large departments of state.

The establishment of the GNU – the government of national unity – inaugurated by the lofty-sounding Global Political Agreement, finessed by the South Africans and SADC, did introduce nominal changes in the secret JOC cabal. Officially the top strategic command became the National Security Council, which admitted coalition leaders. Unofficially, JOC meetings continued, with the definitive exclusion of any tainted MDC members. Some of the JOC intimates suggested a *nom de guerre* for their secret meetings: the Social Revolutionary Council. But the JOC mentality prevailed: power through unity and an avoidance of fratricide, especially in the potentially dangerous days following the departure of Comrade Mugabe. They managed to avoid significant leaks; the main public disputes aired – press speculations – were about who would or who wouldn't salute Tsvangirai and the questions of who supported what potential successors as ZANU-PF leader. It was clear, however, that the JOC debated endlessly the co-habitation deal. Hardliners wanted to finish off the MDC, while so-called 'accommodationists' realized that international, regional and domestic financial pressures dictated a deal of sorts – provided it could be managed. The JOC, however, may not have unified sufficiently to back Emmerson Mnangagwa's long-cherished goal to succeed Mugabe, though his tough securocrat credentials could still win him the day, despite his age (sixty-five) and despite the desire to find a younger technocrat who could regenerate the party.

To sum up the overarching power of the JOC today: in the 1970s, it was a means of Rhodesian command and control. During the 1980s and 1990s, despite being ZANU-PF-aligned, it was less involved with politics. It dealt with military operations domestically and abroad. It tried to keep out of overt politics because of the savage liberation war purges of military commanders who were accused of trying to topple the political leadership. Then, with the inclusion of ZIPRA in the integration of the ZDF and later the fragility of the 1987 Unity Accord, the generals kept their heads down. After 2000, with the increasing dependency on the military to win the elections of 2000, 2002, 2005 and 2008, the JOC combined its former role of running formal military operations with that of politicization of the voters by force. In March 2008 the JOC took charge, without declaring martial law, until the GNU of February 2009. They took but one step back out of the political fray, partly to see how the coalition would work, and to remove a too-obvious direct confrontation with the MDC. During 2010, the JOC reasserted itself with power-broking sessions which excluded the MDC. Relations with the MDC worsened when Finance Minister Tendai Biti, Tsvangirai's second in command, drew up a budget which relegated the military vis-à-vis the allocations to health and education. The JOC saw this as a deliberate snub. A new wave of crackdowns on MDC supporters followed. By early 2011, the security apparatus had been placed on a war footing. The whole of Zimbabwe became an operational zone.

### *Central Intelligence Organization*

Historically, the BSAP, and then ZRP, Special Branch was responsible for internal security while the CIO – which had access to all SB material – concentrated on national security and co-ordinating all intelligence acquired from internal and external sources. The CIO had a number of branches. Branch 1 (internal) was essentially made up of SB officers. The other branches dealt with external operations, military intelligence, telecommunications and surveillance of government officials. Under Mugabe the CIO became the dominant and ubiquitous organ of the state. It was the largest and best-funded intelligence agency, while the police also boasted an intelligence unit, PISI, and the ZNA operated a military intelligence wing. The CIO employed up to 10,000 permanent staff, operating in Zimbabwe and abroad. It was also active in the diaspora, especially London, though it was not as prevalent as the numerous, and nervous, Zimbabwean activists in the UK made out. It also had part-time workers and paid informer networks. Apart from the conventional role of gathering intelligence, it was active in domestic oppression in a paramilitary function. It became notorious for its torture and abductions. Its budget was difficult to estimate because it was supported by secret funds from the president's office. Pay for the rank and file was not good, as some of the junior CIO operatives, informally interviewed by the author, measured their (official) salary by the small amount of sacks of 'mealie' (the maize staple) they could purchase. Despite its undoubted power in the JOC hierarchy, the CIO did not have the same clout as the ZDF and ZNA commanders. Senior CIO officials would try to persuade influential foreigners, especially spook counterparts abroad, that they were the 'good guys', applying the occasional brake on the 'bad guys' in the military and party. They were the pragmatists, they implied, as they had all the intelligence, knew where the bodies were buried (literally in some cases) and understood the need for reform. At other times, the top CIO figures would paint a picture of division inside the organization – hawks and doves, if not exactly ZANU-PF versus MDC. Only the insiders knew the truth and whether this was merely PR disinformation.

### Zimbabwe Defence Force

According to the International Institute for Strategic Studies (IISS), the 2011 figure for the army was 25,000 and the air force, 4,000. Although desertion had been a problem, the actual numbers could be a little higher. The ZDF was configured for a 'two-war' capacity – internal and external, conventional and COIN. The IISS said the ZNA had forty main battle tanks and eighty-five armoured personnel carriers as well as a respectable array of field artillery, but it was difficult to calibrate their condition, given the sometimes poor maintenance, especially since the army had not used the equipment in anger for a decade or more.  The same goes for the air force which still had some vintage Rhodesian kit such as Hawker Hunters and Alouettes. The Chinese, especially, had helped with Chengdu F-7s and Colonel Gaddafi sold Harare MiG-23s at bargain-basement prices. The AFZ also had hired Ilyushin cargo planes not least to traffic its gains from the DRC. Also, the air force had a few serviceable Russian gunships left. The IISS claimed forty-five combat-capable aircraft, although the air defence systems, of various calibres, were not deployed, it said, but the army had air defence capability and surface-to-air missiles. If the IISS was accurate, the lack of a proper air defence system for the air force was odd, because, officially, the ZDF fretted perpetually about the possibility of a British or US-led intervention to topple the regime. Given the national state of alert in March 2011, as well as the obvious lessons of NATO-led attacks on an African state, Libya, the ZDF is likely to beef up its existing air defence systems as well as find the money to shop for upgraded equipment. Harare had spent millions of US dollars on a Chinese ground-to-air defence system, but it was considered very inferior and remained inside a very large warehouse still in the crates in which it was delivered.

Morale is usually more valuable than counting pieces of equipment to estimate combat quality. In the last decade the politicization had inspired an exodus of good soldiers and air men, as had poor pay, inferior accommodation, tribal and clan victimization as well as dislike of the closed-shop fraternity of those who fought in the liberation war. In June 2007, 400 ZNA personnel were arrested for an alleged coup attempt. Some senior officers were court-martialled for a specific plot to bomb Mugabe's residence and overthrow the government; some simply disappeared and others suffered mysterious deaths.

In December 2008 soldiers rioted in Harare when they failed to get their pay from a local bank. After the GNU, and a slight improvement in the financial situation with the dollarization of the economy, the army tried to make sure that the soldiers were paid on time and in a usable currency. The departure or desertion by many soldiers was considered to be a useful safety valve, though some of the better men quit. Also, the integration of some of the youth brigades into the ZNA helped to redress the generational gap, but the retention of senior officers of liberation war vintage, in an active or advisory role, still caused problems for the younger professionally inclined officers and NCOs. Educational qualifications were also lowered, and this was considered to be a negative factor in the desire to bolster professionalism. The departure of skilled pilots had also been a headache for the air force planners. Nevertheless, the ZNA tried hard to impart an *espirit de corps* and regimental pride in their units. The ZNA also gained accolades for their UN deployments, which in 2011 were small – fewer than thirty were stationed in the Ivory Coast, Liberia, Nepal and Sudan.

## The Zimbabwe Republic Police

The ZNA had been the back-up especially during national elections operations; day-to-day enforcement of state security had rested on the ZRP, war veterans and the CIO. Increasing crime rates had not been ignored, but often the police could not attend a crime scene because they had no vehicles or petrol. The traditional role of policing had suffered as better resources went to the paramilitary units such as the Law and Order Section (the 'riot police'), Police Support Unit and PISI. Some policemen did lament the passing of the high standards of the British South Africa Police, and felt they were being forced into the role of enemies, not protectors of the people. Police numbers stood at around 25,000 in 2011. Repressive legislation such as the Public Order and Security Act, which banned demonstrations and some types of public meetings, led to frequent confrontations with law-abiding political protestors and civic associations. The brutal behaviour of the riot police poisoned police-civilian relations, especially in urban areas. Batons and clubs as well as live rounds took their toll of university and MDC protests.

Training for the police was sometimes brutal. A female recruit was beaten to death at Morris Depot, in Harare, in 2008. Shortage of skills and equipment, as well as the omnipresent politicization and maltreatment of those considered not zealous ZANU-PF supporters had led to a breakdown in police procedures. Dockets disappeared. In some cases a victim's (forced) confession would be the only evidence. As with the army, poor accommodation and low pay prompted moonlighting, for example setting up roadblocks to extort money from motorists (though with less subtlety than the British use of speed cameras). The ZRP was scheduled to increase to 50,000 to work on fighting crime not political opponents – that at least was one of the aspirations of the GNU.

Peter Godwin in his book, *The Fear*, examined in graphic details the destructive power of 'the *panga* and penis' on men and women by the militias, CIO and police. The author quoted German-born Dieter Schultz, the Catholic Bishop of Chinhoyi diocese, who was arrested by the Rhodesian Front for his aid to the insurgents during the liberation war. Schultz returned to Zimbabwe after 1980 and was tormented by the actions of those he risked his life for in the 1970s. He said:

> When I am angry in the evening I go to the chapel and I pray for my equilibrium to be restored, to let my anger pass. A third-year seminarian who is to be ordained deacon comes to me and says: 'My father was murdered yesterday, 63 years old, because they suspected him of being a member of the opposition, which he was not. The militia came and beat him to death in front of his wife.' How can one not be angry? And when I phoned the police to report it they said they could not open a docket because they didn't have a photocopier.

## Zimbabwe Prison Service

The ZPS was legally a uniformed paramilitary organization, with approximately 5,000 staff. One of the main institutional problems was the resentment against retired army officers taking over the better jobs. Staff were also seriously victimized by senior officers, but the conditions of prisoners was much worse. Zimbabwe's forty-two prisons were supposed to hold a maximum of 18,000 inmates, but the figure could have been almost double that. Many of them had not been convicted of any crime. Lack of food, brutality, overcrowding, poor sanitation and paucity of medical treatment killed an average of thirty prisoners daily. The bodies were left to rot alongside surviving prisoners.

Zimbabwe's prisons were often death camps, as the MDC's designated deputy agricultural minister, Roy Bennett, found out just before he was due to take up his portfolio in the GNU. He survived but he told the world about the dead, dying and half-living sharing

Sketch by Kevin Woods of his solitary confinement cell in Chikurubi Prison. He is climbing the wall to see out of the top grill. The former CIO officer spent nearly 20 years in Mugabe's jails. (With permission of 30 Degrees South publishers and Kevin Woods.)

the same cell. He was a brave white farmer who fought Mugabe's land invasion, and lost, but was elected an MDC MP for Chimanimani; ZANU-PF promised revenge. Bennett had spent eights months in the high-security Chikurubi prison four years before. He suffered endless humiliation, including being forced to wear a prison uniform totally immersed in human excrement. Later, an attempt was made to drown him. He was a prominent politician, with international backing, so he didn't die, unlike many of his cell-mates.

Death marked the end of the prisoners' suffering, but their bodies would suffer further indignities. Chikurubi prison officers admitted that their mortuary system would often fail. A member of the British embassy staff continued the story:

Of course there was no electricity, so corpses rotted quickly, added to which families could no longer afford to collect and bury relatives. At one point in early 2009, over a hundred bodies were piled in a makeshift mortuary. Rats and flies were feeding on the remains. Eventually the officers were ordered to bury the bodies themselves in mass graves inside the prison.

### The Zimbabwe National Liberation War Veterans Association and the Youth Brigades

The war veterans and the Youth Brigades were shock troops for land invasions and attacks on opposition supporters. The war veterans numbered about 30,000 with about half ready for active military duty at any one time. They were usually armed with traditional weapons – *pangas*, axes, knives and sometimes spears – because conventional weapons tended to be the preserve of the formal military units. Also, traditional weapons were seen as more fearsome than guns, especially by the rural population. The green bombers numbered about 15,000. Some were later integrated into the ZNA, but the younger ones opened the state up to the accusation that it deployed child soldiers.

### Zimbabwe Defence Industries (ZDI)

Arms manufacturing in Zimbabwe dates back to the Second World War. In July 1945 the then government of Southern Rhodesia established the War Studies committee, ostensibly to provide weaponry for the country, but more to fulfil the arms requirements of neighbouring South Africa. Weapons factories were built in the capital (the Salisbury Ordnance Factory) and the Rhodesia Ordnance Factory in Bulawayo. These factories produced a variety of small arms and ammunition and tank spares for Commonwealth forces. The end of the war led to the near-mothballing of much of the production. The 1950s were a time of military harvest as Southern Rhodesia became the armoury of the 1953-1963 Federation, receiving the bulk of small arms, aeroplanes and tanks for the federal military structure. Rhodesian arms' production was resuscitated by the sanctions which followed UDI in 1965. Although the Rhodesians soon developed a complex and effective sanctions-busting programme, the combination of having to pay out exorbitant fees to arms middlemen and the widening war forced the Rhodesians to establish their own defence industry. The late seventies saw a proliferation of Rhodesian military engineering firms which made plenty of money by producing ammunition, infantry vehicles and modified Israeli Uzis under licence.

At independence, the ministry of defence made the case that the country needed a defence industry, particularly since it was seen as the regional armoury against the SADF. The 1983 working paper on establishing a defence industry envisioned various spin-offs, including increased foreign currency earnings, employment for dozens, perhaps hundreds, of Zimbabweans and enhanced military self-sufficiency and capability. The end result was the establishment of the Zimbabwe Defence Industries in 1985, initially under the ministries of defence and industry. Soon enough, the ZDI became the fiefdom of the defence ministry and president's office. The commanders of the ZDF and Mugabe and his inner circle became permanent members of the board of directors. By the 1990s and into the new millennium, the ZDI had become a core component of Zimbabwe's burgeoning military-industrial complex as the JOC joined forces with local and regional businesses to try and drag the organization kicking and screaming into profitability. The ZDI manufactured various items including combat clothing, small-arms ammunition and bombs and organised vehicle repair. It never operated profitably as an organisation, but it provided political and military stakeholders with a conduit for amassing personal fortunes. Some of this fortune may be tied to international drug cartels, not least in South America where the ZDI was accused of dealing, especially with FARC insurgents in Columbia.

After 2000, with Zimbabwe facing an arms embargo from its former suppliers in the EU and US, the ZDI turned its hand to sanctions busting and ensuring that Zimbabwe's military had the weaponry to crush any popular uprising. The military relationship with China was revived in the late 1990s. From 2000-2009, the Chinese remained the largest arms supplier, accounting for 39 per cent of Zimbabwe's arms imports, followed by Ukraine at 35 per cent and Libya at 27 per cent. Slovakia and the Czech Republic also sold small volumes of conventional arms after 2000. In 2004, Zimbabwe was supposed to import twelve Chinese FC-1 combat trainer aircraft and 100 Dongfeng military vehicles in a deal worth US$200 million. The armoured vehicles and assault rifles came via Beira in 2005, but the details of the fighter aircraft were unclear. It may be that the order was replaced with twelve K-8 trainer aircraft which were delivered in two batches between 2005-2006. In April 2008 dock workers in South Africa refused to unload a shipment of weapons destined for Zimbabwe, from the Chinese ship *An Yue Jiang*. The ZDF later had to send cargo planes to retrieve the shipment which ended up in Angola. It was an unusual diplomatic gaffe by an ever cautious Beijing to be caught out sending weapons to a pariah state at a time when arms embargoes on Zimbabwe were being discussed in international forums. How Harare paid for all the

Chinese kit remained an unanswered question though the best guess was the sale of land and mining rights.

The EU arms embargo, which was renewed for another one-year period in February 2011, had limited some European sales to Zimbabwe. Big Russian contracts had not been in evidence since the Congo war, although supplies of automatic rifles had gone ahead after the Hind helicopter deal of 1998. Ukraine provided upgrades, from engines to avionics, for some of the Chinese aircraft purchased. Other non-EU states such as Brazil had not been shy of exporting arms to Zimbabwe. For example, Brazil sold a very large supply of shotgun ammunition – whether it was for hunting or suppressing mass protests was a moot point. Libya and Zimbabwe remained close, but the three MiG-23 combat planes supplied very cheaply in 2003 appear not to have flown operationally, or even flown at all (though, admittedly, plane-spotting around military airfields in Zimbabwe is not a very popular pastime). The Stockholm International Peace Research Institute (SIPRI), the leading authority on arms sales, stated that South Africa, once one of Zimbabwe's principal arms suppliers, had dutifully observed an embargo since 2009, but it warned that Zimbabwe might have been getting some arms from private dealers in the US and UK.

The ZDI was also adept at weapons sales – from 1999 to 2000, its Director, Colonel L. Dube, supplied weapons to West Africa. This was part of a co-ordinated international arms smuggling network which flew in a 68-tonne shipment of guns and ammunition through Burkino Faso and from there into Liberia and Sierra Leone. Zimbabwe's military have ensured that the ZDI remains a private holding with no access to accountability from civil society. It continued to manufacture small-arms ammunition and clothing destined for regional markets. It also still operated closely with the ministry of defence to ensure that when the ministry placed an order for arms and equipment the ZDI was capable of refitting imported equipment for local conditions.

*Zimbabwe National Security Council* (ZNSC, as distinct from the NSC set up under the GNU).

Mugabe set up the ZNSC in 2006. This marked the militarization of the economy in response to sanctions. Military men (mainly retired generals and brigadiers) were appointed to boards as directors or CEOs of the Grain Marketing Board, National Railways of Zimbabwe, Zimbabwe Electricity Supply Authority and other organizations considered to be 'strategic sectors'. The ZNSC was dissolved at the end of 2008, but many of the military elite remained in charge of the commanding heights of the (crumbling) economy.

## The Opposition

Such a formidable array of personnel and materiel comprised the government's security apparatus. By comparison the opposition to the military-industrial complex was tiny. The main opposition groups were formally committed to peaceful change, but they were not defenceless. Both MDC parties had internal security departments, made up usually of ex-soldiers who were supposed to protect MDC leaders and staff from the constant harassment. They also had youth leagues. The MDC organized some local self-defence units, which led to pitched battles with the war veterans in parts of Mashonaland. These MDC groups could not challenge the militarized Zimbabwean state.

In 2008, in response to the national attacks by ZANU-PF, some dissidents in the diaspora, especially London, talked of organizing exiled soldiers into a *Dare re Chimurenga* to wage a 'fourth *Chimurenga*' against Mugabe. Much of this speculation was probably ZANU-PF propaganda, but talk in opposition groups about training in Botswana for a fight-back was so prevalent that it reflected the desperate and angry mood of the opposition if not any real organizational intent, or capability. Of more significance perhaps was the reformation of ZAPU, under Dumiso Dabengwa, but the MDC had stolen much of its thunder, and what was needed by the opposition was national, not tribal, transformation.

How will the military react to the dramatic changes created in 2009-2011 and to the inevitable post-Mugabe era? Despite the power and survival consensus of the JOC, the military apparatus is not a unified body. A large minority, perhaps even a majority, of the junior ranks support the MDC. They look to the future, while ZANU-PF harks back to the glory days of the past. ZANU-PF has long been a politico-military alliance grounded on a supremacist ideology: all political enemies were by definition traitors to the state and revolution. This has been maintained by a close fraternity of serving senior officers and genuine war veterans, albeit retired. The military aristocracy had kept together on the grounds that they must hang together or hang individually. Their allegiance had been weakened, partly because of a pragmatic need to change, even their leader, and because of decline in liquidity – dollarization affected some of the super-rich, despite the recent bounty from blood diamonds. Some of the illegal money supply had gone to improving pay and conditions, at least of the elite regular forces. Just in case, though, an abnormally tight rein had been kept on distribution of weapons, and there were even reports that senior officers feared assassination during major parades. Yet the main driver remained – so long as Mugabe had money and power to offer patronage and allow state looting, then he would keep the top brass on side. As one senior officer noted, 'The opposition can scream all it can, but nothing will happen as long as Mugabe looks after his own well.'

The fears of a putsch in 2007 and the savage reprisals dampened down the ardour for another coup attempt. And the original polarization of the senior officers around the two main factions (Mnangagwa and the Mujurus) appeared to have dissipated. Then there was the internal control; the CIO had replaced the commissars. As one disgruntled junior officer complained, 'There are intelligence officers within the forces ... In the security forces one can not trust anyone. If you're suspected of inciting mutiny, you disappear without a trace.' A coup by junior officers is not an obvious possibility in 2011, though a breakdown in the GNU and a return to widespread violence could spark a violent backlash in the junior ranks, especially if led by a group of charismatic risk-takers. Some of the serving officers, as well as ex-servicemen, could engage or even lead a mass popular insurrection in the manner of the Arab Awakening (even watching televised recordings of Arab uprisings led to arrests in Harare in February-March 2011). That, however, may not suit the Shona culture, especially in a society which has been beaten into submission for so long.

After the formation of the GNU in February 2009, there was a relative lull in military operations for a few months as the new partners in the GNU took stock of each other. It was clear from the beginning that the coalition would be as much about power struggles as power-sharing. Tsvangirai's MDC had done well to ensure that they received the ministry of finance when ministerial portfolios were parcelled out. Over the previous five years, Reserve Bank governor Gideon Gono had dominated the financial landscape and reduced the minister of finance to a cipher. ZANU-PF, believing the finance ministry was a poisoned chalice after a decade of economic destruction, agreed to the MDC-T's allocation of the post. Tendai Biti, one of the most impressive of the MDC leaders, immediately set about reasserting the power of the finance ministry and tackling Zimbabwe's economic crisis. Biti's immediate dollarization of the economy cut the ground from RBZ Governor Gideon Gono who had made a fortune through controlling legitimate foreign currency trading and taking his cut from the black market. The partial resuscitation of Zimbabwe's economy in 2009-2010 should thus bring praise for the MDC-T.

But while the MDC-T was revelling in their new-found soft power, ZANU-PF continued to dominate in the hard power stakes. The GNU agreement had provided for the establishment of four institutions which were designed to rein in the power of the military and open the pathway to improved civil-military relations. The main institutions were: the sharing of the home affairs ministry by the MDC-T and ZANU-PF; the establishment of the Joint Monitoring and Implementation Committee (JOMIC) to monitor and mediate inter-party fighting and security forces' abuses; the establishment of the ministry of national healing to promote reconciliation between rival party supporters; and the establishment of the National Security Council (NSC) in which the security sector would meet with the GNU principals to discuss security.

If the unspoken objective of establishing these bodies was to control the JOC, then the attempt was a failure. The MDC home affairs co-minister, Giles Mutsekwa, was sidelined almost as soon as he took office. A wave of new invasions of the few remaining white farmers' lands occurred from March to June 2009. As ever, many of the invaders were 'war veterans' but more than a few were policemen, some of them in uniform. Pleas by the MDC home affairs minister for the police to respond, stop and investigate and prosecute the perpetrators came to nothing as the police commanders showed that they answered to only ZANU-PF. The MDC replaced Mutsekwa with the more aggressive and controversial Theresa Makone in June 2010. Makone tried to push Police Commissioner Augustine Chihuri to professionalize the ZRP, particularly with regard to possible elections in 2011; but Chihuri showed that he could push back and would not accept her control. Makone's commitment to reforming the ministry and ZRP was also questioned, as 2010 saw persistent media allegations that she and Jocelyn Chiwenga, wife of General Constantine Chiwenga, were close friends.

JOMIC mediation had fared no better. The chair of JOMIC, Minister Priscilla Misihairabwi-Mushonga, publicly admitted in March 2011 that 'There's nothing we can do to … stop this smart coup. We can only write to the South Africans.' The ministry of national healing was supposed to lead a third wave of reconciliation in Zimbabwe (following on from the first wave of the immediate post-independence period and the second wave which followed the 1987 Unity agreement). For a few months in 2009, the National Organ on Healing did indeed begin a process of bringing together ZANU-PF, including some of the perpetrators of the 2008 killings, with opposition activists in traditional–style *dares* (meetings) to discuss admission and atonement for violence. But the organization lacked the resources and support for a truly national reconciliation campaign. Worse still, only nine of the key perpetrators and organizers of ZANU-PF violence participated and there was no authority or mechanism which could compel participation. In addition, no one in the top levels of the military and ZANU-PF were prepared to admit that they had killed hundreds, perhaps thousands, of people not just in 2008, but during the whole decade.

The National Security Council had been established but so far had proved to be stillborn. Originally mandated to meet at least once a month the NSC had met only five times after the GNU was formed. The NSC was supposed to discuss hard security issues, which presumably would include the unceasing attacks on the MDC by the military. Instead, NSC meetings, when they happened, were marked by a lack of any rapport between the MDC ministers and the generals and no substantial discussions resulted. Instead, the real hard security discussions were conducted in the regular JOC meetings which still excluded MDC representatives. During the August Defence Forces Day in both 2009 and 2010, the military – who had lived up to their promise never to salute Tsvangirai – continued to put on a show of unity, pomp and power. Meanwhile, their foot soldiers once again began to ramp up the violence. From August 2010 war veterans were deployed in Masvingo and Bikita districts – the former ZANU-PF heartlands – to soften up civilians through terror campaigns, ahead of the possible referendum and elections in 2011. Villagers were once again forced to attend rallies, MDC activists were attacked by marauding gangs, led by notorious war veteran Jabulani Sibanda, a man who was feared as a key ringleader in the 2008 killings. In an ironic twist, the ZRP often arrested the *victims* of political violence. By the end of 2010 the campaigns had reached parts of Manicaland. In February 2011 soldiers were deployed in Matabeleland and the Midlands; the aim was to close down MDC structures whiles allowing for ZANU-PF to rebuild its own organization in these areas ahead of possible fresh elections. Die-hard Mugabe loyalists in the form of recently retired army officers were moved permanently to utterly dominate the Zimbabwe Electoral Commission, despite the intention of the coalition government to re-constitute a body so crucial to free and fair elections.

The death or departure of Mugabe will not necessarily unlock the Zimbabwean imbroglio. Too many of the serving officers and war vets are too ideologically and materially committed to the status quo to go down without a fight. The problem is they could end up fighting each other as much as the MDC.

# Chapter 10

# Zimbabwe After Mugabe

*The political-military future*

Military interventionism in Zimbabwe was a symptom, not the cause, of Zimbabwe's malaise. The over-arching cause was political maladministration on an epic scale. The military could not be reformed without major political change, and that almost inevitably hinged on the removal of Mugabe. In 2011, it is unclear whether the GNU is the first step on the road to political transformation or a throwback to the ZANU-PF absorption of its ZAPU rival in 1987. Zimbabwe has had a history of coalition governments. Mugabe's first government included members of the old Rhodesian Front and ZAPU. The 1987 merger of Mugabe's and Nkomo's parties was intended to be permanent. The GNU, though, has been a process not an outcome. An accurate historical comparison could be the internal settlement of 1978-79; this was Zimbabwe's first multi-party authority, even though it was short-lived and fatally flawed.

The coalition could easily fall apart and Zimbabwe could sink back into its undeclared civil war. ZANU-PF essentially controlled defence, foreign policy and agriculture, while the MDC Tsvangirai ran finance, health and education. The police portfolio was hotly debated, fudged and divided. Mugabe exercised the hard power, and the MDC the soft. But Mugabe knew that he could probably not survive without the MDC's attempts to improve both the financial and moral image of Zimbabwe. ZANU-PF had declined because of brutality and economic collapse, but unemployment had also undermined the MDC's union base. Despite the real hard power remaining under Mugabe's nominal sovereignty, Tsvangirai's MDC engagement and Arthur Mutambara's balancing act had helped to pause Zimbabwe's descent into total meltdown in the manner of Somalia. The MDC had few options, as a senior MDC member, Langton Bhebe, pointed out: 'People can criticize us for joining hands with ZANU-PF, but if we had not joined, we would have no hands.' The coalition of the unwilling had allowed a breathing space for Mugabe and the country. But how long could Zimbabwe's crisis continue?

*Possible options*

## Waiting for Godot

The waiting for Godot option, or rather waiting for God, meant delaying the renewal of Zimbabwe until the grim reaper dealt with the tyrant. Serious Zimbabwe-watchers had been fascinated by every hint of the eighty-seven-year-old's health. Rumours of various illnesses, especially prostate cancer, and foreign hospital checks abounded. Mugabe's mother lived until almost 100, and Mugabe offered his services as president until he was that age. That could destroy the country completely, perhaps even beyond a possible international reconstruction effort. Instead of playing down his age, ZANU-PF had boasted that Mugabe was the world's oldest leader. In a country where spirits are often revered, even among the urban elite, the old fox had taken to referring to his ghost remaining to ensure his policies were kept intact. He seemed to believe that he could exercise a stranglehold even from the grave.

Mugabe had given no public statement on his mortality or retirement, despite the alleged wobbles in 2000 when he lost the referendum on a new constitution, and in March 2008 when he was beaten by Tsvangirai in the first round of the presidential campaign. Like the mortally wounded El Cid, his military followers propped him up on his horse to keep up the momentum of the crusade. Could Mugabe afford to stay on, even if he called a snap (rigged) election, and ditched the GNU? Although the MDC was considered the gate-keeper to foreign finance, Mugabe's elite had been exploiting another domestic source: the diamond fields.

The discovery of rich alluvial diamond fields in Africa has usually led to war: the Anglo-Boer war, the apartheid defence of Namibia, the DRC, Sierra Leone and Liberia are obvious examples. Zimbabwe's main diamond fields, around Marange near Mutare and in River Ranch near the South African border have been exploited since 2006 and 2004 respectively. The front company structure was intentionally complex, but essentially the deals were run by the generals. Initially, at Marange, unemployed would-be miners flocked to exploit the diamonds, and help set up thriving *entrepôts* over the border in Mozambique. Then the police and army stepped in to organize the spoils. The army rotated its brigades every two-three months to avoid charges of favouritism and to allow the soldiers a chance to boost their meagre salaries. The *gwejas*, as the miners were known in Shona, soon realized that the terms under which they entered into syndicates with the police or soldiers became more and more exploitative. At the start of the diamond rush hundreds of miners were killed in accidents or by military crack-downs. Initially, they were rural unemployed, but soon professional people, with degrees, were forced to seek employment and to submit to the ever-greedy military. The police and army formed separate syndicates; they never worked together. But neither uniformed branch protected 'their' miners from occasional swoops by the feared Police Support Unit.

The diamond extraction was dominated by two main players from the high priests of Zimbabwean politics. In the south, Solomon Mujuru took a major shareholding – leading to jokes about Solomon's mines. In the Mutare area, Mnangagwa was a financial colossus. As was the ubiquitous Perence Shiri, not only a member of the Praetorian Guard, but also Mugabe's cousin. Mugabe refused to abide by the Kimberley Process, despite South African warnings, and continued to allow fake certificates to be used as diamonds were exported to centres in India and the Middle East, especially Dubai. Some of the military commanders were even alleged to have entered into private deals with the Chinese in exchange for arms shipments. Chinese soldiers were also reported to be engaged in the mining itself. The ZDF was originally seduced by the allure of the diamond business in the DRC. The Harare-Kinshasa diamond axis continued after the ZDF exit from the war. The expertise was augmented by the later domestic diamond rush, making Harare a Wild West centre for illicit diamond smuggling. ZANU-PF was sufficiently determined and ruthless to maintain a pirate economy without the MDC mediation, if push came to shove. And not a penny from the diamonds entered the government treasury. In short, Mugabe – without or without the GNU – could stagger on, so long as the Praetorians of the liberation war were prepared to allow him to continue as their front man.

More worrying was the MDC's reaction to the diamonds. Many of the MDC ministers, resplendent in their new Mercedes saloons, had enraged local civic society groups and foreign NGOs by minimizing ZANU-PF's transgressions in the GNU. Tsvangirai was seriously criticized for taking up his position of prime minister when thirty of his senior activists were held illegally in detention. In May 2009 he said that the 'so-called farm invasions' were 'isolated incidents' which had been 'blown out of proportion'. More ominously, in June 2009, at a Kimberley Process conference in Namibia, a junior MDC minister, Murisi Zwizwai, said: 'Contrary to the allegations in the media, nobody was killed by security forces during an operation at Marange.' Human Rights Watch interviewed more than 100 surviving victims of that 2008 operation. Their report concluded that

Soldiers indiscriminately fired AK-47 assault rifles, without giving any warning. In the panic and ensuing stampede, some miners were trapped and died in tunnels. Over three weeks, the military assault resulted in the brutal deaths of more than 200 people. Soldiers forced miners to dig mass graves for many of the dead.

The JOC's control of the diamond bounty meant that the national treasury had been starved and thus prevented even the beginnings of proper financial reform led by the MDC. Obert Mpofu, the ZANU-PF minister of mining, said publicly that he had to get involved with many shady characters, because that was the nature of the mining business. He should know: in early 2010 he went on a personal shopping spree which included the Ascot Race Course and Casino.

The Kimberley Process (KP) organization had tried to get Mugabe to reform. The KP has sent a review mission, appointed a high-ranking monitor, and offered technical assistance. South Africa, in particular, made repeated offers to help, all of which were laughed off by Harare. This had been a replay of the Commonwealth membership fiasco, in that some leaders in the diamond business wanted Zimbabwe to be expelled. Some civil society groups in Zimbabwe argued that, at this late stage in the game, expulsion from the KP would foster greater illegality and human rights abuses. Zimbabwe was not the only diamond huckster. The DRC was also a well-known sinner. But the illegality in Zimbabwe was systematic, conducted at the most senior levels of government and nasty, brutish and long.

## Coup

This could entail a party coup and/or a military coup, especially if Mugabe were incapacitated rather than dead. In the first 1980 cabinet Mugabe used to boast that he had more PhDs than any other government in the world, except West Germany. Many able ZANU-PF professionals and foreign-educated professors – albeit not many talented economists – were still in the government and party. Many were immobilized by fear, lust for power or secure lifestyle, but a time could come when a little bit of the old party idealism could return. The military would have to be side-tracked, however, so a change of leadership from within the party, while Mugabe lived or was not obviously gaga, is unlikely. Various scenarios could be envisaged: the dead Mugabe could be flown to Kinshasa for medical treatment (as happened to Laurent Kabila but in reverse). Any announcement of his death could take as long as the five weeks for the presidential results in March 2008. Though, probably, the generals would move much more quickly than that.

If Mugabe dies in office without a successor, the ruling party factions and allied militias could fight it out among themselves. To avoid this, the military might install a full-blown coup and the MDC leadership would have to flee despite what the SADC troika of South Africa, Mozambique and Botswana would say. Military dictatorship has become unfashionable in southern Africa, but Zimbabwe's leaders have cocked a snook at their neighbours for years. A challenge to Mugabe while he sill lives could prevent a hard coup or a real civil war. The two top contenders in 2011 were still Vice President Joice Mujuru, backed by her husband Solomon Mujuru, the former ZDF commander, and Emmerson Mnangagwa, a serving JOC grandee. The MDC would have preferred a tacit alliance with Mujuru because she was considered more moderate than Mnangagwa, a full-time member of the military aristocracy. Other younger technocrats, in the mould of Simba Makoni (ideally in tandem with the charismatic Mutambara) had also been suggested as potential frontrunners. Breaking the mould will be complicated, because the military have dominated politics intermittently since the mid-1970s, under white and black rule. For Zimbabwe to return to normal politics, whoever emerges as Mugabe's successor will have to woo the military elite. The MDC emphasized improvements in pay, conditions and above all professionalism, while ZANU-PF relied more on patriotism and institutional memories of the liberation war. Once more, it was the future versus the past.

A full-blown military takeover could undermine all parties in Zimbabwe, not just the MDC, although a full-throated junta would probably keep some of the trappings of ZANU-PF to maintain a patina of political legitimacy. Mugabe's rule had made little sense, especially economically, so a putsch would make even less, except as a temporary stop-gap if the country descends into an anarchic civil war. If the transition to a post-Mugabe dispensation were reasonably peaceful, then security sector reform will be a prime element of recovery. Britain is often mentioned as a possible mentor. The British Army did an excellent job in the role of election monitoring then training the integrated army and later provided staff courses in Zimbabwe and in the UK. London may not have the stomach, money, or military resources for a return match. The US Africa Command may help, as it has done in other African countries, and nobody would want the French to get involved that far south. The Chinese would not be tempted; for them military adventurism of the past has been superseded by commercial dictates.

A formal coup has been touted for so long and yet it has never happened. The securocrats kept their man going in 2000. In 2006 the Mujurus, in competition with each other and with their party, were planning a palace coup. They plotted to take over then use ZANU-PF to remove Mugabe and send him into a comfortable retirement. The rumours in Harare were that the putsch would happen in September 2007. The generals in JOC helped to stamp out the alleged Mujuru moves. Solomon was now outside the inner Praetorian Guard, and there may have been some male chauvinist resistance to the idea of a woman, Joice, taking over as party chief. (Mnangagwa had earlier made public his desire to replace Mugabe but was immediately sidelined, albeit this was a temporary punishment.) The generals were also busy later with their intense debate about political change, the possibility of accepting a coalition deal constantly reinforced by South Africa, and also the tantalizing notion of bringing in a fresh generation of men like Makoni, and even the MDC young pretender, Mutambara, whom ZANU-PF was encouraging, not least to divide the opposition.

A coup was also possible in late March 2008, as the defeat of Mugabe became clear. On Sunday 30 March, the CIO went into an all-day crisis session. On that same day, Mugabe gathered his family around him in his mansion in Borrowdale Brooke and informed them he was ready to quit. Apparently his wife Grace went along with this. She wanted to spare her husband further possible humiliations – he could retire with honour. And the condemnation in Zimbabwe was getting to her: at school their son was being taunted by fellow pupils: 'Your father has ruined the country.' Mugabe discussed his intentions with a small group of party chefs.

The JOC intervened, however, although the CIO was ready to respect the vote. After intense differences between the ZDF and ZNA commanders, a formal coup was rejected, not least after Pretoria's intercession. The JOC persuaded Mugabe to go for the run-off instead. Calling off coup discussions by 2 April, the generals concentrated on what would be the final official results for the March presidential poll. Then the JOC handed over to the party caucus. The ZANU-PF meeting took over five hours, partly because party doves had met with MDC leaders and were hoping for a soft landing. The boss's retirement could lead to awkward problems about prosecution. Senior *chefs* wanted an amnesty if Comrade Robert were to leave his post. Pretoria, acting with the US state department, assured them that a deal could be done in return for Mugabe 'going quietly'. If Thabo Mbeki had interceded forcibly at this stage, he could have ended the Zimbabwean nightmare, but he refused to order Mugabe to quit. Despite being kept up to date, minute by minute, of the politburo debate, he did not intervene, except to *discourage* a hard-line coup. The party hawks rallied and the decision was made to hang on and contest a run off, which they knew could be won only by terror.

## South African intervention

Mbeki's quiet diplomacy had finally pulled a hybrid – some would say rabid – rabbit out of the hat: the GNU was finally set up. Mbeki's policy on Zimbabwe was as castigated as his absurd refusal to accept the scientific realities about AIDS. His deference to the older liberation hero, and the general symmetry of southern African liberation movements in the region – Angola, the ANC and Namibia – were also part of the explanation for his snail's pace. So were the sensitivities of the land issue in South Africa: there, thirty times more white farmers had been murdered since 1994 than those killed in Zimbabwe after 1980.

Despite the conventional arguments about party affinities and disputed white ownership of land in both countries, Mbeki's failure to intervene earlier and more effectively in Zimbabwe is still one of the central conundrums in Mugabe's survival. Mbeki's diplomatic inadequacy merely accelerated South Africa's own march to Zimbabweanization. Julius Malema, the firebrand head of the ANC's youth wing, regularly argued that white people who owned land should be treated like 'criminals' because they stole it from the blacks. He said that attempts to return land through negotiations had failed and called for direct action to seize white land. 'We have to take the land without payment, because the whites took our land without paying.' In early 2011, Malema faced a race hate trial for singing the protest song, 'Shoot the Boer', but many leaders in the ANC tolerated, or even encouraged, him because of the popularity of Zimbabwe-style land grabs among the masses. Such was the legacy of Mbeki's fatal vacillation.

A number of issues should be considered besides Mbeki himself, however. For example, the South African department of foreign affairs had eviscerated itself. Many of the experienced whites had been driven out, partly by the reverse racism, but also because of the impossible behaviour of the foreign minister appointed by Mbeki, Dr Nkosazana Dlamini-Zuma. She infuriated her subordinates, black and white, not least with her obsessive privacy about her constant travels. She journeyed less than Mbeki, however, and to even less effect. Another factor was the undue Muslim influence in foreign affairs, even though only two per cent of South Africans followed Islam. A handful of Muslim senior officials, mainly of Asian extraction, skewed policy, especially against Israel, Pretoria's old ally. The ensuing anti-Semitism brought down American wrath. The ANC old guard dogmatically maintained the liberation alliances with Libya, Cuba and North Korea, not exactly countries which South Africa needed to boost its economy. It was in this context of cordial relations with Cold War dinosaurs that allowed Mbeki to empathize with the likes of Gaddafi and Mugabe who preferred to shadow box with the ghosts of long-dead white men in baggy shorts and pith helmets. The old liberation parties, especially the ANC and ZANU-PF, shared fundamentally not only an anti-imperialist ideology of a bygone era, but also they were tarred with a similar racist brush. Anything which threatened their permanent dominance was unthinkable. As the eminent scholar of South African politics, R. W. Johnson, noted: 'They shared much of Mbeki's instinctive paranoia, his tendency to see hidden enemies and a hostile grand design – rather their own mistakes – behind every setback.'

Sufficient expertise survived in Pretoria, especially in intelligence circles, to avoid alienating Washington too much. The CIA pointed the finger at Mugabe for allowing al-Qaeda militants to fly into Harare a week after 9/11 to be fitted out with false Zimbabwean passports. Washington was also concerned about the more extensive use of South Africa for laundering Jihadists with passports and visas, and even allegations about radical Islamist training camps in both Mozambique and South Africa. In response, Mbeki allowed the CIA relatively free rein to operate in his country to investigate these complaints. Also, Mbeki enjoyed hobnobbing in Washington with the political elite, despite his revolutionary ideals.

Another important contextual factor was the decline not only of South African diplomatic virility but also its military strength. The South African armed forces had once been easily the best fighting force in Africa, but in the decade after black rule it had become less capable than Zimbabwe's and even Botswana's forces. The usual litany of corrupt arms purchases, kickbacks, rapid black empowerment, lowering of standards – even for pilots – and general maladministration had emasculated the armed forces, despite the small core of British advisers. The number of generals reached 207 in 2002, after the army had been halved. AIDS was rampant, and not properly addressed, a key issue since the UN did not allow the deployment of HIV-positive personnel on peacekeeping missions. Soon there were insufficient capable officers to operate the ships, let alone fly the Hawk trainers and Gripen fighters purchased as part of grotesquely large arms deals which South Africa, facing no conventional enemy, did not need. Many of the best of South Africa's combat troops and pilots were employed as mercenaries in the rest of Africa and in Iraq. The South Africans, in concert with Botswana, had bungled the military intervention in Lesotho in 1998, a few years later it could not attempt any kind of intervention. Although Mbeki did not threaten military intervention to dethrone Mugabe, the fact that his armed forces were now less combat-capable than Zimbabwe's was an unstated weakness in his diplomacy.

In the final analysis, Mbeki's diplomacy with Mugabe was not just quiet but also highly personal. Mbeki's biographer, William Gumede, insisted that the South African president did not like Mugabe personally. That could be contested because there was evidence of personal warmth as well as immense frustration with Mugabe's obstinacy. Mbeki, in his study, usually crouched over his computer, with his favourite pipe and cognac, would say to confidants: 'Why can't he just leave, resign?' Despite the shared intellectual interests and ideological symmetries, Mbeki wanted Mugabe to reform and then, later, go quietly. Mbeki opposed sanctions because he genuinely felt that the old man might open up a little, if he felt less besieged. Gumede made the argument that South Africa's solo – and dramatically unsuccessful – attempt to save the life of writer Ken Saro Wiwa in Nigeria prompted Mbeki to be cautious and adopt low-key consensual approaches, preferably with African allies. Perhaps, but that argument understated Mbeki's ideological and emotional complicity in ZANU-PF's survival.

A week after Mbeki stage-managed the GNU, he was knifed in the back by Zuma in an ANC palace coup. The shambolic Zuma replaced the buttoned-up Mbeki and immediately shifted policy on Mugabe, whose antipathy to trade unions in general and the trade union leader Tsvangirai in particular irked Zuma, who depended on union support in South Africa. As Stephen Chan graphically noted, 'Zuma is one of only a handful of world leaders who is a polygamist but also alone in his use of song line' – in this case, his theme 'Bring me my machine gun'. 'The giant karaoke machine made flesh' was not about to sing praise songs to Mugabe. In fact, he publicly condemned the man whose time was plainly up. But Zuma still had to tread carefully. Beyond the land issue, South Africa was being increasingly Zimbabweanized itself – power cuts were one ominous symptom, so were the xenophobic riots against Zimbabweans who took over many of the tough, menial jobs in both the construction boom for the 2010 World Cup as well as many positions in the informal economy. An activist foreign policy on Zimbabwe was difficult for the new leader in a region which was still nervous of South Africa's power. Moreover, the ANC itself was mired in corruption. Its politics had been degraded from a liberation organization into a benefits club for the elite, though not as bad yet as Harare's lootocracy. And its once lofty politics had been debased into a soap opera of personalities and vendettas. In short, while Mandela could lead by moral example, Zuma could not. Pretoria stood back and waited to see what the GNU could do – after all, its creation was supposed to be a triumph of South African diplomacy.

South Africa's vote in favour of a no-fly zone over Libya in early 2011 brought the tension out into the open. The ZANU-PF papers went into overdrive, especially the *Sunday Mail*, which described Zuma as a 'liability, not only to South Africa, but also to the rest of the continent'. Mugabe did not rein in his support for Gaddafi, but did order his media organs to stop the personal invective against Zuma. The Zuma/Mugabe relationship was not quiet; to the contrary, the language was heated. Whether Pretoria's new diplomacy could curb Mugabe's madcap despotism was still to be decided. Mugabe's intolerance even extended to musical relations. Thomas Mapfumo, the Zimbabwean singer whose *Chimurenga* songs had provided the soundtrack to the liberation, felt he had to seek creative exile in the US. In 2010, Mugabe was personally affronted by the top South African group, Freshlyground. Their catchy song and amusing video 'Chicken to Change' became a big hit in the region and internationally on the internet. It called Mugabe a 'supernova' but also satirized him with lively puppet imagery. And the chicken (*jongwe*) was a sensitive token, the symbol of ZANU-PF. The government banned a planned tour of Zimbabwe by the group.

## Regional intervention

Mugabe had managed to alienate nearly all his old allies, even the once steadfast DRC comrade-in-arms, Angola and Namibia. Kenya's Raila Odinga, himself a victim of enforced co-habitation, demanded that Mugabe step down and an international peace-keeping force be sent in. After the 2008 election fiasco, Nigeria, Zambia and Rwanda lined up to condemn Mugabe. Tanzania's criticism was a particular blow to Harare. Botswana's President Ian Khama detested Mugabe and made his feelings plain. Moreover, his military background, effective – if small – army (trained by the Americans) and convenient joint border made his opposition a potential threat. Mugabe, however, denigrated Khama as a troublesome half-caste. Many MDC refugees sought exile in Botswana. A government in exile was frequently discussed, as was the use of Botswana as a sanctuary to wage an insurgency. For many reasons, not least the heritage of the *Gukurahundi,* a springboard to popular insurrection fired up in Matabeleland was not, yet, on the cards.

Botswana was not itself a paradigm, despite the worldwide positive marketing it received after the success of the novels and films about the country's female sleuths who ran the 'No 1 Ladies Detective Agency'. The year 2011 marked the forty-fifth anniversary of the ruling party's hold on power. Since taking over in 2008, the Sandhurst-educated Khama had militarized the state. Zimbabwe-style, retired officers assumed key positions in the government and economy. Even the general manager of Botswana TV came from a military career. The cabinet became a JOC-style cabal. Some of the ruling party members defected in 2010, disgruntled with Khama's military style of governance which extolled discipline above all. Whether the new *dirigiste* Botswana is a more potent threat to Mugabe, or its own democracy, may depend on further deterioration in relations with Harare.

Without strong South African leadership, an SADC or AU demarche, let alone military intervention, was highly unlikely. Once again, African leaders were pontificating on the credo that African problems had to have African solutions, and then fail to provide any. Could the leadership come from outside Africa?

### Great power intervention

The Chinese, Mugabe's ally since the liberation war, started to distance themselves politically. Except for aid (and business of course) Beijing grew very wary of Mugabe, despite hosting elaborate state visits for him. The Chinese had sent fighter jets as late as 2005/6 and military trucks, ammunition and weapons in 2006, but they were keen to clean up their act before the 2008 Olympics, especially as far as African tyrannies were concerned. The Beijing pragmatists, although not insisting on any conditionality – the Western mode of trying to tie trade and aid to good governance – started to draw the line at the egregious kleptocracy in Harare. Long-term Zimbabwean-style instability was not good for their new imperialism in Africa. As in Sudan or Nigeria, political chaos could interrupt oil supplies or, in Zimbabwe's case, their growing reputation in Africa.

When international intervention became a hot topic in 2008, the EU had already imposed arms embargoes as well as travel bans and asset-seizing measures against Mugabe and 130 of his leading acolytes. Some foreign activists wanted that extended to the ZANU-PF barons' families, especially their children at school and universities abroad. The US started to broaden sanctions, as did Australia. The EU could have extended business sanctions, especially on mining companies. The UN placed no sanctions on Zimbabwe; the Security Council lacked unanimity, despite China's revised policy. The old arguments against comprehensive sanctions were trotted out, as they had been during the anti-apartheid campaign. It is the poorest who will suffer and smart sanctions take time.

In the northern summer of 2008, press pundits in the UK and the US called for more forceful intervention to save lives immediately. The right-wing British columnist Simon Heffer, opined: 'It may be very embarrassing for whites to intervene to stop the butchery of black tyrants. But if they don't hetacombs of lives will be lost.' That was the *Daily Telegraph*. The London *Times* headlined their scoop on possible British military intervention: the 24 June 2008 front-page headline ran 'Case for military action in Zimbabwe'. The *Times* had been leaked a contingency planning paper from, it claimed, the MoD's 'Defence Crisis Management Organization'. The MoD's job is to plan for as many contingencies as possible – very few are acted on. But they are ready in case Number Ten calls up the MoD at midnight with an urgent request for a briefing. The *Times* commented on variants of emergency evacuations (not dissimilar to the rescue of British nationals from Libya in March 2011). The planners acknowledged the extreme delicacy of British military involvement in a former colony led by a man who was utterly paranoid about UK intervention. The plans included assistance in a straightforward evacuation, but they also mentioned more muscular action to resolve a humanitarian crisis. The softer contingencies suggested placing British troops to guard medical units at entry points in three Commonwealth countries, Zambia, Mozambique and Botswana. British passport holders would have to make their own way to the Zimbabwean border. A tougher version suggested a foreign military take-over of Harare civilian airport. The air support required would have necessitated South African permission and logistical back up. Britain would have had to act as a very back-seat driver, but would provide the unseen command and control to local black Commonwealth troops.

In four pages of coverage, the *Times* quoted Major General Julian Thompson, who commanded 3 Commando Brigade Royal Marines in the Falklands conflict. He said: 'I think the Zimbabwean Army and police force would collapse and the population would treat an intervention force as liberators – but would any of the neighbouring African countries give us flying rights over their territory?' The paper's leader column also pitched in with: 'A civilized world is aware that hand-wringing from the sidelines is no longer a morally fit response to the tragedy of Zimbabwe.' But hand-wringing was the only real option to a British military establishment that had just been bruised in Basra and was taking heavy casualties in Afghanistan.

There it would have rested but for Barack Obama's interest in Zimbabwe. He understood the sensitivities about overt British involvement but the Whitehall rumour machine suggested that he would back-pedal on pressure to increase (and over-stretch) British military contributions to Afghanistan in exchange for more muscular *diplomacy* via the Commonwealth in southern Africa. During the time of cholera in Zimbabwe, when over 4,000 died, it was mooted that Botswana's efficient army and other African military units could escort a convoy of ambulances, with a small protective force, into Harare. Mugabe would have refused anything from Botswana but the convoys would proceed to test the actual resistance to Red Cross vehicles. If the presence of foreign 'medical' forces prompted a spontaneous (MDC-assisted) popular groundswell, more forces could be sent to augment the medical teams. This was a variant of Julian Thompson's argument that a feather would knock over the regime. Or as another *Times* columnist, Martin Fletcher, wrote: 'The Mugabe regime, like a tree hollowed out by termites, is just waiting to be toppled.' Almost certainly the esteemed general and the columnist were wrong. That is why none of the contingencies got off the drawing board, though various intelligence agencies, especially MI6 and the DIS (the Defence Intelligence Staff) did take the trouble to ask Hereford to check out some of the locations for possible exit/entry points and to test the waters in general. The SAS were extended fully on operations bequeathed by Tony Blair's messianic zeal and did not exert themselves unduly, except for one or two operatives who needed a holiday break in sunny Africa.

In the end, in 2009, London did act in the humanitarian crisis but it was to airlift out some of the 17,500 Britons in the country (in 2000 the number of British passport holders was 86,000). The 'Zimbabwe Resettlement Programme' was offered mainly to British citizens over seventy living in residential or nursing homes. About 3,000 were deemed eligible. Many, often literally starving because of the destruction of their pensions, were too proud to accept, but Britain did quietly fly out hundreds of British pensioners, often ailing, who were offered generous resettlement in the UK. It might have been better to deduct these costs from the £45 million given in aid to Zimbabwe in the previous year (2008). Mugabe frequently deployed aid from foreign governments to donate food to his supporters, despite aid agencies' attempts to direct their funds in a neutral fashion. Sometimes foreign aid was simply filched by party chefs.

## The International Criminal Court

In Zimbabwe the prime healing mechanism must be political, not military. Zimbabwe may need to adopt the South African example of Truth and Reconciliation, rather than the Western model of The Hague. The ICC has backfired in Africa, and is often seen as a white man's court, while only Africans – and not the likes of Bush and Blair – are tried for war crimes. The ICC stalled settlements in Uganda certainly and possibly delayed reconciliation in Darfur. Dragging Mugabe or his surviving henchmen to The Hague might relieve a large number of tender consciences in the West, but it would do little to heal the Zimbabwean body politic. Also, despite being an ardent proponent of human rights and agricultural reforms in international forums such as the UN, Zimbabwe did not sign up for the founding treaty of the ICC in 2002. Moreover, the ICC has limited jurisdiction as the gravamen of the offences, the Matabeleland massacres, took place before then.

A Zimbabwean emulation of South Africa's Truth and Reconciliation Commission could avert civil war and salve many wounds from years of repression. South Africa's TRC was deeply flawed but many of the alternative suggestions, for example war crimes tribunals, were worse. The TRC was evidentiary not punitive – victims wanted to know the truth about their own treatment and those of their dearly departed. In Zimbabwe the truth is important because in many cases the victims knew their attackers and often lived in the same area. They wanted to know who gave the orders and why. The Zimbabwean TRC would be a site of cultural healing and cleansing. In African culture it is often believed that that the victim of a violent death returns as a vengeful spirit (*ngozi*) to torment the living. Only when the truth about the assailant is revealed can the *ngozi* rest. How far the TRC would extend – to the liberation war, to the *Gukurahundi?* – has yet to be answered.

Zimbabwe did not create a national healing or counselling programme after the liberation war for any of the traumatized members of the various armies, or for the conflict-ravaged peasantry. On an ad hoc and very local basis, handfuls of spirit mediums and headmen did work with kinship groups to secure the confessions of guilt and repentance from small groups of the more vicious ex-combatants who lived locally and were prepared to attend the informal sessions, where no punishments were inflicted. The ghosts of that war, as well as the massacres in Matabeleland, the violent slum clearances, the often bestial land-grabs as well as a constant pattern of state-sponsored election violence had created a dehumanized culture in Zimbabwe. As writer Trevor Ncube observed, Mugabe 'is responsible for the culture of intolerance where violence is perceived as the only way of settling political differences. Mugabe presided over the perversion of our norms and value system and this will take a long time to fix.'

## *A luta continua*

The struggle continues. This was the war cry of FRELIMO and sometimes taken up by ZANLA. For Mugabe's military barons it is still true. Despite all the pressures, and age, Mugabe appears not have mellowed by early-2011. Domestically, he continued his reign of terror. Worse, in March 2011, he stepped up the military tempo of his domestic war. In the first few months of the year over a hundred MDC activists and politicians had been arrested. ZANU-PF reacted aggressively to Tsvangirai's claim that the senior judges were doing Mugabe's bidding. Hardly a point anyone would dispute. Jonathan Moyo, often Mugabe's personal megaphone, said: 'If these were ZANU-PF judges doing ZANU-PF's bidding, this guy [Tsvangirai] would be six feet under by now.' Many commentators thought that Mugabe was trying to drive his main opponent into exile.

The cue for a coup may not be Mugabe's natural death, assassination or incapacitation, it could be the enforced exile of the MDC leaders and the euthanasia of the GNU. Tsvangirai was saying publicly in late March 2011 that the military usurped his agreements with Mugabe. But the MDC leader also admitted that Mugabe could be 'playing games' with him.

> What is now evident is that some of these actions [security force failure to curb anti-MDC violence] are a fait accompli from a third force within the government, which acts with impunity. You wonder whether there is still control by a civilian authority in government.

Tsvangirai added, 'As prime minister I am accountable for the supervision of all ministers, but there are some who do not report to me but go directly to Mugabe and these include Mnangagwa and State Security Minister Sydney Sekeramayi.' This is a circular argument. The military are men behaving badly, but are they doing it under Mugabe's orders – no matter what he says to the hapless Tsvangirai – or is the JOC acting totally independently of even Mugabe?

By placing the party and security apparatus on alert for a possible snap election, and by ramping up assaults on the MDC, it appeared that Mugabe was encouraging Tsvangirai to finally throw in the towel, after years of provocation. ZANU-PF was busy on a fresh propaganda campaign. One grisly aspect, promoted by the slavish local media, was the discovery, in Chibondo, of mass graves from the liberation war. Although the state of the skeletons indicated they were not from more than thirty years ago, and therefore not victims of the Rhodesian forces, the ruling party made a big fuss of saying that local spirits wanted revenge against whites and their stooges in the MDC. Much more of the same could be expected. The skeleton story was guaranteed to appeal to the rural masses, while George Charamba (alias Nathaniel Manheru) kept up the pro-Mugabe barrage in his excessively convoluted and pseudo-intellectual columns in the *Herald*.

Mugabe still had a large following in Mashonaland, based on tribal and liberation war legacies, as well as short-term bribes such as food aid. But he could never win another national election, despite all the state-controlled propaganda – unless the military used massive force and rigging to keep their man in power. Indications in early 2011 were that the Comrade Mugabe was going to risk everything on a bold and bloody attempt to steal the vote, once more.

Abroad, Mugabe was even more daring – or foolish. In December 2010, he sent an Antonov An-22 cargo plane, registered in Angola, to Abidjan, Ivory Coast. The plane contained tons of arms for Laurent Gbagbo, the deposed president. CIO officials accompanied the consignment of arms. Earlier, the plane had landed in Manyame air base, in Zimbabwe, with small arms, mortars and rockets from China. Some of the shipment stayed on board and was supplemented by stocks from Zimbabwe Defence Industries. The shipment pitted Mugabe once more against the UN, as well as West African leaders and the AU. The UN had 10,000 peace-keepers in Ivory Coast and an arms embargo had been in force since 2002.

Even more controversially, Mugabe decided to break UN sanctions on Iran, according to intelligence reports. Harare did not deny them. Instead, Simbarashe Mumbengegwe, the foreign minister, said the UN sanctions – which prohibit UN members from providing Iran with raw materials that could be used to make nuclear weapons – were 'unfair and hypocritical'. Zimbabwe had an estimated 355,000 tons of uranium at Kanyembe, north of Harare. The foreign minister argued that Zimbabwe needed the cash, and anyway Iran had the right to use peaceful nuclear energy. London and Washington assumed that Mugabe was taking advantage of Western fixation with the crisis in North Africa to try a few sleight-of-hand deals.

Mugabe then came out into the open to defend his long-time friend and fellow pariah, Colonel Gaddafi. That flamboyantly murderous tyrant, who had been in power for over ten years longer than Mugabe, had been one of Harare's staunchest African allies. Gaddafi sent extensive oil supplies to prop up Zimbabwe's plunging economy, and encouraged his Mafia sons to buy up land and mining concessions. As in the DRC incursion, Mugabe apparently did not consult the JOC or even his closest henchman, Mnangagwa, if intelligence sources were correct. Mugabe regarded his relationship with the Libyan leader as a personal debt of honour. If true, that suggested that Mugabe was not simply a docile front for the military, although General Constantine Chiwenga, the head of the ZDF, did personally make the arrangements. It also meant that Mnangagwa may have outflanked his old rival Solomon Majuru, but once more he had been outfoxed by Mugabe. The ZDF sent several hundred serving and retired troops from the commando regiment, and from the Fifth Brigade. They joined mercenaries from Ivory Coast, Chad and Mauritania to try to boost the Libyan regime as it faced popular unrest, and later NATO-led attacks.

Mugabe's public espousal of support for Gaddafi could easily backfire. Western sensitivities may become exhausted by another war in another oil-rich Muslim state, but questions were once more being asked in European parliaments: if Gaddafi must be toppled, why not also Mugabe?

# Conclusion

# Mugabe's Legacy

The attack on the twin towers on 9/11 and the financial crash of 2008/9 shifted the tectonic plates of the international system. Of perhaps greater significance have been the revolts against the tyrants in North Africa and the Middle East. Robert Mugabe nailed his colours to the mast in the defence of his faithful ally, Muammar Gaddafi. William Hague, the British foreign secretary, specifically stated that the NATO-led operations in Libya meant that Mugabe's days were numbered. Britain can do little, but Barack Obama – while reluctant to emulate his gung-ho predecessor – has a proven track record of concern about African dictatorships. He was supposed to have been persuaded to intervene in Libya largely because of his so-called 'Valkyries': Hillary Clinton, secretary of state; Susan Rice, US ambassador to the UN; and Samantha Power, special assistant to the president. Rice was Africa advisor to Bill Clinton when he failed to intervene in the genocide in Rwanda. Power wrote a Pulitzer-prize-winning book about genocide. All three women have unique influence and a proven determination to avoid a repetition of the Rwandan genocide. Hence Libya and possibly Zimbabwe, should Mugabe once more let free the hounds of Hell.

And yet Western statesmen have been predicting – or very occasionally plotting – Mugabe's political demise for over a decade. At the time of writing, the old man is still in power in Harare, and as defiant as ever. A cable sent from the US embassy in Harare to the State Department in Washington in July 2007, via Wikileaks, said this of Mugabe:

> To give the devil his due, he is a brilliant tactician ... However, he is fundamentally hampered by several factors: his ego and his belief in his own infallibility; his obsessive focus on the past as a justification for everything in the present and future; and his deep ignorance on economic issues coupled with the belief that his 18 doctorates give him the authority to suspend the laws of economics, including supply and demand.

Despite his intellectual abilities, Mugabe destroyed his own country, and some of his honorary degrees have been rescinded. Moreover, despite all the massacres and misgovernment, Mugabe still maintained some domestic support and his anti-Western tirades were popular throughout Africa. When the author was working in southern Sudan in 2010-11 any mention of Mugabe would bring smiles and adulation from the vast majority of the southerners who saw the Zimbabwean revolution as an inspiration for their own determination to achieve independence. In the West Mugabe may be a monster, but he remained a model to some in Africa. What will be his legacy when he finally departs from life or government?

It will depend on what history books are consulted. Academics in southern Africa, especially in Zimbabwe, and a handful of fellow travellers in the West, have constructed an alternative narrative, a so-called 'patriotic history'. ZANU-PF is portrayed as the sole champion – past and present – of the independence of Zimbabwe as it faces constant attacks from devious and evil imperialist forces. This alternative history is based on real grievances, not only land issues but much wider perceptions of Western hypocrisy over human rights, not least in Afghanistan, Iraq, Palestine/Israel and the Middle East in general. In Zimbabwe, any opponents of this version of history are accused of 'selling out'. As with George W. Bush's 'you are either for us or against us', it is a Manichean world view. Any attacks on ZANU-PF orthodoxy is tantamount to an alliance with the external imperialist threats and therefore smacks of treason. ZANU-PF apologists state that the Western use of human rights issues is a form of moral imperialism, similar to the old justifications for the colonization of the dark continent. In Zimbabwe you have had no choice but to be a 'patriot' – any dissident views labelled you as a 'sell-out', especially the MDC – or a puppet of the imperialists, and therefore a legitimate target for violence.

Like land, racial inequality is one of the pillars of the new history. At first this was downplayed in the interests of Mugabe's policy of reconciliation. By 2000 this had changed, as ZANU-PF started to advocate a racism which was far more pernicious than anything dreamed up by the Rhodesian Front. Once nearly all the whites, especially the farmers, had been driven out, the main cause of Zimbabwe's ills were blamed on sanctions, even though they were initially aimed at a small minority of party barons. Western, especially British, ambitions to re-colonize Zimbabwe became a *leitmotif*. In reality, the Westminster government was struggling to hold on to Scotland and even Wales, the oldest colony; it hardly had any intentions, let alone resources, to re-colonize Africa. Nevertheless, the duplicity of the British – and the Americans – coalesced with a well-established liberal analysis of Western wrong-doing, exemplified by the abuses at Abu Ghraib, Guantánamo Bay and such practices as illegal rendition and water-boarding. The critiques of well-known radical journalists such as John Pilger played well in Harare. It was in this context that accusations against Tsvangirai of being in the pay of London gained so much violent traction. Thus Tsvangirai's statements that the West should stop Mugabe because of his 'genocide' and that he was 'Africa's Milo?evi?' may have worked in the Western media, but often backfired in Zimbabwe. Such clumsiness might have been explained by Tsvangirai's defenders as a counter-balance to his sometimes toe-curling apologias for Mugabe's behaviour over, for example, the land invasions. Consistency, however, was never a hallmark of the courageous if clodhopping ex-trade union leader.

Western Marxist writers have attacked Mugabe from the left. They argued that he betrayed the revolution by co-operating with white capitalists; thus socialism was compromised right from the start in Zimbabwe. Few white farmers or businessmen in the country would have agreed with this analysis. Some left-leaning University of Zimbabwe academics took Mugabe at his word when he said he was a Socialist-Marxist. Dr Shadrack Gutto and Professor Kempton Makamure were made enemies of the state for saying that the ZANU-PF government was paying mere lip-service to socialism. Kenyan-born Gutto was hounded out of the country while Makamure spent a lot of time researching the insides of police cells.

The ZANU-PF narrative worked in terms of many Zimbabweans who had suffered under white oppression. Their daily struggles for food and shelter could easily be blamed on 'white' sanctions. The ZANU-PF version, although skewed in Western eyes, tugged on many heartstrings in Zimbabwe, partly because of the genuine original grievances. The argument was also developed by clever party-aligned academics, most notoriously by Jonathan Moyo. And because the party had almost total control of the media, especially broadcast media, the message was rammed home, hour after hour, day after day. The fact that so many Zimbabweans voted for the MDC was a telling comment on their sagacity as well as their bravery.

Putting aside the justifications for Mugabe, it is nevertheless an inescapable fact that his rule destroyed his country. Even if, tomorrow, the MDC took over completely and performed perfectly it would take decades, probably generations, to restore Zimbabwe to the levels of the early 1980s. Millions of skilled people have left, most of whom – especially outside Africa – will not return. The country's infrastructure, roads, railways, schools, hospitals and farms, will have to be rebuilt. Rampant disease, of animals as well as people, will have to be confronted. This is a tall order, even assuming the skills and money were pumped in. The mantra used to be 'anybody will be better than Mugabe'. But he could be succeeded by a

ZANU-PF baron, perhaps with more humanity, but less of a grip on his, or her, truculent party. Even if the MDC – both wings – inherited the keys of the kingdom, its performance so far suggests that it may not be more competent than ZANU-PF, although it may well be far less violent.

The first major transition, from Rhodesia to Zimbabwe, entailed the substitution of an efficient racist white elite by an inefficient racist black elite. The liberation war propaganda often deployed an image of the walls of Great Zimbabwe to remind the guerrillas of their country's cultural heritage; the whites preferred the term 'Zimbabwe Ruins', an apt description of the modern state. It is often said, and not just by white Zimbabweans, that Ian Smith was right. He prophesied that Mugabe's rule would lead to first an onslaught on his tribal enemies in Matabeleland and then the destruction of white farms. In this Smith was correct, although his bigoted actions might have made his prophecy self-fulfilling. No right-wing lunatic in the Rhodesian Front, with swivelling eyes and foam-flecked lips, warned that black-ruled Zimbabwe would ever get as bad as it has actually become. Probably, the whites would have fought on if they could have known this, or even if they thought that the British or South Africans would permit Mugabe to win an election. Similarly, if conditions in present-day Zimbabwe had existed in the 1980s, probably the whites in South Africa would not so readily have conceded to the inevitable. The South African military would have hung on, and the civil war would have been far worse, and without the possibility of truth and reconciliation. Afrikaner leaders would have been strung up from lamp-posts if not formally executed by Nuremberg-style courts. So it was better for whites to give in – albeit with too little grace and far too late – in both Zimbabwe and South Africa.

Richard Dowden in his recent panorama of continental history, *Africa: Altered States, Ordinary Miracles*, summarized the Zimbabwe saga thus:

> Mugabe thinks Zimbabwe is his because he took it by force – exactly the same mentality as the brutal white colonists who seized it more than a century ago. His aim, he says, is total independence but Zimbabweans will remain dependent on others' charity for the foreseeable future. In more than forty years Zimbabwe has had only two rulers. Opposite in every conceivable way, Smith and Mugabe have one thing in common. Stubborn and reckless, they both gave the finger to the rest of the world and to their own people. Maybe it is something in the water.

Mugabe would not appreciate his legacy being compared to that of Ian Smith's. And yet it is to Mugabe's credit that he let Smith live comfortably on his farm and in his modest house in Harare, and without little harassment, except non-aggressive police and CIO visits in the latter years, when Smith had been publicly and frequently highly critical of Mugabe, both at home and especially abroad. Indeed, in the first period of transition, Smith was very complimentary about Mugabe's manner and intelligence, during their regular chats over tea. Before his death in 2007, Smith would challenge Mugabe to walk around the Harare townships with him, to see who would have received the most popular acclaim. Smith may well have won his challenge.

Rhodesian propaganda had portrayed Mugabe as a bloodthirsty latter-day Hitler. Whites were preparing for the dash for the South African border when Mugabe won the election in March 1980. Instead, the vast majority stayed, swayed by Mugabe's clarion call for reconciliation. It bears repeating: 'Let us deepen our sense of belonging,' he said, 'and engender a common interest that knows no race, colour or creed.' The words may ring tragically hollow now, but then Mugabe was the popular son of the masses; only he could bring peace, and that is why the vast majority of the Shona people voted for him. Nevertheless, his party still engaged in massive electoral intimidation. Prefiguring by fourteen years the almost saint-like quality of Nelson Mandela's magnanimity, the new Zimbabwean president started well. He appointed a ministry of all the talents, including Rhodesian Front stalwarts. As a former teacher, Mugabe set about reforming the country's educational system, with impressive results, especially the high standards of literacy in Zimbabwe. Later, he helped to end the civil war in Mozambique. And he was cautious in avoiding direct military conflict with apartheid South Africa. If he had also anticipated Mandela's style by remaining in office for just one term, Mugabe's legacy would have been that of a world-famous statesman. Instead, in Desmond Tutu's phrase, he became the caricature of an African despot. So what went wrong?

He may be bad, but he has never been mad. The idea that absolute power over thirty-one years, plus senility, caused him eventually to become demented is not convincing. Mugabe's sober and ruthless determination had always been a mark of his character. He outflanked the original ZANU leader, Ndabaningi Sithole, then imposed his leadership during the final dramatic three years of the liberation war. Opponents were crushed.

He displayed a logical consistency in transforming his country. The white settlers seized the land illegally in the 1890s, and thus inspired the first *Chimurenga*. The second *Chimurenga* of 1965-1979 was partly based upon the historical grievances of the original resistance movements. After taking power, Mugabe waged a third *Chimurenga* against all his perceived enemies:

first the Ndebele, then trade unionists who supported the opposition parties, and finally white farmers and businessmen. Along the way he silenced the churches, media, judiciary, social activists and, especially, the gay and lesbian community.

His greatest crime was committed early in his dictatorship: the *Gukurahundi* in Matabeleland in the 1980s. Estimates vary, but at least 20,000 Ndebeles were killed in the genocide, and many more were raped, tortured and abducted. It is true that South African intelligence backed a few hundred dissidents in the apartheid war of regional destabilization, but the main reason for the devastation wrought by Mugabe's Fifth Brigade was to eradicate the power base of Nkomo's rival ZAPU party. Eventually, Nkomo had to sue for peace, and accept Mugabe's one-party state. The ZANU-PF leader stayed in power by bribing his cronies, particularly in the security services. Mugabe's intervention in the war in Congo helped to bankrupt Zimbabwe, but the mining concessions also made his favoured generals very wealthy.

In many African states, the military, rather than the ballot box, has been the main instrument for change of leadership. This was not possible in Zimbabwe, because of a creeping coup. The generals, police chiefs and the Central Intelligence Organization were absorbed into the inner core of the dictatorship. They would stand and fall with their boss. This suited Mugabe's leadership style. He had always preferred to run the country as though it were still a liberation movement.

The president didn't like being thwarted. Mugabe faced his first major loss of face when he was defeated over a referendum on a draft constitution in 2000. Blaming whites for supporting the opposition, he encouraged his thugs to seize white commercial farms, even though many farmers had been given legal land rights *after* 1980. This accelerated the economic meltdown. A few thousand white farmers were ejected, but hundreds of thousands of farmworkers were also put out of work. Agriculture collapsed. Famine meant that Mugabe's henchmen could control the countryside by centralizing the distribution of food. The cities turned to the Movement for Democratic Change. Mugabe's solution? Bulldoze the urban shanty towns. More than 700,000 city dwellers lost their homes or livelihoods in the 2005 decision to remove 'illegal' structures. Farming had been destroyed, so had tourism. The final straw was to force foreign companies, especially mining, to give 51 per cent control to indigenous black Zimbabweans, effectively a last handout to Mugabe's acolytes.

Under Mugabe, life expectancy was halved, unemployment reached 90 per cent; nearly all the whites and over three million blacks fled the country.

Zimbabwe became a rogue state which threatened to implode the whole region. One of the seven degrees earned by Mugabe was in economics – his last throw was simply to print money (though even esteemed economists, such as Britain's Gordon Brown, did the same). The inevitable result was a world record for hyperinflation.

Mugabe blamed the British government and European sanctions – though they were merely pinpricks against a small number of his robber-barons. The Commonwealth turned its back largely because of human rights abuses. And the international financial organizations deserted him because of chronic financial mismanagement and broken pledges. Some African leaders stood by him, out of a misplaced sense of solidarity, including President Mbeki, who held the economic levers. Then Jacob Zuma's accession spawned a change in the ANC. The trade unionist Tsvangirai became a more attractive option. South Africa's latest moves in Mugabe's long goodbye are still unclear: no news yet on a possible deal for Mugabe's retirement. The MDC has said it wants to follow the South African model of reconciliation, but there may be precious little truth, or justice.

Destroying one's country (and the professionalism of its armed forces) with lunatic policies is not a criminal offence, but crimes against humanity, especially the near-genocide in Matabeleland, are different. Liberia's Charles Taylor ended up in The Hague, but that is a special case. In theory, the International Criminal Court could try Mugabe for crimes committed after 2002, especially the destruction of urban settlements in 2005. The endgame will be political, not legal, however. China's influence in Harare has to be finessed, and South Africa might have to provide rock-solid amnesties, probably in-country, but possibly abroad (perhaps Malaysia), for Mugabe and his top military and police enforcers. This may be a bitter pill for many Zimbabweans, but a peaceful transition is paramount.

It could be a golden – but brief – hour for possible reconstruction. The UN and the IMF will promise much, but do little. All hopes for reconstruction efforts are all predicated on Mugabe's exit. If events turn back to wide-scale violence, as recent clampdowns indicate, perhaps the Commonwealth, as it did in 1980, might just provide a core British-officered monitoring force. The AU is already overstretched in Darfur and elsewhere. The SADC is too complicit in Mugabe's brutal follies. It will take decades to reconstruct the three main pillars of the economy – agriculture, tourism and mining. Is Tsvangirai capable of rebuilding from Ground Zero? Most Zimbabweans yearn for change: anybody can do better than Mugabe is probably the dominant opinion. Mugabe had always been a master manipulator, and stubborn. Now, short of massive rigging and naked use of the army and militias, he cannot win another election. His war machine will probably step in to save him, or perhaps anoint a successor. Whether that would prompt a civil war is an open question.

Another central question remains open, a crucial one for those who want to get rid of Mugabe as soon as possible. Is Mugabe the puppet or the puppet master of his war machine? This book has outlined a remarkable history of Mugabe's ruthless consistency. So why then did he even consider giving up in 2000 and 2008? That is, if the rumours are true. Heidi Holland, a famous observer of Mugabe, explained her belief to the author, in July 2010, that Mugabe has called the shots all along:

> I don't believe the military usurped Mugabe's power in the aftermath of the [first] 2008 election. This is a media construction to explain why we – journalists – were baying for election results over the five weeks and we failed to notice that Mugabe was setting up his army for electoral abuse in the rural areas.

Holland's views must be respected, but the thrust of *Mugabe's War Machine* suggests an alternative view. It has delineated the *fusion* of military and political power in ZANU-PF from the early revolutionary days until 2011, possibly the tipping point of the tyrants's rule. Mugabe may well still be the *primus inter pares* in the Joint Operations Command, the top dog, albeit surrounded by the snarls of younger or more desperate rivals. The vital point remains: it is indisputable that Mugabe and his generals run the show, despite the Potemkin village erected for the MDC. Real change in Zimbabwe can be achieved only when all the JOC cabal members are removed – by elections, sanctions and blockade or forceful external intervention.

And yet. And yet ... The introduction to this book suggested that Zimbabwe's history may not repeat itself, but it does rhyme sometimes. For example, Mbeki did not even approach the moral courage of John Vorster, when the apartheid prime minister ruthlessly shut down supplies to his racist kith and kin in Salisbury to force Smith to deal with his black opponents. Mbeki had all the same levers but not Vorster's *cojones* in enforcing tough love. In another interesting rhyme, Smith's security leaders, especially Flower and Walls, deployed their considerable clout to make Smith settle at Lancaster House, or at least stop upsetting the applecart. Walls, too, as undoubted military supremo, refused to countenance a coup in March 1980, despite the fact that everything was in place. He refused 'to copy the rest of Africa', as he put it at the time. Is it far, far too much to hope that Mugabe's generals, once he is dead or drooling, may step in to stabilize the country until a successor is elected, maybe freely, first within the party and then in the country? In apartheid South Africa, the military and intelligence elites contained elements which were reformist. General Constand Viljoen, in Mandela's opinion, saved the first universal election in 1994. Today the security apparatus is probably the most centralized, disciplined, and efficient organization in Zimbabwe, though that may not be saying a great deal amid the general administrative chaos. Nevertheless, the Praetorians could still fulfil their function: to guard the country from total disintegration. They did so in some measure, and for some of the wrong reasons, in the early 1980s when the country could have been divided in two in a Katanga-style barbarism, far worse than the *Gukurahundi.* In short, military influence, in the absence of democracy, can maintain or restore national cohesion. That has been the sad lesson taught throughout Africa. Arguably, Egypt's military restored some stability in the aftermath of President Mubarak's ousting. It was disciplined and effective and saved lives during the initial protests. Gaddafi's deliberately segmented security machine turned on its own people and created havoc and destruction. Which was the lesser of the evils – Egyptian or Libyan military engagement in politics? Zimbabwe's military machine might – just might – surprise the world and its own citizens. That such a slender straw has to be clutched is an abiding comment on Mugabe's abominations.

It could have been so different. Mugabe could have saved something of his reputation, if he had conceded early and gone into a dignified retirement. Instead, he created massive uncertainty for a transition which could yet become another Libya or Somalia. Mugabe's rule by military force destroyed Zimbabwe. The manner of his departure might yet disgrace the whole continent.

# Select Bibliography

Arbuckle, T. 'Rhodesian Bush War Strategies and Tactics: An Assessment', *Journal of the Royal United Services Institute,* 124: 4, 1979.

Astrow, André, *Zimbabwe: A Revolution that Lost its Way?* (Zed, London, 1983).

Auret, Michael, *From Liberator to Dictator: An Insider's Account of Robert Mugabe's Descent into Tyranny (*David Philip, Claremont, South Africa, 2009).

Barclay, Philip, *Zimbabwe: Years of Hope and Despair* (Bloomsbury, London, 2010).

Bailey, Martin, *Oilgate* (Coronet, London, 1979).

Beckett, Ian F. W., 'The Rhodesian Army: Counter-insurgency, 1972-1979' in Ian F.W. Beckett and John Pimlott, eds. *Armed Forces and Modern Counter-Insurgency* (Croom Helm, Beckenham, Kent, 1985).

Bhebe, Ngwabi and Terence Ranger, eds., *Soldiers in Zimbabwe's Liberation War* (Currey, London, 1995).

Blake, Robert, *A History of Rhodesia* (Methuen, London, 1977).

Brickhill, Jeremy, 'Zimbabwe's Poisoned Legacy: Secret War in Southern Africa,' *Covert Action Quarterly* 43 (Winter 1992–93).

Buckle, Catherine, *Beyond Tears: Zimbabwe's Tragedy* (Jonathan Ball, Jeppestown, South Africa, 2002).

Caute, David, *Under the Skin: The Death of White Rhodesia* (Allen Lane, London, 1983).

Chan, Stephen, *Mugabe: A life of power and violence* (I B Tauris, London, 2003).

— *Southern Africa: Old Treacheries, New Deceits* (Yale University Press, London, 2011).

Chitiyo, Knox, *The Case for Security Sector Reform in Zimbabwe* (RUSI, London, 2009).

Cilliers, J.K., *Counter-Insurgency in Rhodesia* (Croom Helm, Beckenham, Kent, 1985).

Clark, John F. ed, *The African Stakes of the Congo War* (Fountain, Kampala, 2003).

Cocks, Chris, *Fireforce: One Man's War in the Rhodesian Light Infantry* (Galago, Alberton, 1988).

Cole, Barbara, *The Elite: The Story of the Rhodesian Special Air Service* (Three Knights, Amanzimtoti, 1984).
— *Sabotage and Torture* (Three Knights, Amanzimtoti, 1988).
Cowderoy, Dudley and Roy C. Nesbit, *War in the Air* (Galago, Alberton, 1987).
Dowden, Richard, *Africa: Altered States, Ordinary Miracles* (Portobello, London, 2009).
Ellert, Henrik, *The Rhodesian Front War* (Mambo Press, Gweru, 1993).
Flower, Ken, *Serving Secretly: An Intelligence Chief on Record* (John Murray, London, 1987).
Frederikse, Julie, *None But Ourselves: Masses vs Media in the Making of Zimbabwe* (Raven Press, Johannesburg, 1982).
Fuller, Alexandra, *Don't Let's Go to the Dogs Tonight: An African Childhood* (New York: Random House, 2001*)*.
Gann, L. and T. Henriksen, *The Struggle for Zimbabwe (*Praeger, New York, 1981).
Godwin, Peter and Ian Hancock, *Rhodesians Never Die: The Impact of War and Political Change on White Rhodesia* (Oxford University Press, Oxford, 1993).
Godwin, Peter, *The Fear: The Last Days of Robert Mugabe* (Picador, London, 2010).
Gumede, William Mervin, *Thabo Mbeki and the Battle for the Soul of the ANC* (Zed, London, 2007).
Hanlon, Joseph, *Apartheid's Second Front* (Penguin, Harmondsworth, 1986).
Hill, Geoff, *What Happens After Mugabe: Can Zimbabwe Rise from the Ashes?* (Zebra, Cape Town, 2008).
Holland, Heidi, *Dinner with Mugabe: The untold story of a freedom fighter who became a tyrant* (Penguin, Johannesburg, 2008).
Hudleston, Sarah, *Face of Courage: Morgan Tsvangirai* (Double Storey Books, Cape Town, 2005).
Johnson, R W, *South Africa's Brave New World: The Beloved Country since the End of Apartheid* (Penguin, London, 2010).
Kriger, Norma, *Zimbabwe's Guerrilla War: Peasant Voices* (Cambridge University Press, Cambridge, 1992).
— *Guerrilla Veterans in Post-war Zimbabwe: Symbolic and violent protests 1980-1987* (Cambridge University Press, Cambridge, 2003).
Lan, David, *Guns and Rain: Guerrillas and Spirit Mediums in Zimbabwe* (Currey, London, 1985).
Linden, Ian, *The Catholic Church and the Struggle for Zimbabwe* (Longman, London, 1980).

Martin, David and Phyllis Johnson, *The Struggle for Zimbabwe* (Faber and Faber, London, 1981).

—, *The Chitepo Assassination,* (Zimbabwe Publishing House, Harare, 1985).

McLaughlin, Peter, *Ragtime Soldiers: The Rhodesian Experience in The Great War* (Books of Zimbabwe, Bulawayo, 1980).

—, *The Occupation of Mashonaland* (Books of Zimbabwe, Bulawayo, 1981).

Meldrum, Andrew, *Where We Have Hope: A Memoir of Zimbabwe* (John Murray, London, 2004).

Meredith, Martin, *The Past is Another Country: Rhodesia, 1890-1979* (André Deutsch, London, 1979).

—, *Robert Mugabe: Power, Plunder and the Struggle for Zimbabwe* (Public Affairs, New York, 2007).

Moorcraft, Paul, *African Nemesis: War and Revolution in Southern Africa, 1945-2010* (Brassey's, London, 1994).

— *Inside the Danger Zones: Travels to Arresting Places* (Biteback, London, 2010).

— and Peter McLaughlin, *The Rhodesian War: A Military History* (Pen and Sword, Barnsley, 2008).

— and Phil Taylor, *Shooting the Messenger: The Political Impact of War Reporting* (Potomac, Washington, 2008).

Nkomo, Joshua, *Nkomo: The Story of My Life* (Methuen, London, 1984).

Parker, Jim, *Assignment Selous Scouts: Inside Story of a Rhodesian Special Branch Officer* (Galago, Alberton, 2006).

Partnership Africa Canada, *Diamonds and Clubs: The Militarized Control Diamonds and Power in Zimbabwe*, (Ottawa, June 2010).

Petter-Bowyer, Peter, *Winds of Destruction: The Autobiography of a Rhodesian Combat Pilot* (30° South, Newlands, Johannesburg, 2004).

Prunier, Gérard, *From Genocide to Continental War: The 'Congolese' Conflict and the Crisis of Contemporary Africa* (Hurst, London, 2009).

Ranger, Terence, *Peasant Consciousness and Guerilla War in Zimbabwe* (Zimbabwe Publishing House, Harare, 1985).

Reid-Daly, Ron, as told to Peter Stiff, *Selous Scouts: Top Secret War* (Galago, Alberton, 1982).

Sithole, Masipula, *Zimbabwe: Struggles within the Struggle* (Rujeko, Salisbury, 1979).

Smith, Ian, *The Great Betrayal* (Blake, London, 1997).

Stearns, Jason K., *Dancing in the Glory of Monsters: The Collapse of the Congo and the Great War of Africa* (Public Affairs, New York, 2011).

Stiff, Peter, *Taming the Landmine* (Galago, alberton, 1986).

—, *The Silent War: South African Recce Operations* (Galago, Alberton, 1999).

—, *See You in November: The Story of an SAS Assassin* (Galago, Alberton, 2002).

Tendi, Blessing-Miles, *How Intellectuals Made History in Zimbabwe* (Africa Research Institute, London, 2010).

Venter, Al J., *War Dog: Fighting Other People's Wars* (Casemate, Newbury, UK, 2008).

Verrier, Anthony, *The Road to Zimbabwe* (Cape, London, 1986).

Wigglesworth, Tom, *Perhaps Tomorrow* (Galaxie, Salisbury, 1980).

Windrich, Elaine, *The Mass Media in the Struggle for Zimbabwe: Censorship and Propaganda under Rhodesian Front Rule* (Mambo, Gwelo, 1981).

Woods, Kevin, *The Kevin Woods Story: In the Shadow of Mugabe's Gallows* (30°South, Johannesburg, 2010).

# Index